EXACTING CLAM No. 20 — SPRING 2026

CONTENTS

Cover by **Leigh Gore** and **Tyler C. Gore**.

ISBN: 978-1-963846-70-6 (paperback)
978-1-963846-71-3 (ebook)

exactingclam.com
Exacting Clam is a quarterly publication from Sagging Meniscus.

Jake Goldsmith

Envying Artists

I'm not an artist. Occasional sketches and doodles of mine wouldn't usually qualify for the definition of *art*, anyway. Since childhood, I've held admiration and deep jealousy for skilled artists, who could devote effort to work I've always been far too lazy to persevere with. Most art, at least what I admire, requires some training and expertise that my limited pool of energy won't expand to include.

Art at school felt closer to vandalism than creativity. I remember what passed for *still life* were displays of old furniture and decorations stacked in the middle of dirty classrooms, which, if not portrayed, were instead demolished and reconstituted as part of student projects. I was too fascinated by the lost or neglected value of the discarded objects to want to destroy them. Items such as old books and vinyl records were donated as useless junk to be freely used or abused, "for art", which I guess isn't something too many would complain about, and neither do I so absolutely, though the idea at least floats about that some of this abandoned memorabilia would serve a better purpose not being covered in acrylic paint or glued to a wall. I remember this impoverishing some of my creative verve for a while, at least enough for me not to want to do anything productive in art classes, and art remains (most of the time) something I distantly appreciate rather than participate in.

My favourite people are mostly authors. Mostly dead. The history of ideas, or intellectual history, biography, etc, is easier for me to access, and I found that my own experience of illness was better described in words than with imagery or music. As much as it is essential to life, I find it personally more difficult to understand heavy concepts in art, film, painting, sculpture . . . than if laid out in a heavy tome with the benefits of language. This is a philistine streak: my liking of art is often vapid, or ends at the surface world of appearances. Artists describe finer meanings and intentions, yet a cruel part of me, maybe a devil on my shoulder, labels this as a type of sanctimony instead of a hearty expression of a greater thing. I'd prefer to dismiss that judgment.

Anyone sensible who would choose to write about art or artists would do so while knowing more. Most writing about art benefits, obviously, if the author knows the subject intimately and can teach others. Yet there is some merit to my inspiration for this; in that an amateur view of art, or one learning to appreciate painting beyond base notions, is a psychology I want to explore—however indulgent. I want to finally rid myself of the lingering taste of philistinism, where the first instinct upon seeing a painting is no longer dismissive or superficial. I'm not always glib or cynical with art, but there is still part of me that suggests being offhand or snide, an annoying colleague undermining good progress.

Opposing the superficial devil, I have cultivated an interest in artists (interesting people I'd desperately want to be my friends), if less so the acute nature of their craft. Artists with an itch to create, and a talent to do so marvellously, are people I deeply envy and wish to collect. In another life, and with too much to spend, I'd fashion myself as some sort of salon host-cum-art curator, like a skinny British Gertrude Stein. Making up for that inability, I've tried to know artists and support their work, with my limited resources, and a few I consider good friends. Exploring my relationships with them (and exploring, broadly, my own prejudices) may hopefully teach me something.

I met Wendy online some years ago on a tiresome philosophy forum. Despite the aggravating company (many younger people interested in philosophy are insufferable), there were a few, either not so young or not so irksome, who made welcome conversation. Wendy has a background in psychoanalysis and critical theory, yet a life in academia, or as some esteemed scholar, was made infeasible due to neurological Lyme disease. Painful migraines, brain fog, short-term memory loss, and a list of other complex symptoms ensured that the scholarly life she deserved was beyond her. Worse, she's American. Her complex health and dietary restrictions would be far easier to answer outside America, with accessible healthcare and less hidden nonsense in all the food. I should stop short of being some jingoist for European health and nutritional standards.

I spent many hours with Wendy (and her partner, Kooper) in *Red Dead Online*. This game provided a fake, romantic historical America for us to explore as classic western outlaws and vagabonds, roaming a beautifully crafted world of mountains, prairie, and swampland, on horseback, shooting bandits or resting by the campfire. We'd spend (too much) time fashioning our characters, changing their outfits, accessorising their horses or decorating our campsites. The game is a work of art, if only for the graphical design and fidelity. The *assets* are all meticulously appointed. It is a space where lying is okay. Even when the world is dirty, it is pristine and intended. This game became an impressive backdrop, the view above New Austin from Hennigan's Stead or fishing at O'Creagh's Run a substitute for the *real* thing, where illness and distance prevented us from trekking through national parks or taking a boat down the Mississippi. It is easy to argue that this experience is inferior to actually riding our horses through town or eating at a fancy restaurant in New Orleans. In many ways, it obviously is. Yet in the physical world, one can't shoot runaway gangs without severe repercussions, and it takes far more effort to track them down, rather than have them predictably *spawn* near your location, and neither with the hassle of real firearms. My guns were customised with fancy silver Art Nouveau engravings (an expensive affair), and I'm not buying a genuine Krag-Jørgensen bolt-action rifle any time soon, let alone decking it out in filigree. If you are hurt in the game, you drink a tonic, eat some seasoned meat, and all is well—a dream. My *avatar* was a distinguished older gentleman with a great silver beard, dressed in a fine sage green 'Londonderry' collector's outfit (while it should be *Derry*, the game is set in 1898; so we might forgive the naming—and the outfit is so swanky that almost no name would deter me). Playing as an older man in an online game is a novelty and a rare sight. It is fun to think of someone so long in the tooth flooring a gang of upstart youths. If we forgive me for being maudlin, it allows me to play at something else I won't get to experience in real life either. I won't ever grow a big bushy silver beard, and I won't see my twilight years. Kooper dressed his cowboy in all-black (including the horse), and Wendy went for big hats. I'm still sore about how the game was treated (by its enigmatic creators), a waste of potential from one of the world's largest game developers, practically abandoning its art for money or opaque reasons it will never communicate. Forgetting the lost potential, it remains a gorgeous world to inhabit for some time. I'd much rather meet around a virtual campfire, next to my dog and my horse, than sit in any conventional setting on a Zoom call. Video games can be pathetic or kitsch, and I'm more critical of their basic mechanics than most, but they may still be poignant. Playing wasn't some shallow or throwaway experience, and the virtual space allowed us to mediate our conversation and eventually meet in person. Neither am I ever going to the *real* America—health and logistics make that impossible. I have to make do with a simulation, and America is best in the movies anyway. Art that is an interactive experience, shaped by our input, customised and tinkered with, is common enough to go unappreciated; in expendable games from a cynical, often callous industry. Yet imperfect people are always making good art. They make enough terrible art, arguably more bad than good, and may still provide a ground for our own superb moments. If something flawed can still overcome modern disillusions, then it is worth some respect. We can forget that art can be great even when its authors are inferior or risible, reading nonsense into discourse that isn't there or supposing stupid meanings for their creations. We read our own nonsense into work as much as any banal or nauseating artist. But that shouldn't always distract from the creation.

> "Even in the midst of the most remarkable experiences, we still do just the same; we fabricate the greater part of the experience, and can hardly be made to contemplate any event, except as "inventors" thereof. All this goes to prove that from our fundamental nature and from remote ages we have been—accustomed to

lying. Or, to express it more politely and hypocritically, in short, more pleasantly—one is much more of an artist than one is aware of."

—Friedrich Nietzsche, *Beyond Good and Evil*

After years of digital correspondence, Kooper had the opportunity to research Freud (at the Freud Museum) in London as part of a study trip, which was the opportunity for both Kooper and Wendy to finally escape the US for some time and stay with me in Suffolk for a couple of weeks, between their artistic and educational adventures in the city. The weather remained sunny and welcoming throughout, and our previous communication, whether in virtual forests or in less gamified settings, lightened any awkwardness or discomfort. I met them, and I already knew them. From what I recall, Kooper enjoyed his time in the city more than Wendy did. Wendy's condition precluded much tolerance of the dirt and pollution, even if she wanted to revel in the urban scene. Wendy enjoyed the countryside peace of Suffolk as I would. Cities are only good to visit for brief periods. I value nature and air too much for any urban life to be tolerable for long.

Unburdened by the constraints of long-distance communication, we could freely discuss artists and authors we loved. Baltasar Gracián, Montaigne, La Rochefoucauld, Nietzsche, John Ruskin, Raymond Aron . . . Wendy painted Keats' House and the Freud Museum, always drawing something; a serendipitous purchase of a secondhand book allowed us to discover the Welsh painter Frank Brangwyn. We visited churches, Sutton Hoo, and quaint county towns along thin English roads that have surprised and inspired travelling Americans for years. The biggest 'culture shock' for them, I think, was the everyday infrastructure so different to the large and overwhelming American sprawl. Any customs, references, ways of speaking or other eccentricities they already knew through me or were not particularly surprising.

Infrastructure is always working against us, or at least its ceaselessly inept operation doesn't help. Wendy lost all her luggage on the way back on a flight with no layovers. She found it again, though not before rummaging through the airport with little help from staff, who seemed to be unaware of their own surroundings, let alone the concerns of any passengers. I'm surprised anyone can fly anywhere without some debacle. Less a well-oiled machine and more an un-oiled beast. All the airports I've known have been undignified. Some duty-free chocolates and perfume won't make up for losing your belongings or demolishing wheelchairs. Singapore is supposed to have a pretty one that I won't see any time soon. I can't travel by plane without the aid of oxygen. The more I hear about airports and their sins, the less likely I am ever to be in one again. Airports are like cities to me, with a type of intimidating intrigue that's better appreciated from afar, and if I have to immerse myself in the mix, I start to lose my head.

As an aside, and I can't help but include it, there's something unintentionally funny about so many people passing through one space, the expectations of typically weary travellers, what is required of them, or what might suit their fancies . . . A friend of mine asked: Is there a more miserable, isolated existence than that of the single copy of *Infinite Jest* that resides interminably in the WHSmith at Luton Airport? That's going to be stuck there for some time. By now, it is just part of the decor. While we all like to jest, doing so infinitely is probably unseemly. I'm sure the airport patrons must feel the same way and, as such, neglect to pick up the book. Also, I don't think *Infinite Jest* is a book one picks up on a lark as a casual read on a busy day commuting. Reading such a tome requires intention. I never go around with such things as intentions or notions. That's dangerous and possibly even vulgar. I instead wait and see what direction seems most appropriate at any given time. And reading David Foster Wallace is ill-advised in Luton.

I should apologise for my snobbery about city life. In many ways, it is a good recommendation that people live closer together in traditional, walkable urban centres, rather than cluttering and building on yet more pleasant land. Wendy and I share a distrust of cities, airports, and other urban bastions, as they can't help but inflame our health, precarious as it is. It is old advice that the ill go for convalescence in nature, and I can't fault it. Though I'm not going to roll around in mud or walk through nettles, I'm not built for that either. I'm aloof from too many walks of life. Cities have virtues, but I prefer them in paintings.

Outside the difficulties of urban life, relaxed in the country, I'd watch Wendy draw and use her small watercolour palette to paint brief sights and moments in her sketchbook. She would complain that whatever she had just interpreted to the page, whether a passing shot at old houses on the Aldeburgh coast, or the gribblies and faces in cathedral cloisters, on the move and transient, was inadequate and didn't catch the scene in the way she desired. Yet from my view, or my mother's, or from someone unaccustomed to artistic training or craftsmanship, the sketches all had a beautiful, fleeting virtue. If I wanted a replica, I'd take a photograph. Photography isn't perfect; its pretence of realism is flawed, but the barrier to entry is lower, and for most laypeople and philistines, it will capture a satisfactory portrait of a moment.

We are easily satisfied, likely too easily. Wendy's sketches were all immediately recognisable to me, and she was illustrating sights I was intimately familiar with, places I have seen countless times, where I live, that she was seeing only once, with a cursory glance. My own tastes favour inexact drawings and quick tracings. I love doodles and something brilliant created in a few minutes or seconds. Wendy underestimates her ability to impress others, but I won't say her standards are too high. She can do more, learn more, while her previous forms are not unsatisfying or wrong. So-called better artists, in the popular imagination, get by on far less and with much less work.

Amateurs can produce great art, much as they may also produce great philosophy, or, more attuned, helpful and better effects on the world. With more artistic or philosophical training, one has a greater chance to produce great work, with more resources and experience at one's disposal. Such a wherewithal, though, doesn't automatically mean one will make the best or correct choice, or live the best life. Ask a professional philosopher to define liberty, and they may recall everything notable said on the subject over the past 2000 years, while an unprofessional bystander will rely more on intuitions and what's immediately available in the culture. A trained artist is more likely to produce a worthy piece than someone who rarely holds a brush and who hasn't heard of Monet. Yet amateurs can still surpass professionals; they may be better people, or give us a more interesting answer—the chances are just less so in their favour. Many of us know people who haven't spent time in professional education but are nonetheless more ethically sound than expert scholars. A satisfactory answer relies not just on wherewithal and a scope of information, but on intuitions and prejudices. Sometimes years of study don't reveal intuitive imagination. In this way, the layperson can be a 'better' artist, with the right mix of disposition, attitude or influence. Expertise matters, and education may help, but not always so directly.

We attended an event called *Sketch Fest*, with local artists and workshops along the River Deben, where artists learnt to paint water, boats, and birds in the picturesque setting. At the end of the day, many of the artists, amateur or professional, displayed their sketchbooks on a large table for everyone to peruse and appraise. Wendy's effort, her first time painting boats and water, was well-admired. I overheard it mentioned well enough to be significant among the other books, with enviable company. Wendy was still doubtful.

I suffer from the same vulnerability: I feel ill, scant, and no amount of validation and respect, authentic and reliable, gets through the noise that says you're not doing well enough for too long. The volume of cynicism is always greater. We are woeful, always trying to please ourselves while constantly sour at our attempts—as if under our own twisted despotism. We don't cope with trying to please ourselves, and yet we have little strength, if any, to rid ourselves of the need. We hate our own flaws and also anything that might diminish them. If we remedied our complaints, then what would we have to speak of? All of it is too much for us; we will find discomfort whether we are quiet or loud. Few get rid of the mess, and those who say they do, all *enlightened* and at peace, risk lying.

Wendy's art is the best refutation of my uncultured view. The craft and process of her art are partly an act of remembrance, a way of restoring memory and marking one's life creatively when words fail, and when language becomes a lesser faculty. Though not remembrance exactly. It is not about being exact. The most important thing about Wendy's art is the thing itself, the process, disorderly, self-referential, less so trying to declare something beyond reach, or less so an end; nothing so neatly packaged. The presentation itself, confused and upsetting, becomes more critical than a concluding message or something ideal. Wendy's education in semiotics means there are always allusions, something more, and something hinted at, but there isn't a definite article. Certitude is nowhere here. Attempts at an absolute (epistemological, representational, transcendental, rational) are sure to fail. Imperfection, cliché as it is, aware of its own unawareness, the permanence of imperfection, is the point. Or at least *a* point.

I'm familiar in my own way with occasional lapses of reason or complete perplexity, induced by illness or my strange constitution. As much as I value words and text most in explaining myself, this doesn't mean I think they are the best way to do things: rather, it is the least bad or least incompetent for my needs, while greatness is impossible or beyond me. Wendy has to make use of a different medium, facing a similar difficulty. Most of the time, I am not coherent, at least in my own thoughts. Words have the benefit of time, reflection, and editing to capture a better view of my intent over speaking, which requires immediacy and is less accommodating of distractions. Sometimes it is complicated to talk because my health is always erratic and disturbing me, so I'm not reliably coherent or cogent in ordinary conversation. Most people are bad at the art of conversation and stutter, interrupt, or become overwhelmed, struggling to process words or access basic functions. No amount of reading, diligent training, or excellent preparation helps you when you're overburdened and lost in the moment. A single misplaced word can throw a conversation off track. Whoever you're speaking to gets the wrong idea entirely, and then it is all a mess. Anyone does well if they can slow down and engage in conversation less hectically. Much of the time, we have an idea in our head of what we want to say next and desperately want to get it out, rather than properly listening to our interlocutor. What's most important can easily be lost in the heat of human interaction. Wisdom is often only recalled in hindsight. "Memory is often unruly, or stupid." People are always passionate beyond and before their limited ability to be reasonable. Writing is better for deeper conversation as one has time to reflect over each choice of word, while in spoken conversation you're under immediate pressure, distracted by objects in the room, or smells, or just being uncomfortable in one's own skin at that moment; so I can't be as eloquent or articulate in speech as I may be in writing, most of the time. Painting, or music, can express something where words are lacking, though it is still imprecise and false. It is familiar to us to pursue overwrought concepts like authenticity and individuality, especially in art. Sadly, the most common forms of this pursuit are cheap, corrupted, insipid or shallow and show an inflated sense of competence. This incoherence can be tragic or hilarious, but admitting incoherence should be more common. Often, I disguise how I'm feeling by acting whimsically or just being quiet. I find it hard to compose myself and act in a half-convincingly human way. I'm vitally awkward, weary, and never truly comfortable in any situation, even if I look content or unperturbed in some seemingly benign circumstance. This isn't a rare sentiment, and yet we fail to acknowledge it—forget understanding or acceptance.

All this, I gather, is something I acutely share with Wendy. Her art tries, in some way, to express that discomfort and impossibility, either with a laugh and levity, or more sombrely, making use of the medium within her own constraints. If anything, Wendy's particular condition, with much pain and distraction, only compounds this feeling and makes language, speech, or text and recording oneself in book form, even more onerous and tiring. I don't want to give the impression that this is all so serious and grim. There is lightness and humour, which is best at regulating despair or misanthropy. Wendy's work can be loose and subtle while also pointed and decidedly funny, whether it is a light, delicate watercolour of a garden, or a cunning joke about parasitic ticks. It takes little imagination to find solidarity. Wendy's project to record her life with art, the journey, learning and watching her progress through different styles, finding what suits her best, has been a delight to see, and it is a joy to watch a good friend make their mark on life.

I first contacted Mette Ivers in late 2018. Part of my reason for trying was extraneous to art and more to do with her history, and history generally. I wanted to do some informal research on Albert Camus, and the chance to talk with someone who knew him was enticing. Yet the pretence felt rude, and I was wary that this might be a common invasion of her privacy. Mette is an accomplished artist and illustrator, at the time of writing still well and active at 93, yet, in an all-too-familiar story, has been overshadowed by the famous men in her life. For a while, it wasn't so widely known that the 'Mi' in Camus' private correspondences was her, where she was indeed one of Camus' lovers. Romance is subject to much slander and gossip, and I sincerely wanted to avoid any crass or common insinuations. Later, Mette married the famous cartoonist Jean-Jacques Sempé and was again a footnote in an important someone's life and not as much, at least in typical perceptions, a distinct entity one mentions without speaking of her past associations. I somehow commit the same sin, even when I'm trying to dissect it rather than maintain it. There is a routine feminist message here, one we take for granted, where a woman, however talented, appears second to a great creative man. Sylvia Plath became more renowned than her husband, in one of the few counterexamples, while a wife or girlfriend is typically relegated in some way.

Mette once told me about a time when some visitors came to her home while she was married to Sempé. Art from both of them lined the walls, and it was likely a privilege to see the home of two artists, with their work together, in a cosy, familial space. Yet visitors would ignore Mette's work in the presence of the renowned Sempé, with his covers for *The New Yorker* and popular posters.

"When I was married to Sempé and had invited some friends home, they only looked at his drawings on the wall. Mine didn't awaken the slightest interest . . . That's how it is, Jake. Living or not living with a star, your work has no real value if you are a woman. For my illustrations I was paid much under the pay of a male illustrator, no more talented than me . . ."

Again, this is obvious or rudimentary, yet it doesn't mean a lack of respect or gratitude toward talented men. My love for Camus and his work is undiminished, yet justice says we should expand the canon. It is a stupid impulse to dethrone the old guard of men for new faces. Genuine inclusivity means standing alongside giants, not just on their proverbial shoulders, and not misguidedly vanquishing them.

I read an interview Mette gave in 2019 and raised the subject with her. She knew well enough, and through real experience.

"You noticed that in the short presentation of my interview, it ends with the names of my two "great men" . . . I asked the author of this short presentation (a woman!!! (in 2019)) not to mention them. She couldn't! No! It would have been so much better if we mentioned them, what a spotlight on the ant that I am! Misogyny is ancestral, thousands of years old, and women themselves are steeped in it. And the woman in the article loves and admires me!!! You know, Jake, I passionately admire the work of Camus. I'm not in competition. Sempé is also a valuable artist. But you yourself were struck by this quote from my prestigious private life. And it shocked you. Like me . . . My work is an independent and personal thing. You're right, [Maria] Casarès is also flattened in her being by her relationship with Camus. We are all enslaved by this pervasive stupidity. Our leading men are like feathers in our caps . . . And endorse our artistic stammering . . ."

Too obvious. Only a fool might deny the truth. We live with a surplus of fools for whom even the most innocuous feminist tract is untenable. This isn't even the fifth or sixth wave, or whatever wave we're currently surfing. Unfortunately, this isn't as obvious as it seems, and it is a mistake to think ideas are somehow natural or expected. An understated feature of the history of ideas, or ideology, is that thinkers and thoughts we believe we are consciously opposed to still seep into casual acceptance. Ardent anti-feminists will take as a given ideas from Wollstonecraft without interrogation or realisation, while still maintaining positions opposed to perceptibly modern or contemporary discussion. Most of us don't realise what we accept or borrow from others, even if we oppose them. The idea that primary rudiments of feminist thought should be so obviously true is part of a Fukuyama-esque gambit or delusion, or to be more precise, an outmoded notion that good liberal and enlightened ideas are part of a natural teleology; organic, automatic, accepted and inevitable—with whatever opposition they have somehow being an aberration. This idea still infects us, or influences us (if we're choosing a less aggressive verb), even if we reject it; such is its permeation through culture. We have faith in *good liberal notions*, their goodness notwithstanding, as if they would be *common sense* or clear and elementary moral standards. Instead, alas, we can argue things are true, but that does not make them obvious. We still need to litigate and make a case for something. I re-read Frederick Douglass recently, and by today's standards his thought appears seamless, or so self-evident that it should *go without saying*. Instead, it still needs to be renewed. A superior assumption of obviousness is unlikely to lead to moral or political progress. Considering this, Mette's point may not be new, but it needs renewed affirmation.

Besides that, I would correspond with Mette semi-frequently over the following years, at first asking questions about art and her history (she's long enjoyed Voltaire, Montaigne—authors we've both enjoyed much since youth—Madame de La Fayette, Edvard Munch, numerable others), and eventually as a type of pen pal discussing the news and recent events as they happened in the U.K. and France. Knowing my ill health, she would send comforting messages that served as needed reminders and validation. Spend more time in gardens and find nature wherever you can. Without platitude or cliché, which become easy default modes, it is worth sending such reminders and finding the strength to keep going—especially during the tougher years of the pandemic, with many being less careful or concerned for vulnerable people (either vulnerable through disability, illness, age, etc), affirmations towards life were more necessary. It is also worth speaking with people much older than you. Right now, I am in my late twenties, foreboding as that is considering my condition and the dubiousness of my surviving long, and speaking to a nonagenarian artist gives a needed perspective absent from those closer to me. I find myself prematurely aged and irritably, if privately, scowling at bright young things taking life at a pace far too speedy for me to ever engage with. All generations are too mean to each other, and it is better to be more discerning.

Younger people have always seemed emotionally distant to me, or rather, their emotions are in a distant place that is harder for me to reach. I appreciate a wide breadth of humanity, though when I was younger, I would prefer to speak more at length (or more substantively) with older people. Youth is peculiar. I share youthful wants, or no lack of immaturity. Other common youthful desires (or vices, if we are rude) that require great energy and enthusiasm towards adventure are less obtainable. Being older doesn't necessarily mean being sedate, but being sedentary is more common as we age, and I share a kind of elderly reticence. My limitations mean that being active and daring have always been less appealing modes of being. I can filter between social circles and niches with some ease, where class, age, or gender bother me less than they may others, as I don't enthusiastically subscribe to any full membership. However, this means I'm more alone, or lonely, than happily on my own. Here is my prejudice: age should ideally mean experience and wisdom (which only makes it more disappointing to have lived long and not learnt much), so I value being older. If a group consists solely of the young and has no advice from other generations, then I'm suspicious, just as I would be in the opposite scenario for similar reasons. Ignorance and a failure to keep one's thumb on the pulse are understandable failures with age. Youth is more often cocky, overzealous, rude, and while these positions are never absolutely unwarranted, and may be helpful, we get enough of them. I don't trust friendships just as I don't trust think tanks that are too narrow in their scope of ages. We are aware that age is used as power, with the old taking advantage of youth, though this is less of a concern for me. I have zero desire to punish youth or leverage it. I'm still young. Imagining myself as an older person only to wield power over youth makes me feel sick. Many of us comprehensibly, with just reasons, see connections between the young and old as exploiting vulnerabilities; as elder abuse or the opposite. All of this can colour our view with an intelligible yet obscuring lens. Still, I am peculiar. My own wants are innocent, yet it looks like I protest too much. I put so much effort into circumventing our concerns or fears that I seem odder than others who don't investigate themselves. An innocuous, or even a healthy situation—a diversity of rich platonic friendships—looks off just for being uncommon. Its reasons for being uncommon are then not entirely spurious. After all the fretting, I have written extended paragraphs trying to justify something that should be common among a healthy civic culture—the sharing of knowledge and experience. Friendships with others much older than us link us to another world that is slowly disappearing. Let's not turn this into anything perverse. We should put more effort into rebuilding communal and social bonds, rather than sequestering ourselves into like denominations. A narrower life of fewer friends (of every variance) makes us less creative as well as less ethical. For those reasons and more, it is worth being brave, sometimes foolish, and meeting a range of people beyond the digital simulacrum or our imposed limits.

In November 2024, I finally travelled to Paris to meet Mette. I've said before that I dislike travel. My worries could be assuaged if trains, train stations, and airports weren't so aesthetically unpleasant and crowded.

The first place we went after meeting outside Gare du Nord was straight to Montparnasse Cemetery. I had been in 2018, and I wanted to make a kind of pilgrimage to see Raymond Aron and Samuel Beckett (again). A pilgrimage appears less significant without any religious affiliation or ceremony. Aron's family tomb is Jewish (despite his secular, assimilated life), and Beckett's is plain, almost unadorned. We weren't silent or seriously reverential, nor solemn, meditatively contemplative, or upset. My French is terrible, and so we spoke in well-articulated, deliberate English; slower, making sure to enunciate and pronounce words with more care for Mette's sake. Cemeteries and graveyards are worth walking in more often, as long as our sentimentality isn't too tasteless. We somehow think that if we aren't religious or dogmatically attuned, experiences like this are lesser. That they hold less weight, or that they are otherwise pointless without some apparently profound spiritual or metaphysical connection. This gives the *committed* too much credit, as if events can only have any significance if they are divine or extraordinary. We don't need a great sense of spirit or communion to take pleasure or any feeling from events. Virtue, morality, love, wonder, grief, and the whole range of human emotion precede dogma, and this is true whether we are dogmatic or not. The religious are better for it if they know that their feelings exceed dogma or official direction, and that their world doesn't shatter into nothing if they no longer hold one dogma or another to be true. Neither are the irreligious, wandering religious spaces, cancelled out of any virtue or significance unless we subscribe to the most inhuman and bureaucratic forms of religiosity, which border on being fascistic if they exclude others from human categories and experiences they know they should belong to. For the most extreme, simply exploring a church for artistic, aesthetic purposes alone (without prayer) is blasphemy. This isn't something to recommend to believers, or anyone. Exploring the world can't be a joyless, *administrative*, managerial affair, whether one accepts God or not. Anyone who relies too much on theoretical principles, especially incontrovertible ones, risks being lost, even fanatical, when those principles are shaken. Thankfully, for the less zealous, what's beneath our lofty ideas saves us. We shouldn't be left with nothing when principles fail. Anyone studious enough can render the world unobtainable and unknowable, easily upending theories and received teachings. Investigate life thoroughly enough and there is no security. Yet we aren't all running around headless and damned. We survive as our virtues, our conduct, our inmost reasons, outlive later justifications. Reasons are invented to excuse our actions after the fact. I need not go further, I don't care about God, and this isn't the time for that sort of philosophical deliberation. I still care about feeling, life, intimacy, and wholesomeness, even when we are otherwise so lacking in knowledge, when so much is beyond us. Freud said that we will still face ". . . the difficulties which the untameable character of human nature presents to every kind of social community." This isn't a solely negative situation. Human nature, why we think anything worth seeing, why we visit gravesites without any promises of salvation, why we do anything despite death, and why we are good or bad at the bottom of all deduction, can be traced and dissected to a fair degree. But in the final analysis, it is beyond us, no matter our views or beliefs. We can say we believe something, really think we believe it, while doing nothing of the sort. What lies behind our motivations, any sequence, code or scheme, is irreducible, lost in the depths, and no amount of spiritual woo or scientistic pseudoscience will unveil it. We don't give up life because we don't understand it. What hubris suggests we can work it all out? If we somehow did perform the greatest act of genealogical or archaeological investigation into human action and found the sure reason why we do anything and magically knew our way, with all mental states reduced to formula, all life subjected to organisation, it is unlikely we would find it satisfying or even human. We suffer from exposure. We would be void, mentally and spiritually ossified. The lights in all our rooms would be lit, and we would hate it.

After visiting Montparnasse and thinking too abstractly about the limits of human understanding, I walked around Paris (or rather, I was pushed by my tired mother in my wheelchair, as walking around Paris would be much too tricky). My mum had never seen the Eiffel Tower, but we didn't care to climb it (too long, too tiring) or view it so closely, with our noses pressed against the iron. Something she had never seen before could still be hackneyed and overdone, overexposed in tacky images. At the same time, sometimes even the most gimmicky-seeming landmarks have a good essence behind their exploitation. The object subjected to crowds isn't itself debased, though its overcrowding and saccharine treatment by vain tourists is (often) debasing (at least to grumpy people like me, anyway). In these situations, where having a complete experience of a landmark would be wasteful of one's time and weakened by the abundance of others, it is enough to view something from a distance, taking in the presence of an object without seeing *how the sausage is made*, where over-tourism or long queues make the experience a chore, losing its mystery. Maybe we just wanted to avoid a full-blown case of *Paris syndrome*, and we're living in denial to preserve the magic? For some, being in the bustle is part of the joy—but I'm too impatient and fragile. In a world with fewer and fewer original experiences, or where quintessence is rarer and rarer, we have to find different ways of seeing sights (or sites) that keep the romance. Be that by avoiding the Hell of other people by visiting when nobody is around, or being satisfied with seeing something from afar. We don't always have to be so close to something, although this works when the thing in mind is a tower visible from everywhere. The Mona Lisa is another question, where the sheer profusion of people viewing it, with no time to sit with the painting before moving along, makes appreciation more elusive. A museum with too many people is worse. I don't just have a reactionary aversion to crowds; the time to study and value all the objects is rarer if things are too boisterous. Maybe I should be less misanthropic? Smaller museums, or those outside of visiting hours, maintain their charm.

Mette's apartment was stereotypical, though in the way that's appreciated. High ceilings, on the fourth floor of an old building with a tiny elevator shaft lodged between the spiral staircase. In her youth, Camus helped her acquire a picturesque apartment with beautiful tiles. The building's age made installing an elevator between the stairs impossible, so she moved once the steps became too burdensome. Her newer apartment was still lovely. Her studio was also stereotypical, with tall bookshelves, canvases, paintings, spilt paint and easels. These spaces are familiar to me in the sense that they are common in media, while not personally familiar (at least anymore). Throughout my high school education, my form group spent time in the school's art block, rotating annually between messy art classrooms. I didn't like the smells or the rotating cast of strange materials and supplies stored there. This studio lacked the scent of dirt or of so many people coming and going—paint everywhere, disorderly, yet clean. The view from the window was also superior: a classic Parisian street rather than musty school grounds. Art on the walls surpassed most—subtle figures, drawings, portraits and illustrations. The small washroom had frames and little paintings too. My own downstairs toilet at home has two large paintings my sister and I made in nursery school on the wall adjacent to the loo. I have no idea what they are supposed to be, or what my four-year-old mind was thinking as it splotched large blobs of paint on the paper to watch them drip. I remember the easel was red, thick and plastic. I remember exactly where the room was, too, where I composed the Pollock-like piece. Art in toilets and bathrooms often features nautical or marine motifs: fish, shells, dolphins, and boats. I guess water makes the association fitting, while bathrooms being nautical is still not an immediate connection, but a secondary one. It all goes to the sea anyway . . . The best bathrooms I've been in had fishy motifs, crustaceans, or molluscs and clams. They're comforting, blue and breezy, and somehow make the room smell nicer by a sort of spiritual association. Non-nautical toilets smell worse and are less welcoming. All this rumination comes to you when you piss in a new space, though it is soon forgotten when you get to food and socialising.

I hope to go to Paris again someday soon, eating from local delis and boulangeries. Vainly, I think I appreciate its history and ordinary life more than the average tourist or idle flâneur, even if I remain within the central arrondissements as a safe and casual observer. I still don't approach having some fetish for dirty places, or some reverence for maligned cityscapes. The city can still make me shiver or cringe. Friends or family are required to guide me around or supervise my health. Mette is more storied company than most, and while it is maudlin or veering on kitsch to say . . . it is still a wonder to know someone of her calibre and her age, and daunting to think of our (limited) time. She gifted me a painting, a Mediterranean house, which reminded me of the houses I saw in Provence when I first went to France in 2018. Why such houses impress our imaginations is obvious. They have charm and warmth, and British weather struggles to recreate the conditions. A while before, she sent me a copy of *Poucette* by Hans Christian Andersen—a recent edition she had illustrated. I forgot where it was for some months as I had put it inside a box for its safety, as if locking it in a vault. I could understand, for a moment, why collectors with too much money hide the great art they buy (or squander it out of public view), fearing theft or damage. The book is now within easy reach, and the painting hangs proudly on the wall. Sentimentality is permitted.

I first knew of Riva Lehrer when her memoir *Golem Girl* was submitted to the inaugural Barbellion Prize. I created The Barbellion Prize, a book prize for disabled authors, in 2020. The underappreciation of disabled authors is surprising (given their historical prevalence, from Kierkegaard to Virginia Woolf, etc.) and then immediately unsurprising, given common attitudes and disadvantages. The prize was *a hit*, as they say, for the three years it operated before its current hiatus (as of writing). My own health meant being a primary administrator of the prize was not sustainable for very long, and I would need more organisational support to keep the prize going, which should be forthcoming. Regardless, the judges for the first year were enthusiastic about Riva's memoir, and it helped her in some way, she admits. While the prize is in part a tribute and homage to the English diarist W. N. P. Barbellion, it also exists to *represent* disabled authors. That word is too common and overused for my liking, but my sensitivity to clichés or platitudes shouldn't overstep an elementary point. Riva's art, especially in portraits, has much to do with representation, with all its flaws and deceptions.

Riva told me that one of her "lodestars" was Alberto Giacometti. "Mainly his drawings are about the attempt to see, and the failure of seeing. That reality can only be glimpsed. A drawing like this, for me, is an act of severe honesty; the subject is built of notations, human vision at its most ambitious and most fallible."

Riva has spina bifida, a visible disability, which means a lot when confronting a judgmental public that condemns so much at first sight. My own ill health is often, instead, *invisible* to casual or uninformed observers, before excessive coughing or inelegant interruptions pierce the fantasy. With all their variances, these conditions shape how we are seen, stared at (often and suspiciously), and how we portray others. Portraiture can be a subversion of how we stare and ogle at others. Riva usually paints fellow disabled people in ways a rude public can find disturbing just for their regularity, for being seen, lingered on, studied and investigated, and without venom or wariness. She shows love, tenderness, and an unsparing honesty instead.

Riva was casually asked, innocently by a friend, who should portray her in a theoretical film adaptation of her memoir. I half-remember a long, poignant conversation with her about it during one of my hospital admissions, and the layered contemplation the question provoked for her: about self-image, the perception of disability, logistical challenges and a weight of other concerns.

The motivations behind this reveal confused priorities that may turn crude or vulgar. Live-action film is typically, without considered thought, deemed the pinnacle of artistic expression for any story or for epitomising a person; despite how other media show strengths and weaknesses that may pay a better compliment. A book, a radio show, a stage play, music, animation, a video game, all these are different modes with different specialities, different capabilities, with distinct features that mean a book can do what a film cannot, a film can do what a book may find unworkable, with further determinations the further you go. Video games are inherently interactive and so may tell stories and exploit mechanics that cinema cannot constitutively provide. Yet, the implicit prejudice in favour of film and being *cinematic*, for all of cinema's fine qualities, means games (or at least the most expensive ones) still often strive to be much like films but with some minor interactive elements. In our hierarchy of art, we place film above all else, particularly live-action film with all the trimmings. That a 2D animated television series can portray action or nuances that a 3D film cannot, and vice versa, and that a book can do what a game could never do, and vice versa, is barely considered in popular culture. Even if we can note obvious differences, we still hold on to this creative pecking order: film is best. The incessant drive to remake, remaster, and redo practically anything in a *film adaptation* betrays not just the economic concerns of film studios and producers, but also key aesthetic notions that have diffused through culture. The bias likely derives from a jumbled mix of preferences for *realism*; it is not my place to dissect all the reasons why; we can simply take notice of it. Do we really, really need a *Golem Girl* biopic film? Memoir captures life in ways a film can never do. Rather than a myopic hierarchy of artistic media, we need a filter for what each does best or not in each case.

The desire for *adaptations* can be benign yet also perverse. Each time I see a biopic adaptation of real life, a celebrity biography made for television, a war film, a historical epic, or the life of Miles Davis, I feel something minimally uncomfortable, or at least, even in the most commendable and awesomely directed cinema, that *something is wrong here*. Paintings portray real, non-fictional events, as do books, yet many film biopics have a particularly lurid or disturbing effect, something that can be cheaper or more profane. Any art can be uncomfortable, which isn't an argument against it, nor for its tighter regulation, but I still harbour this tense suspicion. I think in books, or paintings, there is a greater licence in non-realistic and imaginative interpretation, which can somehow be fairer to real events, without the photorealistic pretence. Yet with an added pretence, an added façade, showing real environments while telling a fictional story, an eerie sense we can feel in the portrayal (or misrepresentation) of real things can be disarmed. Film can be brilliant and surpass these impressions. Yet, considering the dramatic incitement to have recent events and people shown in this way, a way considered best for inclinations towards realism (a simulacrum of realism of course, always slightly off), with how we so habitually crave to dramatise recent crimes and recent deaths, this isn't always an urge I think is healthy or appropriately adjusted to coping with our affairs. Not that it can't be, I'm always equivocating, but this is my prejudice. The appetite for these representations, so sensational and explicit rather than not dressed-up for prime time video, not in showy images, where we really must *see* something, is not always a good way of seeing. To adapt something means we make unkind choices, careless additions, and omissions. We delight in some things in a way that's untoward, or doesn't render life, often frightening, tragic or disturbing, in a way that gives respect or better appreciation. I can like something gaudy or even tasteless, yet I can also feel different things simultaneously. Great art can still leave a wearying impression, making us doubt its purpose. Let's be short and less verbose: a biopic risks being disrespectful. And while anything can be callously produced, I'm more often feeling this in the presence of a screen than on a page or canvas. I won't call on anyone to stop anything, but the sentiment still haunts me in some unsure way.

My friend Kooper reminded me: ". . . the medium of film is unlike other media in that it can produce a more uncanny effect by making present a past reality and making certain audiences feel like they are witnessing the people and events in question themselves. Film is akin to dreams in its ability to trick viewers into hallucinating reality. All film is based on illusion, but that's not to say other media are more reliable."

This sentiment is likely part of my trouble. Film has the potential to be more uncanny than other media, I'd cautiously say. It can cross greater boundaries than, say, photography and encourage more blithe engagement. Then consider how many bad, multi-million-dollar biopics there are of important figures. If one is wary of being misunderstood and misinterpreted, then the possibility of being crass and impertinent is magnified. Riva's intimate worries about poor film representation are shared, while I'm sure I've gone down a mental spiral beyond her primary concerns. Pristine, unfiltered understanding is impossible; dull attempts to strip away and get at the essence of something can be tragic, funny, or ridiculous. Still, we at least don't want to be presented in such a poor light, or so uncannily, that others get a violently wrong idea and we start to feel sick about ourselves. We know some things, terrible events or the inner workings of our private lives, are beyond the reach of art: whether they are great works of art or not.

". . .we watch television programs and we say: 'Sorry, but it isn't it.' And when we are asked: 'But what is it?', we find ourselves unable to respond. What we really wish to say, what we feel we must say cannot be said."—Elie Wiesel.

I'm reminded of Agustín Fernández Mallo's objection. The objection to writing, or painting, or film about intimate subjects isn't necessarily aesthetic or moral. I don't feel prudish or morally outraged over sex, war, death, or complex inner lives shown in art. The art can be *technically* amazing and finely crafted, even. I instead sense a residual inadequacy. ". . . because it seems absurd to me, sex is like dreams, it cannot be ported into the representational mode, it never comes out well on the page, or on-screen, in either place it ends up untrue, ridiculous, or naff, or trivial, or laughable, or childish . . .".

There might be some merit, if not total and never absolute, to the idea of *where one cannot speak* and remaining quiet.

One of the more practical concerns in *adapting* Riva for the screen is choosing the lead actor. Employing non-disabled actors for disabled roles isn't absolutely bad, or impossible, or necessarily wrong, and by many reckonings is *easier*, but instead becomes an issue of labour rights or access to employment. Particular disabilities leave one with less energy or time to do anything, and logistics alone can make employment difficult. However, it is still true that disabled actors are denied work they could plausibly do, where less consideration is given to structural disadvantages that could be conceivably mitigated. Yet a disabled actor who fits Riva's appearance may not exist. Do we employ CGI to make the character more alike, or would a more surreal route, with Riva portrayed as a fantastical *monster* and with exaggerated practical or digital effects, be better for a hyperbolic view of others' warped perceptions? Or does that risk obvious offence? We can rest on the idea that it is *okay* or unobjectionable after enough finesse and deliberation to represent something. With any moral concerns eased, we still cannot say what must be said. Riva reminded me of a complex, delicate reality, where a proposed biopic representation of her would always be insufficient in some way. We are having to measure various practical, ethical, and aesthetic demands that have no clear, impeccably appropriate answer, and we will always have to make some form of trade-off or uneasy compromise in representing her, or in the finer portrayal of her story.

My connection to Harriet Memory is slightly confused—or, fittingly, my memory is in question. I knew her vaguely through mutual childhood friends, and I discovered her art relatively late. Everyone I have written about previously is distant or abroad, and I dislike that I don't live in some alternate world where everyone is closer to me. So an opportunity to know an artist who at least lives in the same country is helpful. There is no shortage of local artists in swish middle-class art galleries near me, yet I still struggle to meet strangers, regardless of the fortuitous connections I've somehow made above. My tenuous connection to old acquaintances and a couple of recommendations made saying hello less inconvenient or laborious, as a *sort of* stranger is at least easier to speak to than a total stranger.

Unlike with the above artists, I am less familiar with her or her work, though this provides an opportunity to explore how art can foster new acquaintances, or rather, arrange renewed links with one's past through mutual connections. Being so local to me also means access to shared national and regional knowledge, and I can work on building greater local roots instead of distant relations with people I can so rarely, or maybe never, meet. I've said already, illness adds a fundamentally anxious and unsure dimension to any physical interaction. I always want to make new friends and cherish friendships as essential to a better life. Somehow, I've found this easier with people terribly far away than with people on my doorstep. Aristotle said friendship is ". . . most necessary to our life . . . no one would care to live without friends, though he had all other good things." I'll accept his authority (at least here). I'm long tired of society's undervaluing of friendship as an institution, where it is by some means considered, on some unimaginative hierarchy of relationships, below the upper tier, lesser, or somehow optional. This is unthoughtful and frankly boring. We should be more open. Besides my own weariness or lack of confidence, there are sociological reasons for our poor form. It should be simpler to reconnect with old friends with the ease of new technology, yet without an organic or apparent reason for doing so, this is uncommon. We're more likely to be suspicious of being sold some pyramid scheme rather than think someone innocently wants to say hello after a long while, if contacted out of the blue by some half-forgotten school friend. This is an indictment of modernity and its disenchantments. I share dozens of mutual friends with Harriet from childhood, many of whom I occasionally wonder about in an offhand way, or I'd be happy to encounter randomly in the street, yet doing something as straightforward as sending a message to them, asking how they've been doing since we last spoke, feels clumsy and awkward. Past friends remind us of youth and, consciously or not, of disagreeable memories we'd rather forget. Yet one can't grow intellectually, emotionally, socially, without going through *odious incarnations*, if we're quoting Proust. I don't house any especially awful, let alone any criminal or repugnant past mistakes, but for many people, youth is at least a bit embarrassing or regrettable. Years pass, and most of us surely become very different personalities, hopefully wiser and more worldly, while we can simultaneously reject our past and acknowledge its necessity for our development.

I hold far less value in the idea of art being a lonely activity than I used to. Stereotypically, art requires, or has been made within, conditions of solitude and distance from others; with the fear that company or too much engagement with others' art will impress upon one's own work. I find that the recent books I have read seep into my vocabulary. I then involuntarily adopt them as my own, sometimes with a keen memory of their source, though often in a haze where a secondhand phrase becomes my own in a process of (wilful or sincere) forgetting, or oblivious osmosis. If I am not careful, I become a parrot, but then it is more important, in my mind, to be honest about our influences and not be ashamed of being infected by others. I first read the word 'verisimilitude' in Kafka. It would be graceless of me not to owe him.

More importantly, I would be a far weaker person, intellectually, if I didn't have, say, the articulation of Leszek Kołakowski on the fluidity of ideological allegiances (similarly, aesthetic allegiances), where there is a recognition of being *ideologically beautiful* (not a phrase of Kołakowski's, although fit for our purposes). We can think of ideology negatively, as in dogmatic and intransigent, extreme politics, but ideology is more: not a set of boxed and controlled conceptual categories, certainly not a dull list of policies, but a loose sense of ideas and dispositions, epistemologies and emotional inclinations, that float about culture and history, fluidly and pluralistically, that influence us whether we like it or not. We are all, in some way, more *conservative*, or liberal, socialist, anarchistic, authoritarian, or of any other lineage than we know or acknowledge. We are made outside of our control, all implicated by any idea with any power in our culture. Fittingly, speaking of unconscious meanings, we are all to some degree Freudian in the way we frame and think about the mind, personality, beliefs, desire . . . We are, in some measure, as I have said before, emotionally Fukuyamaean, whether we are intellectually well-disposed or actively opposed to such notions, as ideas penetrate culture (and us) beyond our conscious will. Individuals don't often invent ideas; they give names and shape to what already exists. This applies just as much to aesthetic bias or affect. Images, less articulated than considered beliefs, hold sway over us beyond our reckoning, and this doesn't have to be negative or some imposition on our lives. Artists can sometimes vulgarly express a wish to be alone and special, as if their work must stand on its own or must be created without interference. They envy others as much as the talentless envy them, and can grow susceptible to a lonely arrogance. I can't discount the idea that solitude, a lack of engagement, distance, and rejection produce masterful art. Life requires relief from the presence of others, even forgetting other lives. Yet I am less attracted to solitary living or solitary expression as I once was (and when I was more committed . . . there was a youthful narcissism that framed this). Graham Greene once said that a writer engaging with other writers discussing the craft of writing, as much as fellow writers were his friends, was a masturbatory act. I think this is unfair. We want to remain our own personalities, think for ourselves and stand unassisted, but we can't so seamlessly reject other lives. If we don't want to be in full agreement in an aligned community, we should at least aspire to a more commodious living. Misplaced pride makes us not want to owe others, and it is foolish to want wisdom all by oneself.

It is not the case that I am interested in literally collaborative art, where two authors or two painters write in the same book or share the same canvas, but I am less moved by the image of the artist in solitude, which becomes a type of tedious affectation or hackneyed banality. All of this text is in some part a lonely experience, as writing so often requires solitude and quiet, physically on one's own and without the immediate distractions of others. I am nonetheless more receptive as I age and brood over my life to a shared, even mawkish or saccharine, corny or cheesy, solidarity and exchange with others when viewing art. This is a departure from my usual temperament, which is poorly socialised and self-pitying.

Getting closer to the point, the above extended deliberation comes from envy. Harriet works with *Art Safari*, an organisation that hosts exotic painting holidays and workshops, as well as the aforementioned *Sketch Fest* event I attended with Wendy. As someone without any painterly talent, I enjoy a secondary fulfilment in being surrounded by skilled painters, but also jealousy and resentment at my own inability. If I am not careful in mediating my emotions, then the artist's life, viewed from the outside with an idealised filter, glorifying in the vision of *the artist's retreat* and one's profession, let alone their vocation, being art . . . hazards becoming some flashy ego ideal one invests in to escape reality. If one is less privately aware, we can succumb to fanciful imaginings in which another's good life makes one's own more tolerable. When I wonder, either committedly or off-handedly, what my favoured life would look like, what I would do without limitations or if not prevented by illness, my wish resembles these creative lives: art as one's profession, venturing to faraway places to visit elephants and awesome landscapes, and not just painting for myself. I'd like to teach, or at least advise and guide others. Outside my imagination, I lack the knowledge and the stamina to learn, or I am sluggish, so I make do with knowing others, or even voyeuristically appreciating them. Jealousy is often bitter and rarely elicits pity or sympathy. Yet, if it is recognised, interrogated, tempered into shape, and aware enough of its own ill, refusing to give in to mean temptations, then we can see that it is born of appreciation. Our self-interest doesn't need to be selfish. It can evolve into gratitude. Many artists will be quick to tell you that their lives are not romantic, picturesque, or calm, and that they struggle with the same obvious afflictions and more that we all do. The tortured artist is such a common stereotype that it becomes irritating. I have less time for the morose, alcoholic or degenerated artist, with their life of woe. If I am careless, then I grow judgmental of pretentious musicians and their silly clothes, or their excessive pageantry, or their tacky lyrics. I shouldn't be so rude. I admire painters more for what I see as a lesser pretension, but then that can be stupid of me; as if painters don't behave just as wildly, with as much potential for sanctimonious drivel. Paint is poisonous; don't get too close. Thankfully, there are enough good and great painters (and musicians) that we can ignore the bad ones (as hard as that can be), and my ideal picture isn't totally divorced from real life. I'm rude about the morose artist as they are closer to my own natural disposition, so my lashing out is also a form of self-dismissal. Or I have consumed so much depressive art and literature that I begin to lose sight of its merits; its familiarity rears contempt or apathy. The art, or specifically the paintings, that I approve of most don't resemble my ordinary emotions. As well as quick sketches, I gain the most enjoyment from paintings of animals and the natural world, in happy settings or avoiding bleakness, which I guess is why Harriet's work is so appealing to me. It shows a life that is decidedly not mine, and reveals a simultaneously bitter but gracious aspiration.

I gifted Wendy one of Harriet's paintings, a delicate piece of a dormouse. In doing so, I wasn't just being nice. I was trying to somehow connect the artists in my picture library in the outside world, as well as hand a local present to an international friend. In truth, I struggle to say more without sounding banal and cloying. I can be cynical; we love things selfishly, as they relate to us, and if I prefer my friends to myself, then that aligns with my own tastes. We are self-regarding, even vain, and without that preference, we wouldn't be true.

I have a small collection of books about friendship. It has been a repeated motif in the earlier sections, and it is through friendship that I prefer to explore art, rather than alone, despite the art I partake in (if memoirs and essays can somehow be considered *art* in the same sense as novels or fiction), being, again, a mostly lonely enterprise. *The Norton Book of Friendship* is prized on my shelf. When I enjoy paintings of lonely figures, such as Caspar David Friedrich's classic *Wanderer above the Sea of Fog*, I like to imagine myself just behind him, accompanying him on his journey. I engaged with that painting more significantly after first reading *Ecce Homo* by Friedrich Nietzsche, my 1985 Penguin Classics reprint of which featured the wanderer on the cover. Indeed, though I wouldn't recommend this to anyone new, it was the first work of Nietzsche I read as a young boy (I loosely recommend reading *The Gay Science* first and being of a more experienced age to appreciate him better, and avoid clichés or immature caricature). I read as if he were in direct conversation with me, lecturing as an older man, and with me surely missing all the nuance or subtext without good guidance. Through the solitary act of reading, I felt a type of communion, not of physical community, but of shared associations and tangents. I rarely get to speak about Nietzsche, or anyone I appreciate more (Montaigne, Aron, most recently Georg Christoph Lichtenberg, etc) in a way that isn't me self-interestedly monologuing. Art, or scholarship, is better in dialogue with friends.

I've written about friendship and its importance, how it is undervalued, and the difficulty of making new friends (physically, not through a digital facsimile of human interaction). Yet it doesn't matter how much I pontificate on the matter if I'm useless at doing anything practical. Some of this isn't my own fault. There are social forces that contribute to our poor ability to communicate, maintain, or start friendships, and these forces are somewhat beyond individual whims. Yet we still have some responsibility to be ethical humans and try to be good friends with one another. My own hankering, or aesthetic ideal, is a robust group of regularly seen friends, all with a type of creative brilliance that I can bask in. Besides sociology, it is my own biology, a substrate of discomfort, that prevents me from being sociable. For my whole life, I've felt I've had to pursue or chase any relationship, with little coming to me on my own, with poor results unless I put in some (rather emotionally arduous) work. This isn't an unusual or original thought. Maybe the price of admission for some to keep friends means putting in this effort, though it is still tiring. We may have 'low maintenance' friends who we barely talk to, but can easily rekindle conversation with after a long absence. Life is busy, and this dynamic has an implicit understanding. I love lots of people dearly, but I don't get to see them often at all. Yet we also need high-maintenance friends, people who call after us regularly, who check in most days, and the level of stamina these relationships require is not appreciated. We quickly spoil them. The best life is impossible without friendship (as I've already reiterated), and I'm heartened by lifelong friendships, or deeply envious of them.

All this said, I still hold a fundamental weariness, or tension. I want to be social and immerse myself in social situations, but my health often fails. I'm never at ease, which makes everyday interactions difficult. I become far too eager to pursue some form of reciprocity, and when effort isn't returned, I feel cast astray. I want to enjoy varied, deep friendships with a wide breadth of humanity; old, young, men and women, yet what we may call 'common dynamics' or popular notions about how people are (or what they are supposed to do) make this harder. We start believing in intentions that don't exist, or we lack confidence and become distant. The now-ubiquitous 'ghosting', as the youth call it, which hurts more because of the ease of communication, happens among lovers or friends, and we can't find a more honest approach, which might be culturally unavailable. If you try to break the taboo, you come across as either too earnest or leering.

We are ill at ease with this paradigm, as it were, and we recognise, at least in part, that this unfriendly behaviour is a vice. Yet the answer to the vice is just as terrible, as it requires a type of uncomfortable honesty or self-reflection. We cope neither with the discomfort of our afflictions nor with the task of curing ourselves, in other words. We are wretched, as La Rochefoucauld would say. Let's not be the sort of "nose-snuffling, cynical man", as Barbellion scolded, who takes too much pride in a kind of depraved knowledge, as if he has laid bare human nature and revealed all as selfish . . . That's too easy; we can be cynical about cynicism. Still, and yet, we see follies. We invite drama and slander; we wade willingly into a mess. I know few who have performed enough interrogation of either life or self who really take lessons to heart, who know when to be loud or quiet, to be moderate or immoderate when it best suits, who know how to respond always in the right tune or key. Anything I say sounds dissonant. Put me in any situation, and I'm half-dazed. Intelligence doesn't work; imagination is scarce. Centuries of art and literature, all studied in the finest detail, and the most banal acts of community, our constant subjects, are still insolubly awkward. So much is strange about how we spend our time. As we struggle to do anything, we take the path of least resistance, which means carrying on as we were, satisfying nobody. We can always say we are too busy and use that as an excuse to keep to ourselves. We may well be too busy, but it comes at a cost. We are all very busy working away and with less of a good life to show for it.

Most of us, if we interrogate our wants and desires, find ourselves in contradiction. Either side of our contrary desires is true, simultaneously, where we affirm and reject our inclinations or prejudices all in the same breath, or believe two things at once: entirely possible, not wrong or unnatural, yet still unsettling. I write again about friendship, and I concur again with La Rochefoucauld (who is becoming more and more of a touchstone of mine—I should be careful) that true friendship can be harder to find than true romance. Friendships are essential to a good life, I repeat *ad nauseam*. And yet there is still something I must admit to myself if I want to be honest. All the above is true, I value friendships in many cases more highly than romance or eroticism, while I am still a desperate, yearning and laughable romantic. I adore women, beauty, and all the superficial elements of female presentation as much as I do our richer, inner lives. Women captivate me. I imagine myself helplessly in their hands, fawning and slightly pathetic.

I don't put myself out there, in the worldly sense. I don't talk to strangers very often, and I certainly don't proposition anyone randomly, without a proper reason. My life is too alienating, or I am too self-defeating. Being ill prevents internal comfort and prevents me from accessing the type of effortless surrender, rather than foolish seduction, that I would prefer in any social engagement. Friends are difficult enough. The whole artifice, the imposed way we are determined to engage with each other as sexual beings, or lonely souls seeking common cause, is somehow daft, absurd, atrocious and frightening. And then there's the fact that I'm failing, as in my health is ever on a downward track. Trying to convince myself that I am a person worthy of romantic love feels silly when I can't do much, and my life is too precarious to live in a substantial union.

Anyone describing the usual romantic troubles common to so many of us finds themselves met with rote responses and dull clichés. All this has been said before; why repeat it? In some way, I blame other men for making love a more treacherous affair, being so hurtful and vulgar. I can't imagine myself as a woman wanting men to approach me, given what many men have to offer. Regardless, I can't be stuck with sociological explanations or personalities beyond my control. A crisis of men (and fake solutions to male ennui) isn't something to get into now.

I am still utterly useless at social intercourse, let alone any other. Trying to engage with life, talk with others, and form meaningful relationships means overcoming a range of technological and social obstacles I have little time or energy for. We have not just outside machinations but my dreadful id to deal with. If I begin to find a particular woman enthralling, I'm soon lost. My time is over-occupied by daydreaming (and this sounds like all the regular cant—all the regular, overplayed talk), and with little way to organically, without some degree of insufferable discomfort mediated by clunky, inadequate mediums, speak to anyone with clarity or finesse. I value clear, proper communication. I'm still bad at it. So much of what passes for communication now is a shortcut, or a type of electronic cheating that renders real speaking as something not at our disposal. If I try to say what I want more severely or in detail, I may be seen (justifiably) as some indulgent freak or a tactless buffoon.

This contemplation looks tangential and possibly irrelevant, yet it is a type of study of aesthetics where we might find a better answer, or better presentation, for all these difficulties that some book of rules or analytical disquisition is unable to provide; too sterile and robotic. In art, we can reach for an attentiveness, to try and grasp meanings and circumstances in a way that isn't always immediately understandable to us, much as a poet can express something unconscious and not just of their superficially intended purpose. I don't care for art or aesthetics as some successor to religion, but to attempt towards a type of wisdom, or perceptiveness, that isn't found elsewhere. Beauty isn't just about looks; it means a beautiful life. And a beautiful life is harder to come by without the wonders of art as well as the wonders of friendship, in tandem, where we can try to divine the world. I memorised a quote from Ford Madox Ford's *The Good Soldier* as soon as I had read it, and had the temerity to have it preface my memoir. "We are all so afraid, we are all so alone, we all so need from the outside the assurance of our own worthiness to exist."

All this internal conflict is a vice; the overcoming of which requires greater discomfort, or spirit, I fail to attain. Part of me then wishes to give up on love, or romantic feelings anyway. They cause so much grief in their failure to be satisfied that I can half-convince myself that stoic asexuality is possible. But then I'm only lying to myself, or acting ridiculous. I can't help yearning in the morose, one-sided, sickening way that I do.

I imagine a long life, family, a home, love, things I see among my peers that, while not easy, still appear as regular, ordinary, normal. I envy them.

None of my artistic friends here has wealthy *patronage*. Rich people used to be patrons of artisans and the arts. They would pay for bespoke tailors and fund opera houses and libraries. I don't wish to be romantic, but rich people no longer do this. Arts and craftsmanship are now preserved, barely, by a niche, depoliticised middle class with eccentric interests in artisanal goods: clothes, fragrances, architecture, or whatever else. Class, in the old definition, patrician elitism, is more obscure and deeply impoverished. Rich people now don't have 'class', or style. They don't rely on the best artisans to preserve their prestige or invoke status. They favour gaudy brands whose prestige is in the commercialism of their name, *fashion* in the worst sense, no longer talented or exceptional. For all that was wrong with 'old money', much of the arts relies on elite and moneyed sponsorship. And if the rich don't care for this, or don't know of it at all, then valuable craft and expertise dies—without sustenance.

The political right used to be home to elites, meaning cultural and intellectual, artistic elitism, or snobbery. At least the snobbery had talent behind it. Now, elites are rich but vulgar, dress poorly and have no taste for arts or culture. And they wear silly hats. Simulated poverty became an expression of *authenticity* that insults the poor, as if their aesthetics were appreciated by the wealthy but not enough to remunerate them financially, and gives the rich a reason not to invest in *high* art. Poverty is destructive, undignified and cruel, and it is better that we properly reduce both poverty and inequality. When the ultra-rich play as poor people in fancy dress, it gives credence to the idea that being *genuinely poor* is somehow authentically excellent and good. They romanticise poverty and, in so doing, make poverty, to some degree, not a concern to alleviate.

If one's primary goal is to make fatuous amounts of cash, then we won't make the best art. The best art, shown historically, requires spending an extravagant amount of money you won't get back—at least sometimes. The most extravagant art in history, in temples, churches and museums, didn't see a swift return on investment. You can make great art with little money, but I'm no rote leftist, and it is rash to say art doesn't need large pockets. Trade and business, the patronage of capital, gives us the opportunity for spectacular art that will live in posterity, yet this is only the case if we have other concerns besides efficient money for its own sake. Without religious, social, or cultural motivations, if money is primary rather than secondary, then art is depreciated. Old capitalists, even old feudalists and kings, gave us great art. Now they don't. Today, the world's richest are enthralled by finance for its own sake, or by power, but without regard for the public good. They are perverse, profoundly selfish, artless, neurotic technophiles. Past times were brutal and antihuman, yet they still provided us with elite patronage of the arts and well-funded craftspeople. They are brutal now, yet with fewer and fewer aesthetic justifications.

All of this meandering writing is an attempt to uncover a connection, or even create a new mythology for myself. We lost mythology, though I never really cared for it. The past was never so *unclouded*, and we have always had delusions. Today's superstitions are much like the past's, with whatever differences in artifice or detail, and new delusions are invented daily. The past appears irresistible but offers the same lamentations we have now, while we've developed a greater vocabulary for our complaints. It is probably better to realise that past figures felt a similar level of dire trepidation for the future as we do now, and I might (intellectually) lean that way. Yet, the speed of current developments gives anxiety a new sheen. Returning to a kindly pastoral past is something a few of us act out, in affected ways, with various self-flagellating restrictions on technology—a type of anti-science-fiction. Our technology, obliged rather than optional, speeds along at a rapid clip, offering uneasy dismay more than any real excitement; never mind pleasure. Addressing any of that at a societal level is beyond individual whims. Technology doesn't reverse itself. We can maybe react to it healthily, with the growth of local roots and community, and, with luck, avoid the tasteless flavours of nostalgia or desperate hankerings. The concept of renewed community or revitalised friendship risks becoming a therapeutic fetish, where, instead of *real community*, with all the honest ideals of support and social sustenance, our failure to mediate conversation correctly (despite the utility of modern communicative technology) means we fail to attain anything. Our ideas about love and friendship remain as images, empty simulacra or aloof possibilities, where the failure to organise anything properly results in indulgent dreams and resentment. Localism, if it is some *-ism*, can be reactionary or fascistic, closed to outside help, insular and rude. While we fear the impacts of ecological destruction or worldwide trends beyond our ken, and may want to retreat from the wider world to our local sphere, looking inward, to our nearest neighbours, it is of little use if this becomes a neurotic fantasy. Any idea can degenerate into terror. Yet I don't wish to be some *herald of catastrophe*, as much as I dislike claims of salvation. Hyperbolic exaggeration is a type of lie, and still a lie even if it leverages truths. As much as the world seems predictable, with all the data and balances on offer, history still offers us fewer settled convictions—*historical tendency* notwithstanding.

The truer, personal root of all this trouble is my own expectancy, not just wider expectations. I'm closer to death and clumsily reaching out to past acquaintances, finding any connection I can while anyone else is too busy or unaware of my indulgences. My fixation on art, or my attempts to appreciate it more than my cynicism allows, *material* and human in the basest ways, is a last-ditch effort to find meaning or solace when anything transcendental, metaphysical, or mythological seems unconvincing. I've previously called this a 'material sensualism of friendship'. I'm sure it would appear just as unconvincing to those who believe in elevated positions I reject, yet the alternatives of nihilism or cruel misanthropy are worse than unfulfilling. I oscillate too much between positions; our own descriptions and internal schemes can't show us some actual 'external world', 'in itself'—something that might approximate Nietzsche's position. Yet I can't accept deniers of truth, nor do I accept robust *platonisms*. This may be weak and spineless, as if I float between any allegiance and can't find any ground to land on. I'm seeking refuge, then—with people and moments outside all that philosophical mess. I have enough of a mind to ponder aimlessly, but not enough to find any solid foundations.

Envy doesn't mean I resent anyone's success. When I'm jealous of artists, painters, musicians, I wish I had their talent and possessed their energy for my own private world. I don't envy their success or their fame. I'm not bitter at anyone else's victory, I'm indulgently angry at my own lot. I love others' achievements. I've never been ambitious or wanted much in the way of material fortune, and only a very meagre or limited vanity. I would be doing much the same as I am now if I had any larger measure of prosperity or money, which is essentially retirement and rest. If one has enough money to buy an island, retire, and quietly sip margaritas for the rest of their life without intervening in the world, and instead uses vast resources to speculate, move and shake the world, then they're a wretch and a fool. I live like an elderly retiree, which I accept as fine compensation given my slim chance of ageing. I envy talent as I wish I could create more within my narrow frame and with my inadequate time. I dislike admitting it, but I'm not just upset at the world. I feel a type of poisonous anger that is more like grief, that *reduces all to indecision*. Why am I so pathetically desperate to cultivate friends? Why am I so difficult? I cry about it. For as long as I can remember, I've been haunted by illness and rendered perpetually tense. I sense a terror that reduces me to raging confusion and worry, that I keep quiet for my own sake as much as for not upsetting others. It can sour a conversation and eventually become boring. Whimsy or humour is better. I react violently to good stories about overcoming ill health because they look insulting, as they won't apply to me. I envy others who get the chance and the reprieve. I envy joy, love, and happiness. Not that these are alien to me, but I rudely consider myself deprived of them, as if some cruel god decided I've had enough and can make do with loneliness and a spluttering death in some uninviting hospital. They don't bother with paintings like they used to in the new hospital. The old one still held on to sentimental notions and quaint artifice, but they make cleaning harder, and only a few mawkish bores would care anyway . . . A hospital should be less fearful, and they haven't cracked that yet.

One envies other lives for the subterranean reason that makes all life so difficult: death. Other lives embody the lost chance to live a different life, discover talents, to find romance, friendship, family, creativity, and sometimes the best life on offer is vicarious, by proxy, and unavailable to you. To occupy my own time, I write, more as a type of narcissistic self-interrogation, and I would want to write even if I were not ill. Regrettably, the impetus to write, for me, comes predominantly from being ill and as such writing *in extremis*, which I don't recommend to others as some sort of artistic sustenance. Better art and more time for art are more readily available if one is healthy. I don't often envy the psychology, or ethics, or attitudes of healthy people. I envy their endurance, their ability, their good luck, and their time to cultivate art and beauty. They get to live at a different tempo. Yet I also envy artists who are in similar situations. They have spent their time better, so I grow jealous. Accepting death is a dance. We have not just a personal reckoning but a general, universal one. Immortality would be terrible and morally averse, yet a longer age means more space to grow. Illness is a vital part of life, just as crucial for the well as for the ill: it will affect them whether they're aware of it or not. The best art, I think, is made with some tension and is intimately aware of fragility. It is still better to have enough free space and good health; to not be so constrained. At some point, it is better to come to terms with the thought that it would now be acceptable, or not so terrible, to die. This is better than the alternative refusal or negation. And we can make a banal point: we would not make great art, make any meaningful mark on the world, live wholly, love, notice beauty and tenderness, if we were not fully human and therefore limited beings who all eventually die. At some point, even, we are lucky to have the opportunity to die; and as much as we hardly accept it, we are better for it.

On illness, I write too much "on the impulse of the moment . . . like pouring water from a bucket", if we misappropriate Goethe's observation. It is organic and reflexive. I prefer to end any writing on a warm note, even if my primary mood is sombre. So, I'm grateful to have known everyone here. They make life welcoming and more hospitable. Art suffices for life. Sometimes it is enough, whether life is beyond its reach or not, to make fear less imposing.

Cevin Soling

Apocalypse How?

A Reassessment of Adam Parfrey's Apocalypse Culture Books

History is littered with apocalyptic predictions. Even today, public squares often include the followers of millenarian faiths incessantly chanting, "Repent! The end is nigh!" Many predictions of doom are dismissed as crackpot when they are made, such as the dubious 2012 Mayan calendar prophecy that the world would end upon the conclusion of the 13th b'ak'tun. On the other end of the spectrum, the Y2K global devastation due to a computer bug failed to materialize despite a significant media buy-in. However, many notable people have provided specific dates for Armageddon, including at least two popes, Martin Luther, Christopher Columbus, Cotton Mather, Emanuel Swedenborg, the Shakers, the Jehovah's Witnesses, psychic Jeane Dixon, Jim Jones, Pat Robertson, Nostradamus, Jerry Falwell, Sun Myung Moon, Grigori Rasputin, and even Isaac Newton.

While we can look back and laugh at these predictions, doomsayers are not always wrong. According to Homer, the Trojan priest, Laocoön, correctly predicted the fall of Troy. It is also reasonable to assume that someone in Pompeii, Krakatoa, and other annihilated locales must have insisted that their days were numbered shortly before the devastation. The problem with human extinction is that you cannot interview prophets when no one is left behind to say, "I told you so."

Writer and editor Adam Parfrey proffered a novel approach to prognostication. Rather than announce the coming of the end of days, he accumulated a collection of profoundly disturbing offerings created by psychopaths, schizophrenics, and paranoid malcontents in his two-book *Apocalypse Culture* series. Parfrey also included essays that he and others drafted on individuals displaying preternatural behavior. In a brief preface, Parfrey contends that the apocalypse will arrive soon in the form of an ecological catastrophe. Much like the unusual behavior exhibited by rats, weasels, snakes, and centipedes days before a catastrophic earthquake, Parfrey claims the depravity documented in his books represents the kind of aberrant behavior one should expect shortly before the world comes to an end.

Apocalypse Culture first appeared in bookstores in 1987, and *Apocalypse Culture II* was released in 2000. Reviews of older texts such as these are typically occasioned by a milestone such as an anniversary, the death of an author, or the publication of a new work that calls for a retrospective. In this instance, the review is prompted by something much more meaningful—the fulfillment of a prophecy. The prophecy of *Apocalypse Culture* was indeed prescient in that the apocalypse did arrive, but as is typical of the art of divination, not in the form presumed. The world persists, but a culture capable of producing meaning has died.

The *Apocalypse Culture* books include the worst kinds of deviant ideas and behaviors. Participants in serial murder, pedophilia, and depraved brutality are given authentic, often first-person voices, replete with disturbing pictures. It is not for the faint of heart. This includes me: I have no problem skipping violent passages. I do not need to read the advocacy of castration by someone who engaged in self-mutilation, where Parfrey was kind enough to provide images. I do not need to see the photos of Fakir Musafar's masochistic and grotesque impalements, nor do I need to read Issei Sagawa's sexual fetishizing of a young woman he murdered and cannibalized or to read the self-congratulatory monologues from actual psychopathic serial killers. But I can appreciate its function, nevertheless.

The works effectively remind us that humans are a violent species in a way that the crime section of newspapers falls short because, thankfully, the media, for all its failings, typically does not indulge in presenting the self-righteous justifications of perpetrators. Parfrey claims, "Murder is the primary engine of our culture, the spark plug of the entertainment industry dressed up with pretensions to a moral high road: newspapers, magazines, novels, true crime books, music movies. Murder is the fuel guzzled by the large bureaucratic labyrinth behind judicial, police, and prison industries and its secular limbs—law, firearms, all of them." It is easy to forget that it is a recent development for many of us in the First World to be largely shielded from these horrors. A talk I attended by a funeral home worker whose job was to retrieve corpses reminded the audience of just how rare it has become for many people to see a dead body. From a historical vantage, this is anomalous. Death is everywhere.

Some of the pieces in *Apocalypse Culture* are the stuff of nightmares, and a random search through pages will lead to a gruesome image of a desecrated murder victim or a scene of mangled flesh much more often than chance should allow. One reviewer on Amazon wrote, "It takes a lot to shake me, but I felt dirty after reading it." I get it. Even though many of the books' images are often crappy degraded photocopies, they are still sufficiently repulsive.

Explicit violence comprises only a fraction of the material but intimated violence permeates much of the remaining subjects, which include eugenics, conspiracy theories, deviant sexual practices, and apocalyptic visions. Parfrey warns in the preface to Volume II, "Paying no attention to the material presented here does not eradicate its existence." Chapters are short, and other than the gore, many are entertaining, thought-provoking, and informative.

I encountered *Apocalypse Culture* shortly after its release and assumed it was a compilation of salacious materials presented for miscreant and prurient interest shielded by a specious claim that the offerings were, in fact, representations of apocalyptic times to provide a flimsy philosophical justification for its existence. That hypothesis cannot be discarded entirely, but even if one disputes Parfrey's earnestness, the content would still demand some form of reckoning.

Although Adam Parfrey views himself as a kind of anthropologist and thus separates himself from his subjects, he nevertheless falls within the camp of augurs predicting the end of the world. In a 2002 interview with critic Mark Prindle, he claimed, "The planet is overpopulated, and with that overpopulation comes the ruin of the planet. The melting of glaciers, the overproduction of radioactive and other toxins. Overfishing. The ruination of species diversity. Deforestation. The prospect is not a good one, not one that makes me want to add to the problem by reproducing . . . In the not too distant future, I see a fight between people in vastly overpopulated areas for water and food."

Despite this, much of the writings can and should be dismissed as evidence of mental illness, as opposed to a new phenomenon that can be used as evidence of a coming catastrophe. Since the dawn of mankind, humans have had to address how to deal not just with people who are irreparably sick but also depraved. What encroaching ecological decimation would account for Leilah Wendell, who writer Chad Hensley reports "doesn't make love with just any old bag of bones; the rotted cadavers she fondles become possessed by the Angel of Death. The desiccated body comes to life in Wendell's embrace, reanimated by the spirit of this supernatural being."?! Mental illness would seem a more likely culprit at first blush.

As is the spirit of the *Apocalypse Culture* books, everything must be one step beyond. Wendell is not just a practicing necrophile; the act for her is spiritually transcendent. In other chapters, that kind of ecstatic enlightenment also permeates the self-justification for murder. Some of these psychopaths are literate and capable of describing and even defending their actions without any moral burden, but that should not lead one to conclude that their behavior is a symptom of a broader condition unless these perverse spectacles are contagions—and they might be.

Beyond the repulsive carnage, the bulk of the books are comprised of thought-provoking pieces, many of which come from dark places. The most enjoyable are the essays that are commonly written off as conspiracy theories. For example, Ron Steele, who is described as an "investigative reporter and prophetic author," notes, "In Michael Jackson's song, 'We are the World,' there are things which are very sinister. He said that God has shown us how to cast stones into bread. Well he [God] *never* said that. That was Satan's first temptation to Jesus when Jesus was out in the desert for forty days, fasting. The deception is there, and you really have to look hard to see it."

It is easy to write off something like that at first glance as a blunder, except Michael Jackson was an exceptionally devout Jehovah's Witness, so it seems highly unlikely that that was a mistake. Given that the song was a global phenomenon, the assertion was sufficiently troubling that I had to check the lyrics, but there it was. If the confusion was deliberate, it is hard to ascertain the intent, which is precisely what makes this kind of thing fun to read and contemplate.

Similarly, Michelle Handleman and Monte Cazazza's "The Cereal Box Conspiracy Against the Developing Mind" asserts that the marketing of sugary breakfast cereals is part of a plot to indoctrinate children into a life of consumerism. "Advertising intervenes between people and their needs, separates them from direct fulfillment, and urges its victims to believe that satisfaction can only be obtained through the symbolic magic or grace of its commodity." Hard to argue with that, but the passage goes many steps further to someplace off the map.

They begin with the thesis: "Cereal boxes are designed to hold young ones in thrall as they progress through the normal transitory stages of orality and anality." Um, OK. Their analysis of the Cocoa Pebbles artwork leads them to conclude, "The first perversion comes with the concept of Barney and Fred engaging in a ménage à trois in oral consumption of Pebbles (the name of Fred's daughter)." If that was not insanely disturbing enough, they add, "The clincher is the giant cereal bowl before them with a hole bored out in the center with the aid of Barney's 'drill.' From the sphincterish hole, large brown blobs are shitted out." There is quite a bit of imaginative reading in here, although I did track down the cereal box in question, and I concede the uncanny resemblance to excrement coming out of an anus. However, it would seem to me that would inspire children (and adults) to avoid the cereal unless they are marketing to kids with coprophagia.

The books are at their best when they engage in fresh ideas even if they reek of paranoia—or perhaps especially so because that imbues the writing with a frantic sense of urgency. Paranoia is about drawing connections between seemingly disparate phenomena. Sometimes, the associations are tenuous, and the conclusions are absurd, but other times, the revelations are novel, exciting, and sublime.

Author Jonathan Vankin observed, "In 1998, every major news organization devoted millions of dollars and most of its time to cover the Clinton-Lewinsky dalliance . . . At the same time, Exxon and Mobil, two of the world's largest oil companies, were in the process of merging. Their union created the world's largest corporation whose product affects every aspect of life in modern society." Lest one thinks this is an aberration due to public infatuation with salacious stories, Vankin notes, "The media has generally applauded corporate mergers—the bigger, the better. And no merger is more laudable to the media than a merger of media companies." Even for those of us who rail against major media, it is hard not to feel sickened by the implications of the degree to which we are manipulated by the forces that subjugate us.

One must keep in mind that this kind of content was not broadly available to the public when the first volume was pressed. At least one notable influence was the punk rock fanzine *Search & Destroy*, which had already morphed into RE/Search Publications. While there is some overlap between the two—artist/musician Boyd Rice and performance artist Fakir Musafar make appearances in both, RE/Search was more about counterculture than deviant culture. Tattoos and piercings are relatively tame compared with *Apocalypse Culture II's* glossy full-color depictions of a naked Shirley Temple smiling and standing in front of a giant swastika while masturbating with a riding-whip and a Blalla W. Hallmann's painting of Hitler standing on corpses peeing on little girls. Again, not for the faint of heart.

When *Apocalypse Culture* arrived on that scene, reviewers ignored the book for six months until substantial sales for a counter-culture product—55,000 copies—prompted editors to relent. The book was surprisingly well-received. *Readercon* awarded Apocalypse Culture Best Nonfiction Work of the Year. Novelist J.G. Ballard declared, "Apocalypse Culture is compulsory reading for all those concerned with the crisis of our times.

An extraordinary collection unlike anything I have ever encountered. These are the terminal documents of the twentieth century," and Edwin Pouncey of NME wrote, "Parfrey has edited a new book of Revelation, a collection which is almost as awesome and terrifying as the original biblical text."

In 2000, Volume II was released. The sequel is more of the same, but it is also a vastly superior collection with a greater diversity of content and higher-quality images. There is no shortage of body mutilation and gore, but where the first volume focused more on abnormal psychology, this second volume leans slightly more toward conspiracy politics. Even with the internet flourishing at that time, the content was still disturbing, although the shock value had diminished.

As the title suggests, the apocalyptic nature of these books is explicitly advertised as the unifying theme. The contents are intended to be glimpses of the apocalypse that arises due to overpopulation, the destruction of the environment, and the burgeoning battle over scarce resources. For what it is worth, the scientific community largely rejects Parfrey's Malthusian scenario of exponential population growth and limited food. This does not obviate environmental disasters such as climate change. In either scenario, the apocalypse that Parfrey envisioned has not yet arrived. However, Armageddon can emerge in another form—and, in fact, has.

Parfrey's cast of characters is indicative of a different kind of pathology. The books testify not just to the proliferation of the rejection of all social norms and the dark forces that seek to undermine societal cohesion but also to the ubiquitous emergence of unbridled narcissism. This is the expression that I contend reveals there is another kind of apocalypse upon us—that of culture. As social critic Neil Postman said, the death of a culture arrives when it becomes "trivial." Despite desperately fearing the arrival of such a state, Postman curiously only intimates the nature of cultural triviality in a subordinate clause in his seminal text on the pathology of triviality, *Amusing Ourselves to Death*. This he does by proffering a comparison with the trivial society depicted in Huxley's *Brave New World*, which is "preoccupied with some equivalent of the feelies, the orgy porgy, and the centrifugal bumblepuppy." To translate, a trivial culture has no redemptive qualities. It is driven by an endless, insatiable desire for entertaining distractions and has no capacity to manufacture meaning. Parfrey's catastrophic prospect of environmental doom becomes irrelevant in the face of cultural triviality.

By way of example, consider the surgeon tasked with scooping out the larvae from Sylvia Plath's cheek when she was hospitalized after her unsuccessful suicide attempt. The fate of these maggots is never something anyone considers. Their existence is trivial at best—parasitic at worst. But what if those maggots produced breathtaking art and experienced profound love that inspired them to work toward attaining goodness in their interrelations? Their extermination would then be tragic. From a planetary perspective, humans are parasitic creatures, but we have the potential for redemptive qualities.

The cultural apocalypse is the eradication of any possibility for redemption. This does not apply to the entirety of humanity, just to the specific cultures fixated on indulging narcissistic impulses. In this regard, Parfrey documents extreme forms of self-indulgence. He recognizes this feature and notes, "The reader will soon begin to notice a preponderance of material from individuals who have the audacity to consider themselves their own best authority, in repudiation or ignorance of the orthodoxy factories of Church, University, or State. The constructions of these folk researchers may often seem wildly amiss, laughable, disreputable, but are more revealing cultural barometers than the acculturated pabulum of compromised and corrupt professionals." This assessment is particularly astute because Parfrey recognizes that narcissism emerges as a self-defense mechanism in response to the absence of legitimate moral and expert authority. He goes awry by concluding that the cause is external physical factors involving the depletion of natural resources as opposed to a perverse cultural trajectory fueled by technology's capacity to feed people's desires more efficiently.

Parfrey's selections are cherry-picked and anecdotal, but they can nevertheless be used effectively to show that the institutions that are supposed to be the guardians of culture have failed. For example, he includes John Hinckley's letters to Jodie Foster while the two were students in college, which were used as evidence in his trial when he attempted to kill Ronald Reagan. Hinckley wrote, "Dear Jodie, Did you see that scumbag on the t.v. last night? He thinks he's so smart and safe behind all those bodyguards, but I've found a crack in his armor and the crack is big enough for me to slip through to fame." Hinckley's poems were also included: "My fist keeps you down / Knuckles cross over yr eyes / You feel it? me I tear skirt / falls—thighs paste across / the dash—My fist / See!"

My first reading prompted me to ask, "This guy got into Yale?" Upon reflection, my response is, "This guy got into Yale." The elite institutions are so debased that, of course, a marginally literate deranged predator would be enrolled. This is the same university where riots erupted because a professor assumed the students were mature enough to choose their own Halloween costumes. This is precisely the distinction between individual psychopathy and social degeneration. While Parfrey fixates on the former, I contend the latter should instead be viewed as evidence of the apocalypse. The cherished institutions no longer exist to elevate. They have been commodified and exist to validate and comfort the psyches of those who enroll.

Like a sorites paradox, there was no specific moment when the apocalypse arrived; instead, it has been brewing since the advent of postmodernism. Jean-François Lyotard, who coined the term in 1979 but was not published in English until 1984, described the philosophy as "incredulity towards metanarratives." In practice, this amounts to an assault on objective truth. Things have only gotten worse since then as the pathology of postmodernism has taken hold. According to Nietzsche, the death of God meant that in the absence of an objective authority, all things are permitted. However, secular humanism stepped in and provided a rational basis for morality to persist. Postmodernism obliterated all of that by rejecting reason.

Concurrent with Lyotard was the birth of demographic marketing in the early 1980s. This meant consumers could be segregated so that they would only be exposed to the things that interested them. The result has been a narcissistic feedback loop where consumers can select their sensory input and the information they receive. Not only did this result in news outlets becoming explicitly biased in response to their audience predispositions but educational institutions were also debased with the traditional canon of literary giants being erased. With no universal cultural referents other than advertising slogans, tribalism was the inevitable consequence. Truth has become "my truth." Empirical evidence had been replaced by "lived experience." Academic research is no longer about knowledge but has been replaced by activism. Clearly, something is amiss when peer-reviewed journals accept hoaxes that fit their political agenda, including one submission that plagiarized *Mein Kampf*.

The internet has been a boon for the cultural apocalypse. It removed the gatekeepers who suppressed from public discourse the voices of those who are devoid of introspection and seethe with rage at anything that challenges their ego or fails to produce immediate gratification. Its collective capacity has also been complicit in making vile bigotry a social norm under the guise of social justice movements that provide absolution through the pseudoscience of intersectionality. These factors fuel the ego, reject universal morality and any consensus of objective truth, and negate any notion of meaning. As Michel Foucault, one of the architects of the apocalypse, noted, all that remains is power.

Parfrey observed, "I keep thinking you can get to the bottom of human behavior, that it can never get any more sordid or pathetic, but I'm always wrong." Similarly, the depths of stupidity promulgated by academic institutions know no bounds as Harvard proudly celebrates Ph.D. student Kareem Carr's conclusion that 2+2=5 on its Department of Biostatistics web page. Given the centrality of this objectively wrong assertion in George Orwell's *1984* as evidence of the capacity of totalitarian systems to propagate blatant falsehoods and successfully demand their acceptance by an oppressed population, one can only guess what the department heads were thinking. But unlike inspecting cereal boxes for subliminal artwork, there is no fun in this process. Parfrey looks to individuals for expressions of depravity, but the real horror comes from the excrement spewed by esteemed institutions.

Postmodernism has populist buy-in because it insists on the validity of everyone's uninformed and uneducated opinions. This mentality is devastating when evaluating art and affirms the final death knell of culture. In the absence of objective standards for art, no philosophy can come to the rescue and restore meaning to existence. The works of Shakespeare cannot be better than the output of Danielle Steel in a world where there is no objective better. There is nothing to aspire to in our narcissistic bubble except appealing to the moving target of fickle tastes. Every incoherent utterance is equal in merit to creations by the most skilled artisan. You like what you like, and whatever you like is good because you like it. This deranged perspective should be positioned next to Apocalypse Culture's child molesters and Aryan Nation apologists, but instead, it is mainstream, endorsed by the plebians and the elite.

Parfrey's index of pathology does include an essay that calls for rejecting art, which is an egalitarian inversion. Instead of every artistic expression being potentially worthwhile, none are. John Zerzan's "The Case Against Art" echoes Plato's assertion that art, as a representation, distances people even further from the ideal forms. "The primary function of art is to objectify feeling, by which one's own motivations and identity are transformed into symbol and metaphor. All art, as symbolization, is rooted in the creation of substitutes, surrogates for something else; by its very nature, therefore, it is a falsification," writes Zerzan. The premise of this essay, however, is fraudulent. The function of art is to enhance communication for the purpose of bringing people together.

Zerzan's essay can nevertheless serve as a reaction to the new zeitgeist. Art in the apocalypse has been commodified and negated. A duct-taped banana is called art, and more aptly, for this moment in history, quite literally nothing—advertised as an invisible sculpture, is art. The items were marketed and sold for large sums under the pretense that they are art, but art cannot be created when all output is deemed a matter of subjective taste. We cannot express a love of goodness because there is no objective goodness.

Critic Adam Groves noted on the 25th anniversary of the original publication of *Apocalypse Culture*, "The whole thing is now quite dated, due mostly to the rise of the internet; I doubt even Adam Parfrey could have foreseen how the cyber-verse would so completely usurp his book by providing freaks and weirdoes of all stripes with an infinitely more expansive forum." Ultimately, Parfrey's text is important because while it still possesses some shocking elements, it is rapidly becoming quaint. Whenever the environment can no longer sustain human life, tragedy will have been successfully averted because culture is already dead.

Kurt Luchs

Listening to the Grass and to Charles Simic

We often hear someone described as "a citizen of the world," a silly, empty phrase that usually seems to refer to a person who can afford to jet all over the place without any particular purpose. But in the case of Charles Simic it is the literal truth. Born in Belgrade, Yugoslavia in 1938, he and his Serbian family were among the millions displaced by World War II. They suffered hunger, physical danger, oppression, and the no less severe psychic oppression of being without a real home for years on end. This traumatic formative experience must surely be at the heart of the sense of strangeness and permanent dislocation so central to his poetry.

By 1954 their situation had become dire enough that they immigrated to the United States when Charles was sixteen (his father had come over first, followed by Charles, his mother and his brother). After a year in New York City they relocated to Oak Park, Illinois. He finished high school there and several years later was drafted into the U.S. Army, ironically becoming one of the soldiers who had made his early life so miserable and unsettled. Afterwards he was drawn back to New York and graduated from NYU in 1966.

He had already been writing poems for years, quite excellent poems that were not in the least tentative or immature. He had been forced to grow up quickly, almost at gunpoint. Perhaps because of this he appeared to arrive on the American literary scene fully formed. You could say that his further development as a poet did not involve any significant changes in outlook or approach, only a never-ending quest for greater concision and evocativeness. Has any other writer done so well with English as a second language except for Vladimir Nabokov? I don't think so.

Although Simic's first full-length collection *Dismantling the Silence* would not arrive until 1971, he had already published two chapbooks with *Kayak*, at the time one of the half-dozen most important literary magazines and small presses in the country. His first chapbook, *What the Grass Says* (1967), is as good as anything he ever wrote. With another writer this might be a way of saying that his later work failed to live up to the early promise. With Simic it is simply an acknowledgment of how great he was right from the beginning. According to AbeBooks, a copy of this rare treasure will cost you anywhere from $75 to $505, and let me tell you, it's worth every penny.

The title of *What the Grass Says* comes from a line in the poem we'll be looking at here, called "Evening." This free verse poem is outwardly simple and direct, like most Simic poems. In this original form it consists of three stanzas, the first containing four lines, the second containing seven lines, and the third containing five lines. Later, as we shall see, he cut the last line before including the poem in *Dismantling the Silence*. Here's the first stanza:

> The snail gives off stillness.
> The weed is blessed.
> At the end of a long day
> The man finds joy, the water peace.

There's a lot to unpack here, even at this early stage. The first two sentences are so short that, at two lines, the third sentence almost feels like an epic. It would be easy to say, wait a minute, Mr. Poet, and start questioning things. Isn't the snail always giving off stillness? In what sense can a weed be described as "blessed"? To do so, however, would be unseemly and also beside the point. He's clearly setting the scene here and establishing the mood.

Yes, the snail is always giving off stillness. The little hermaphrodites can sleep for up to three days. But maybe the poet didn't notice the stillness until evening came. The weed could be called blessed in several ways. First of all, for surviving another day without being mowed down (could this also be one reason the man "finds joy"?). And secondly, for merely being part of the idyllic tableau despite its lowly status as an unwanted plant (again, I feel there is an intentional if unstated parallel to the human). Joy can be found in many ways. There is the honest joy of work completed, implied by the "long day." And also the joy of setting aside mundane concerns to enter into the spirit of a special moment at day's end, like the water that has found "peace," presumably because the wind has died down and it is no longer rippling.

The second stanza starts by seeming to reinforce the quiet pastoral feelings of the first stanza. It calls for everything to be "simple" and "still." But then it also calls for everything to be "Without a final direction." Why the sudden note of uncertainty? Well, things are about to get darker rather quickly:

That which brings you into the world
To take you away at death
Is one and the same;
The shadow long and pointy
Is its church.

What else does evening bring besides stillness and peace? Lengthening shadows. And these inevitably turn the mind toward the great mysteries of life and death and whether there is anyone or anything behind it all. In other words, the meaning of it all. Only the poem is much more nimble than my prose. It doesn't present the shadow as an overt symbol of anything but rather as a thing-in-itself that happens to embody these resonances. Because that's what humans are, that's what we do. We aren't snails or weeds or even water (at least, not more than sixty percent).

The third and final stanza offers yet another turn that, to my mind, synthesizes the feelings of the first two stanzas. It integrates the quiet stillness with the shadow:

At night some understand what the grass says.
The grass knows a word or two.
It is not much. It repeats the same word
Again and again, but not too loudly . . .
The grass is certain of tomorrow.

The idea that nature continually speaks to us is something that science, indigenous cultures and ancient wisdom have in common, though from very different viewpoints. The image of the grass having a simple call, like a bird, is straightforward, charming and distinctly inventive. Which is to say, typical Simic.

It does raise a question, however. In the first stanza the overall stillness and the peace that the water finds suggest that the wind is not blowing. The breeze, if there was any during the day, has subsided. So, is what the grass says a sound, like the sound the wind makes blowing through a field? Or is it another silence? It could be either. Or both. Sometimes the wind picks up again in the evening as a result of the temperature change. Sorry, I'm not purposefully trying to be too literal here. That's not the best way to approach any poetry, especially Simic's. I simply wish to understand how he created this wonderful poem and how it works its magic on us. Contemplating this poem makes me think of that marvelous Robert Frost couplet, "The Secret Sits": "We dance round in a ring and suppose, / But the Secret sits in the middle and knows."

I'm all right with letting questions remain questions and ambiguities remain ambiguities. One thing I do know is that the original last line is a clunker, an awkward bit of tacked-on anthropomorphism that adds nothing and subtracts a good deal of the mystery. I can hardly believe the line made it into the chapbook that took its title from the poem. Simic was dead right to cut the line when the poem was reprinted in *Dismantling the Silence*.

The business of revising one's work after it has already been published in a book can nonetheless be tricky, as another example from Simic shows. I'm talking about the title poem from Dismantling the Silence, which first appeared in his second *Kayak* chapbook *Somewhere Among Us a Stone Is Taking Notes* (1969). When he put it into his first full-length collection it was unchanged. By the time of *Selected Early Poems* (1999) he had lost faith in the ending and tried to fix it. As of course it was absolutely his right to do. Yet in my humble opinion he mucked it up horribly. Thanks to the internet and Kindle and used bookstores we will always have the first version to look at so we can make up our minds. At the end of a long day, that is what brings this man joy.

Kurt Luchs

Mr. Monotonous

He only has two songs, the black-capped chickadee,
more than, say, Debby Boone or Vanilla Ice,
but still, not much of a musical storehouse.

He takes his name from the five-note cry
chick-a-dee-dee-dee
which makes him sound
like a tiny high-pitched flying Sinatra
in a Beatnik beret.

This time of year, though, they're nesting
and all he seems to have in him
is the little two-note tune
fee-bee
the first note up, the second one down,
over and over,
and that's when I call him Mr. Monotonous.

All right, we get it, you have eggs,
you don't want them to be stolen,
and you're proud you can still
get the missus with child.
Get over yourself, go eat a seed
or an insect and try to have a vocabulary
larger than that of a Chicago alderman.

I hate to tell you, Mr. Monotonous,
but the mourning dove has a song
every bit as limited as yours
only much more beautiful.

She is singing now too
and it's the strangest thing,
something no one intended
and I know you have nothing to do
with each other, yet somehow
you sound so much better together.

Thomas Walton

Unsavory Thoughts

A Brief Note on the Human Species

By the time we reach a certain age, we start to notice patterns in life. We start to recognize things as things that we've seen before. When this happens, it allows us to have a more measured response to things. A less emotional response, or, at the very least, a response that is not only emotional. However, by the time we reach this point in our lives, we're usually old. We're old and it's time for us to check out. It's time for us to die.

This seems almost by design. Not "Intelligent Design," but a design of the species to help us survive. It's possible that we have to remain in the dark, ignorant, we have to stay dumb long enough to regenerate the species. If we become too intelligent, too reasonable, we would ask ourselves, "what really is the point of going on?"

She Goes to Estate Sales

We were at the bar. In her kitchen. The counter that we call the bar. We were drinking coffee. Outside the rain was swirling in a light, mist-like drizz. I guess it was January.

"Ellen's coming over for dinner tomorrow night?" Liz said.

"Oh," I said.

"Why 'oh'?"

"I don't know," I said. "She's just not my favorite person, I guess."

"She's nice," Liz said, "and I don't see her very much since she moved out of the neighborhood."

"I know," I said. "It's nice since she moved."

"That's not fair. There's nothing wrong with her."

"I know," I said. "You're right. I can't place it. She is nice, and there's nothing necessarily wrong with her, but still . . . something about the way she's . . . I don't know, I can't explain it. There's just . . . you know."

"She stays too long, I'll give you that. But even so, I think she means well."

"She definitely stays too long. She never leaves. You practically have to kick her out."

"She's a good listener," Liz said.

"She's not very interesting."

"And you are?"

"You know what I mean . . . she's too sincere or something. I can't figure it out. The conversation is always so serious with her. So solemn. Remember the time she kept talking about her dog?"

"Yes . . ."

"It was your birthday, for gods sakes."

"That was too bad," Liz said.

"And it just had the dog flu or something like that."

"The dog flu?"

"Isn't that what you said?"

"I said it had distemper."

"Okay, distemper."

"That's what Ellen told me. She said distemper."

"Anyway, the point is, the dog was just sick and she ruined your birthday because she was so upset because she thought it was dying."

"It's true," Liz sighed.

"No offense to the dog, but . . . she shouldn't have come."

"No, probably not."

"She's too heavy for me. She has no sense of irony. Or sarcasm. Or something. I don't know what it is, but she's boring."

"That's not fair."

"Yes it is. She almost seems proud of it. She's pretentiously boring."

"Stop."

"Ostentatiously boring. She's extravagantly boring."

"Okay, that's enough," Liz said.

"I'm sorry but there's something egomaniacal about how there's always some terrible drama she's upset about. Some terrible melodrama. Shitty things happen to all of us. You don't have to go talking about it at dinner parties."

"I know, but I invited her, so . . ."

"What is that called? Munchausen Syndrome?"

"I think so. I don't know if it's full-on Munchausen but it's something . . . Anyway it doesn't matter. She's coming to dinner tomorrow night, so . . ."

"I wish she wasn't," I said.

"Well she is. I invited her. I ran into her at the park and we don't see her much anymore."

"I realize that. I like that we don't see her much anymore."

"Don't be mean."
"Well . . ."
"Also, she said that she and Scott are having problems . . ."
"Oh, great."
"Stop," Liz said.
"Fun! I'm really looking forward to hearing about her relationship issues with Scott. What an exciting Saturday night!"
"It'll be fine. She's nice."
"I know she's nice, but . . . Can we at least make negronis?"
"She said she's not drinking for a while. That whole Dryuary thing."
"Oh god."
"I know."
"Why is everything so trendy now? Were things always this trendy?"
"Probably . . . But who cares, *you* can have a negroni."
"You're not going to have one?"
"I don't know. I might. It depends on how upset she is about Scott."
"Wow . . . this is gonna be a great night . . ." I took a sip of the coffee, which was no longer hot. "Maybe we should invite Nacho and Tanya," I said.
"I don't think so. They'd just steal the show. Ellen wouldn't get a word in."
"All the more reason."
"That's not fair. Ellen is a good person."
"I know . . . I'm sorry. I'm sure she is."
"Why are you so annoyed with her?"
"I don't know. I can't figure it out."
"She's a good listener."
"Uh huh."
"And she has a good heart."
"Okay . . . whatever that means."
"It means that there's nothing wrong with her. She's my friend."
"I know, I'm sorry. It's just that it's Saturday night and . . . well, I mean it's Ellen. If it was anyone but Ellen it would be fine."
"What if it was Sarah?"
"Which Sarah?"
"Sarah Lozenge."
"You're right, that would be worse, but at least she drinks."
"I'll make Bolognese . . ."
"Oh wow, you're bribing me now."
". . . and garlic bread and a Caesar."
"Fine."
"Great. It'll be fun."
"I doubt that, but at least the food will be good. And I'm making negronis."
"Sure . . . It shouldn't be a big deal."
"I know, I'm sorry. I don't even know what it is about her."
Liz took a sip of her coffee. "And just so you know ahead of time, she said her dog passed away."
"Oh god!"
"I know, it's sad."
"Sad? It's terrible. She's gonna talk about her fucking dog all night. Unless she's talking about her problems with Scott, or how great she feels now that she's sober . . ."
"That's not fair."
"I'm really looking forward to it." I grabbed the pot of coffee off the stove and poured some into both our cups.
"You know, she goes to estate sales."
"What do you mean?"
"She goes to estate sales. I think that's what it is."
"What what is?"
"Why you don't like her. Why there's something weird about her. She goes to estate sales."
"Wait, what? You think I don't like her because she goes to estate sales? I didn't even know she goes to estate sales."
"Well, she does."
"Okay?"
"You know those people who are always going to estate sales even though they don't need anything . . ."
"Okay? So she goes to estate sales. So what?"
"So what? Well, I think she goes early, too. Like first thing in the morning."
"Uh huh?" I said.
"Like she waits in line for the sale to open."
"Okay?"
"Yeah. She's like, a regular estate sale goer . . ."
"A regular estate sale goer . . . is that a thing?"
"Definitely. It's a *whole* thing. An *entire* thing. It's like a cult or something. But I don't think anybody talks to anybody else. There's no god, of course. People just wander around in other people's houses. Usually a dead person's house."
"Jeezus."
"I know."
"Are you making this up?"
"Nope. She goes to estate sales. I think that's what's wrong with her."
"Wow."
"I know."

"Wait," I said, "you mean she goes to estate sales since her dog died?"

"Both before and since."

"But she's so young."

"I know."

"She's, like, thirty-five, right?"

"Something like that . . . she's definitely not forty."

"What does she buy?"

"I don't think she really buys anything. Like I said, she just wanders around looking at people's things. Walking through all those houses, going through their kitchens, and closets, and basements. Touching their clothes. Smelling things."

"That's kind of crazy."

"I know."

"That's kind of batshit crazy."

"I know."

"Why didn't you tell me?"

"I don't know."

"I'm gonna ask her about it tomorrow night."

"I don't think we should."

"Why not?"

"I think it's a secret."

"A secret?"

"I think. Maybe not a secret, exactly, but she told me a while ago . . ."

"And she asked you not to tell anyone?"

"Not exactly."

"Okay?" I said, confused.

"I don't know, maybe it would be fine to ask, but . . ."

"But what?"

"But I don't know. It just seems like something we shouldn't talk about. She might be embarrassed about it."

"But it's the most interesting thing about her. I'm actually kind of looking forward to it now. Besides, it's either that or Scott. Or the dog."

"True."

"Or her sobriety. I don't really want to hear about Scott."

"No."

"Or the dog."

"No, but he passed away."

"Thank god."

"Be nice," Liz said.

The rain was coming down harder now, and there was a crow on the roof of the building next door. We both saw it land. The coffee wasn't nearly as good as it should be. Not as good as the idea of having the coffee.

"She goes to estate sales," I said.

"That's what she said."

"Maybe tomorrow night I should make other plans."

Portrait of My Wife in the Garden

I love gardening. Not weeding, but gardening. Actually, I don't really even love gardening. I just love being in the garden. Doing nothing. I love looking at the garden, from within it. The gray sky and the garden. Sitting on a bench beside a poppy that hasn't yet bloomed, its orange lips just beginning to pout.

Sometimes my wife will join me there. In the garden, on a bench beneath a gray sky.

"I would like to get one of those garden signs that have an icon of a dog defecating," I said to her one day. One day when she'd joined me in the garden. "The ones that say, 'No Dog Poop In The Garden, Please.' I would like to get one of those signs."

"Maybe for your birthday," she said.

"Oh what a gift that would be!" I said.

"Nothing but the best for you, dear." She was wearing a red-and-black wool flannel shirt, a button-down that had once belonged to an ex-lover of hers. I'm not sure she knew that I knew that. Every time she wore it, I thought of him, her ex, who owns a café on Dolores that I despise and won't even walk by, much less buy coffee from.

My wife is very kind. Much kinder than I am. And I was thinking how much I love how kind she is, despite her wearing her ex-lover's shirt. I was thinking this as I shoveled away a pile of dog shit from a clump of as yet unblooming day lilies. When I said to her:

"If you get me one, will you have it say, 'If Your Dog Poops In My Garden, I Will Cut It Open Lengthwise, Pull Out Its Intestines, And Use Them As Fertilizer . . . Please.'"

"That's terrible," she said.

"No no," I said, "not if it says please. It would have to say please."

She winced, there in the garden, beneath the gray sky. There in the garden wearing the red-and-black wool flannel shirt.

Kat Meads

Nelle Harper Lee, Character

In the words of a woman clearly uneager to be cinematically portrayed, Nelle Harper Lee wrote to poet Ralph Hammond: "There will be no end of hoo-hah with two movies coming out about (Truman). In my old age I must yet again be prepared to duck."

She's referring to the films *Capote*, released in 2005, based on Gerald Clarke's biography, and, fast on its heels, *Infamous*, released in 2006 and based on George Plimpton's oral history, *Truman Capote: In Which Various Friends, Enemies, Acquaintances, and Detractors Recall His Turbulent Career.* (Plimpton went to Monroeville to interview Lee for the book but was told she was in Maine, playing golf. He later learned she had been in town but dodged him.)

Capote earned Philip Seymour Hoffman a Best Actor Oscar for his portrayal of the writer and a Best Supporting Actress nod for Catherine Keener, who played Harper Lee. The *Infamous* cast starred Toby Jones as Capote and Sandra Bullock as Lee. Douglas McGrath, *Infamous*'s screenwriter and director, was wrapping up the editing on his film when *Capote*, directed by Bennett Miller from a screenplay by Dan Futterman, hit theaters. "We could have rushed to finish and come out at the same time," McGrath told the *Hollywood Reporter*, "but nobody seemed to think that was the right idea. Dueling Capotes."

The two are very different films. *Infamous* extensively covers Capote's New York life with the rich society women he dubbed "The Swans" as well as his time in Kansas, researching what would become the "nonfiction novel" *In Cold Blood* about the Clutter family murders and their murderers. In keeping with the film's oral history (or "participatory journalism") source material, there are "testimonials" (as they're called in the script) by publisher Bennett Cerf, rival Gore Vidal, selective Swans, Harper Lee and others. In these segments, seated before a not very convincing rendition of a glittery New York skyline, characters confide to an unseen interviewer. In an early version of the script, the Capote character also explains himself in testimonial fashion, but someone thought better of the strategy. No Truman testimonials appear in the film.

Infamous, the rangier movie, is longer by some 20 minutes, features multiple flashbacks, favors jump cuts, and covers more of Capote's life. It also mixes comedy with drama. (McGrath started his career as a *Saturday Night Live* writer.) The bewilderment of the people in Holcomb when Capote and his trailing scarf blow into town is played for laughs, underscored by a jaunty score. In an overdone joke, the town folk repeatedly call Capote "ma'am." Unlike *Capote*, *Infamous* addresses Capote's and Lee's writing struggles following the bestselling success of his *In Cold Blood* and her *To Kill a Mockingbird*. Of the two films, *Infamous* is more sentimental in both its rendering of Capote's attraction and attachment to murderer Perry Smith and in its presentation of the hardships of the writing life. Bullock is tasked with articulating that difficulty in a testimonial: "I read an interview with Frank Sinatra in which he said about Judy Garland, 'Every time she sings, she dies a little.' That's how much she gave. That's true for writers, too, who hope to create something lasting. They die a little getting it right." Other Bullock lines challenging to pull off: "One must remember that at the center of any bright flame is that little touch of blue," and "I've come to feel with great heartsickness that there were three deaths on the gallows that night." (The actress is, however, spared a nobody-can-measure-up-to-daddy speech that appeared in an earlier version of the script.)

Miller's film, *Capote*, is a moodier, more austere, bleaker and more consistently somber work, set, with few exceptions, where the crime occurred (Winnipeg standing in for Holcomb, Kansas), an isolated place of vast fields and gray skies and unnerving emptiness. In both films, Harper Lee figures prominently, the friend who accompanies Capote into the wilds of Kansas as his research assistant in the winter of 1959. The real Harper Lee was more than eager to go. *To Kill a Mockingbird* was at long last finished though not yet published. She had time on her hands and an interest in crime in general. Her friend asked for her help, and she gave it. And for her time and trouble, she was paid $900, plus expenses.

On the press junket for *Infamous,* the ever gracious and collegial Bullock remarked: "Catherine Keener and I were laughing, it's taken two of us to play Nelle Harper Lee, and we probably still haven't scratched the surface of who this extraordinary woman is." Both actresses were asked if they had attempted to meet with Lee prior to filming. "I never met Harper Lee, nor would I ever want to because of the choice she made to live out of the public eye," Bullock responded. "I have enough respect for her not to have trotted over that line." Keener had other ideas. Her "first thought," the actress admitted, was "to march right down to Alabama and knock on her door." Then she heard the author "wasn't keen on people making a movie in which she was included" and refrained.

Both Keener and Bullock had the background creds to pull off their believable Southern accents. Bullock, Virginia-born, had the additional advantage of Alabama relatives living in the vicinity of Monroeville. Keener's father was raised in North Carolina. Keener herself grew up in Florida. Physically, neither actress resembles the sturdier author who, according to Tom Butts, ex-minister and long-time Harper Lee friend, was "not a dainty person." Although Lee's "manliness" is referenced in *Capote* by Capote's partner Jack Dunphy, nothing about Keener's person or portrayal of the character substantiates that claim. In reality, Lee was two inches taller than Capote, 5'5'' to his 5'3". The Bullock/Toby Jones stats (5' 7" and 5' 5") run closer to the facts. Hoffman was, and Keener is, 5' 10." To help carry off the illusion that the actor was a tinier man, the suits and coats Hoffman wore in the film were reshaped and pulled in at the shoulders.

For the most part, Bullock and Keener wear coats, skirts and sweaters in the wintry palettes of black, brown, and dark green, with Keener's wardrobe being the more tailored and flattering version of the two. Keener's hair is fashionably waved; Bullock's short, layered cut with bangs more closely approximates Harper Lee's true hairstyle. In a bit of business that didn't make the final cut in *Capote*, Hoffman "tries to spruce up (Keener's) limp scarf" while murmuring "Oh, Nelle, you poor thing." Keener's Lee needs no sprucing. More effort goes into showing *Infamous* Lee's indifference to fashion and preference for comfortable togs. Throughout the film, Bullock wears ankle socks, usually gray. However, in Capote and Lee's first scene together, the two seated on a New York park bench, Bullock wears white ankle socks with black flats.

Regarding those white socks.

According to *The Mockingbird Next Door* author Marja Mills (a book reviled by Lee—we'll get to that), after watching *Infamous,* Lee wrote to director McGrath "something along the lines of this: 'You have created a creature of such sweetness and light and called her Harper Lee that I forgive the socks.'" If the "something along the lines of" quote can be trusted, Mills, in reporting it, appears to have taken the comment to be a straightforward, unadulterated joke. No Southerner would miss both its scold and acidic irony. The "sweetness and light" cliché is most often applied to those never-give-offense females who demonstrably lack critical thinking skills. Fair to assume Harper Lee did not consider herself one of that crew.

Although the unfolding investigation of the Clutter murders propels both films, how Lee and Capote work together to find the stories beneath the story is a critical part of the mix. Both films spotlight the closeness of their friendship, the deep knowing that underlies their bond. As observed by Dolores Hope, wife of Clutter family lawyer Clifford Hope, the real Harper Lee "sort of managed Truman, acting as his guardian or mother." Neither film goes with that interpretation. Both cinematic Harper Lees are in Kansas as helpmates. The difference is in the shading: Keener comes off more partner than secondary. Bullock comes off more self-effacing.

With the exception of a single scene, there is much affectionate indulgence of Capote by Bullock's Lee, an indulgence that covers his quirks, his misreading of situations, his self-centeredness, his need to shine. When he's feeling discouraged, she bucks him up. On the street, she takes his arm. When Jones's Capote embarrasses her—as he often does—Bullock dips her head, glances sideways, faintly smiles. On those occasions when she chides, the chiding is gentle, forgiving. The single break in pattern occurs after a long day in Kansas as the two characters write and type up their findings. The cause of their heated spat is the revelation that Capote now thinks of his book as a "novel" that will apply "fictional techniques to a non-fiction story." "Reportage means recreating. Not creating," Bullock's Lee argues. "The truth is enough." The squabble ends in a standoff, the scene concludes. Neither the disagreement nor its cause is again mentioned.

Keener plays Lee as a tougher personality, self-contained and self-sufficient, someone who sees more than she discloses, nobody's fool. Her loyalty to Capote is less absolute, less blind. There is tolerance but no blanket approval. She is there for Truman and will, on occasion, play the noninterfering spectator to his shenanigans, but her character also, with something closer to disapproval than exasperation, notes Capote's over-the-top manipulative games in Kansas as he woos sources. In large part because of the measured restraint of Keener's performance, the two scenes in which she lets loose and joyfully cackles (one celebrating the news that Lippincott will publish her novel) are particularly fun to watch. Throughout, her wit is sharp, dry, pointed. "Pathetic," she tells Capote in their first scene together on the train to Kansas after realizing Capote has paid a porter to flatter him. As they drive toward the Clutter farm past acres of fields, Keener at the wheel asks: "This make you miss Alabama?" "Not even a little bit," Capote answers. "Lie," she replies.

Although Keener has fewer lines of dialogue than Bullock, she gets some of the film's best. (As in *Infamous*, there are Harper Lee speeches in the script that got axed, including this doozy: "You remember when we were kids? I had no idea what a homosexual was. But I knew whatever they were, you were one of 'em.") Wise to all her pal's tricks, Keener's Lee primarily ribs Capote in private, but in an indication of how comfortable the two have become in the company of lead investigator Alvin Dewey and wife Marie, at a Christmas Eve gathering at the Deweys' home, a smoking, drinking, laughing Lee mocks, by echoing, Capote's brag that he has "94% recall" of everything he reads, forcing Capote to laugh too.

Even so, she will only put up with so much. At a party celebrating the release of the film *To Kill a Mockingbird*, after finding a very drunk, self-pitying Truman stashed at the bar, she demands: "And how'd you like the movie, Truman," walking away when Capote fails to respond. Again and again in *Capote*, the character of Harper Lee serves as moral conscience and clear-eyed truthteller. After the killers' execution, when Capote telephones Lee for comfort, she delivers something else: "They're dead, Truman. You're alive." When Capote whines: "There wasn't anything I could have done to save them," she refuses to let the self-deception stand: "The fact is, you didn't want to." Yet even in lay-it-bare *Capote*, Lee's well-known prickliness (her "notoriously peppery persona" in Monroeville native Erin Hall's phrase) and salty tongue ("the saltiest tongue on earth," according to friend Claudia Johnson) go missing. Such omissions wouldn't have occurred by chance. Prickly, salty-tongued sidekicks tend to divert attention from the star.

What neither film omits is the extent and value of Lee's assistance to Capote in Kansas, further confirmation of which can be found in the 150 pages of typed notes Lee supplied Capote, now held in the Capote archive at the New York Public Library. Divided into ten sections, the notes are organized around the town of Holcomb, the Kansas landscape, the Clutter crime, the four victims, the two Clutter daughters who lived elsewhere, interviews (some of which Lee conducted without Capote), and the trial, in which Lee not only summarized the court testimony but psychologically profiled the jury. Along with objective facts, Lee interspersed opinions, impressions and judgments. Lead investigator Dewey rates a "handsome." Prosecutor Duane West is considered "a slob." The "Christian books and magazines" alongside Herb Clutter's easy chair amount to "modern religious crap." Bonnie Clutter was "probably one of the world's most wretched women . . . stomped into the ground by her husband's . . .efforts to regulate her existence." Daughter Nancy's "family life was ghastly." Killer Perry Smith resembled "a small deacon . . .prim." His partner-in-crime Richard Hickock confounded Lee by appearing "so poised, relaxed, free & easy in the face of four first degree murder charges."

In Cold Blood, published in 1965, was "never meant to be a joint project," Lee told Claudia Johnson. Nevertheless, Johnson and others close to the author subsequently reported Lee felt hurt and betrayed when Capote's only acknowledgment of her contributions came in the form of a dedication shared with Jack Dunphy. Asked by Capote to do so, Lee had read the manuscript pre-publication. "She was written out of that book at the last minute," Johnson maintains. Lee's objections to Capote's blending of fact and fiction, as dramatized in the *Infamous* scene between Bullock and Jones, were not immediately known to the outside world. In public, for many years, she remained a staunch supporter of both the book and Capote. Only later, as their friendship frayed—and with greater frequency following Capote's death—did she give vent to long-held grievances against her onetime friend, calling Capote a liar and, as reported by Marja Mills, a "psychopath."

Why did the friendship fray?

In the PBS *American Masters* documentary about her sister, Alice Lee explained: "It was not Nelle Harper dropping him, it was Truman going away from her."

Lee herself gave different explanations to different people.

To Claudia Johnson, Lee denied that the friendship had turned "sour" because Capote "did not acknowledge her contributions to the book." It soured because "for the last twelve or fifteen years of his life," Capote "seemed hell-bent on destroying everyone who had ever loved him."

To Donald Windham and Sandy Campbell: "Truman did not cut me out of his life until after *In Cold Blood* was published . . . Our friendship . . . had been life-long, and I had assumed that the ties that bound us were unbreakable."

To Wayne Flynt: "I was his oldest friend, and I did something Truman could not forgive: I wrote a novel that sold. He nursed his envy for more than 20 years."

The two authors did not mend fences before Capote's death in 1984. Yet Lee made the cross-country trip to attend Capote's memorial service in Los Angeles. Among the others paying their last respects, Alvin and Marie Dewey of Garden City, Kansas.

T*o Kill a Mockingbird*'s immediate and tremendous success profoundly shocked its author. "It was (like) being hit over the head and knocked cold," Lee told Roy Newquist of New York's WQXR in one of her last interviews. Published in 1960, the book's initial popularity was many times compounded and extended by the success of the movie adaptation, starring Gregory Peck, released in 1962. "My baby sister that we thought would have to be supported all her life could buy and sell us all at the drop of a hat," Harper Lee's other sister Louise ("Weezie") wrote in amazement to a family friend. When, in 2009, Lee filed a lawsuit against her former agent, her book royalties, as reported in court documents, exceeded $9,000 a day.

In the early going of Lee's altered existence, she was still able to write humorously to friends about her status change. To John Darden, two months after the publication of *To Kill a Mockingbird*, Lee wrote: "I have been to the four corners of the United States and back: In Kansas, where Truman Capote & I spent a bleak winter solving 4 murders for the New Yorker; . . . in New York, where I became Famous; in Connecticut, where the Famous go to get used to it; in Easthampton, where the Famous go after they've gotten used to it" and more in that vein. In such communiqués, she gives the impression of being overscheduled and lingeringly bewildered, but the crankiness and bitter resentment from continuous intrusions into her private domain have yet to set in. For four years, she dutifully made the rounds, promoting both book and movie, and then she was done. As sister Alice explained in the PBS documentary: "As time went on, she said that reporters began to take too many liberties with what she said. She just wanted out . . . she felt like she'd given enough."

In 1947, following the success of *The Glass Menagerie* and four days before the even bigger hit *A Streetcar Named Desire* opened on Broadway, Tennessee Williams published an essay titled

"The Catastrophe of Success." In it he mournfully admits: "You cannot arbitrarily say to yourself, I will now continue my life as it was before this thing, Success, happened to me."

Harper Lee, it can be argued, gave it her best shot.

When Lee settled in to watch a "bootlegged copy" of *Capote*, sent from Los Angeles by Gregory Peck's widow, Veronique, Truman Capote had been dead for more than 20 years. Lee herself was experiencing age-related difficulties, including pronounced hearing loss. At age 79, she was watching Hollywood's rendition of her 33-year-old self.

Working the remote was Marja Mills, a former *Chicago Tribune* reporter who had moved into a rental next door to the Lee sisters on West Avenue in Monroeville. Because Lee had trouble hearing the dialogue, Mills frequently stopped the tape to repeat the actors' lines. From this on-the-spot witness, we learn that Lee declared the movie Clutter house "nothing like" the actuality, which was "sort of modern." (Stock photos of the Clutter house show a yellow brick ranch with multiple picture windows.) Lee laughed loudly at the idea of a movie premiere party, wondered "why filmmakers make so much up in movies about real people," thought Hoffman's portrayal of Capote "uncanny" and predicted his Oscar win.

But what, what, what did she think of Keener's portrayal of herself?

If journalist Mills inquired (and how astonishing if she did not inquire), Lee's response is not recorded in *The Mockingbird Next Door.*

Among the tidbits Mills did see fit to include in her memoir/biography are descriptions of the "musty," cluttered, book-piled, unairconditioned, outdated house the author, when not in New York, shared with her older, lawyer sister Alice, the "baby" sister occupying what had been their father's larger bedroom. The world-famous writer, we're told, still typed on a manual typewriter, loved catfish, potato "logs," McDonald's coffee, golf, small-stakes gambling, college football and feeding ducks; had a habit of stabbing the air with her index finger to make a point; had a "temper"; and "when something set her off could get creative with her cursing." If she'd had too much to drink, she dialed up acquaintances and "chewed" them out. She got her hair cut in the kitchen of a retired beautician. She bought clothes at the local Walmart and washed those clothes at a laundromat in Excel, one town over from Monroeville.

In Mills's explanation, the Lee sisters' "decision to let me into their lives as fully as they did had not stemmed from one grand declaration but, rather, was a gradual process."

In 2011, having gotten wind of Mills's plan to publish a book, Harper Lee issued a statement through her attorney refuting her cooperation in any such project and unambiguously denying that she had "willingly participated in any book written or to be written by Marja Mills" or "authorized such a book."

Following *The Mockingbird Next Door*'s 2014 publication, Lee again released a statement to the press: "Miss Mills befriended my elderly sister, Alice. It did not take long to discover Marja's true mission: another book about Harper Lee. I was hurt, angry and saddened, but not surprised . . . Rest assured, as long as I am alive any book purporting to be with my cooperation is a falsehood."

Marja Mills's literary agent countered that Mills had "the written support of Alice Lee . . . and prior to Harper Lee's stroke in 2007 she had the verbal support of Harper Lee."

On a break from her life and career in Chicago, a young journalist moves next door to two elderly sisters in a small Southern town.

Sounds like a horror flick pitch, does it not?

Caroline Clark

Behind the Scenes with Gerald Murnane: A First Reading of *Inland*

As I read *Inland,* I think back to a conception of the poem that Osip Mandelstam and Paul Celan both shared, the latter adapting it from the former. That of the poem as a message in a bottle sent out in the hope a reader will find it washed up on a shoreline at some point in the future. Although the narrator (or implied author, a term Murnane uses elsewhere) of *Inland* claims to dislike the 'idiot-sea' and associates it with poetry, this image of writing as a message in a bottle chimes with his thoughts on how his writing could get sent out into the world:

> . . . someone in future may find one of these pages drifting and may take it for a page of a book.

What's more, the three-part image of poet-message-reader hinges on his most treasured preposition: 'between'. The book, these pages, as he calls them, exists *between* the writer and the reader. He is conjuring the contents of the pages into being before his eyes and ours, though only we, reading in real time, know it has an end, whereas he, writing in real time, feels the infinite ahead:

> While you read you are sure of coming to the end of the pages. But while I write I cannot be sure of coming to the end.

At times the writing in these pages seems to be directed to a specific reader, such as the woman editor he imagines awaiting his pages in the Calvin O. Dahlberg Institute of Prairie Studies. Towards the end of the book, the reader becomes a different woman he knew as a child, as the narrator tells us, this book started with a letter to her. The book attempts throughout to set up various ways for the narrator to approach his reader—real or imagined, with such ties forming and dissolving before our eyes. This writer-reader relationship is always foremost and a prerequisite for any writing to happen:

> I could not think of words without a reader.

The word, for this writer, is dialogic and can only exist between the two. As he conjures up his desired reader, we, another kind of reader, must go along with him. At other times he suddenly addresses us, the general reader, dropping the previous set-up to announce:

> Now, you still read and I still write but neither of us will trust the other.

He prepares us:

> I am going to write for some time, reader, about myself standing in the garden . . .

Assures us:

> I am far from having forgotten you, reader.

Plays with, or demands of, us:

> But who, in any case, do you think I am?

Always reminding us of our connection with the book between us:

> . . . since you are reading this page at this moment.

What fuels this book, powering it forward, is the writer's seeking out of the other, the reader.

I am not concerned with defining this as a novel or non-fiction or otherwise. Elements of biography and fiction fleet across the pages like the thoughts that pass through our minds all day. Elsewhere Murnane has suggested that what he writes are essays, and with this he frees himself to wander over any imagined borderlines of genre. He plays with the possibilities of that thing in the middle as though with a Rubik's cube, gliding from story to something else. He can hold all the sides of the thing in his mind: rather he can speak from several sides of it at a time. Simultaneity is a truth he draws us to.

Whatever it is, his is a kind of writing I greatly admire: one where the writer admits the reader behind the scenes. The scenes of what? Beyond the set-up of the monologic self directing itself to the blank page, beyond the simple accumulation of material, of 'aboutness'. I sense this behind-the-scenes quality also in Clarice Lispector's writing, in her addresses to the reader and her existential investigations. Writers who are a mystery to themselves are my favourite kind, occupied as they are with a study of self. In both writers I find a purity of writing, nothing superfluous, never narrative-driven, all is being laid bare. There is here a sense of the writer-narrator filtering, remembering, unfolding and conjuring material into being, going over it again and again.

What adds to this sense of a behind-the-scenes are Murnane's references to the process and timing of writing these pages. He cuts through the pretence, gets behind the façade of writing, and brings the reader behind the scenes with him.

But what do we find there? Personal geography, whereby the self is established by places real and imagined.

> Let me tell you, reader, what I consider you to be. [. . .] Your body is a sign of you, perhaps: a sign marking the place where the true part of you begins.

All the places we have read of in books, he tells us, leave an impression on our selves. Whatever places we have seen or remember seeing or dreamed of seeing 'appear on the map of the true part' of us. The map of the places of our true selves. This map is not full:

> All those empty spaces, reader, are our grasslands.

And in these grasslands are our possible selves. Here we have body, place, self, geography and potentiality all in one.

Instead of narrative there are passes over the same ground, with each pass yielding something new. For him, depth with layers and rootedness is king. Poetry is like the waves of the 'idiot-sea' while prose is 'grassland movements'. How to understand this 'idiot-sea'? In a book also published by And Other Stories, I read:

> The transformations of the self are the business of the lyric poet.

This is a quote by Günter Eich in Lutz Seiler's book of essays *In Case of Loss*. If I put these two things from different books read on the same day together, it gets me somewhere helpful. It gives me an insight into what I've been doing for the past thirty years and what Murnane isn't doing here.

As a poet, I have been occupied with the nature of self in the lyric mode, exploring (swimming in?) the unknown. Murnane's concern is not with the transformation of self. He is a writer of fixed geography and his task is to take in the layers that exist contemporaneously.

> . . . the chief pleasure of my life, which is to see two places I had thought far apart lying in fact in one place—not simply adjoining one another but each appearing to enclose or even to embody the other.

and

> I will match landscape with landscape.

The principle of multiplicity guides or inspires his central way of being:

> I learned that no thing in the world is one thing; that each thing is two things at least, and probably more than two things. I learned to find a queer pleasure in staring at a thing and dreaming of how many things it might be.

He revels in the potential multiplicity of things. If he were a poet of the idiot-sea we would be talking about metaphor. But for him this is ridiculous. Metaphor. Why call one thing another, for him they can be both or more.

As he looks into complex layers where what could/would/might have been exists alongside the actual present, he conjures himself into imaginary situations to see what might happen there. Then he speaks as if these things were real, before suddenly snapping (us) out of it.

Most of all the narrator of *Inland* likes the moment of being *about to* write something and imagining himself in the place of another so that he can *see* things from a different angle. Here is a mode, a tense, a potentiality that inspires him. It brings the writer and reader together in the moment of something being written, and combines with his idea of multiplicity. Until a thing has been done, it exists in all its states of possibility.

> I had been about to write what I have just written, but when I stood between my table and the window I thought for a moment what my reader would have thought if he had been reading the pages where I had read the words *my reader*. I had thought for a moment what a man would think if he saw himself clearly named on a page he was reading.

In *Inland* background is foreground. The narrator is concerned with location and direction, where the most prized, significant descriptors are the flanks of whatever lies between: all places are given as being located *between* two points, usually rivers. We the reader track and mirror his movements as he seeks out relationships of betweenness: tracing maps, seeking out pairs, mirrorings, signposts to follow. He starts with the ground, the place and puts a name to it. Indeed, he loves a good place name: the Great Divide, Climax, the Great Alfold, Ideal, Dog Ear, Oral. Disappointment Creek.

In one version of his future he imagines having studied the languages of specific places, the 'soil-of-speech', which gives rise to particular ways of speaking:

> . . . I might have become a scientist of the depths of languages. I might have learned that a language grows from roots and soil just as grass grows. I might have followed the dialect of my native district down to its roots. I might have studied the soil and even the rock under the language of my homeland.

Gaining an insight into his own language, he dreams: 'I would become at last a scientist of my own writing'—reclaiming that most treasured place from which he was taken as a child, his home.

Indeed, language is so intertwined with place that he finds his bearings not just by a language of place, but a language that *is* place:

> When I hear the silence that comes between my own words sometimes, I think of prairies or plains—as though all my words are being spoken from grasslands. But whenever I hear the silence that comes between the first five and the last two of the seven words spoken to me by the girl from Bendigo, I think of depths.

The energy of potentiality that pulses through these pages stems ultimately from the unsolvable mystery of the other. He can never know the intention with which precious words were said to him via a go-between when he was twelve. As he meticulously picks over a girl's declaration that she likes him 'very much', he lays out an analysis not of sentiment, but of language. As I read those pages I feel something shifting in my brain: I am slightly altered. I feel, not for a first time, but in a new way that language is real and shapes and creates and goes forth. And there is eternity, ongoing time: 'an action that can never have been brought to an end'. And as such he manages to impart to us an immense sense of loss without using any emotive language. We suddenly find ourselves in a place where communication is happening.

And now we are in a sacred position:

> The words I have just written are written as though to a go-between. But a man who writes on pages such as these can only have for his go-between his reader.

Towards the end he talks of a final mirroring. Each page between us is not a window, he realises, but a mirror. Perhaps then, I think, each reader completes *Inland* having read and looked into it. It becomes part of our individual geography: one that is moulded by the landscape of another's mind. I read-watch in wonder as he seemingly conjures this book from behind-the-scenes: a place only he can go but only if he knows we are here to receive his reports from back there.

Alice Lowe

In Portland, Maine

1.

In Portland, Maine, "down east" is up north. If you're not native-born you're "from away," and the weather is always the topic *du jour*.

2.

The Maine Mall opens early in inclement weather for walkers, mostly seniors, who stroll, stride, or speed around the inside perimeter to the upbeat tempo of fifties music blasting from loudspeakers. I live in Southern California—this is a first for me. I power walk, loop-de-loop within the mall's confines on a cold, drizzly October morning. I sing along with the Everly Brothers and Jerry Lee Lewis as I zip past slower walkers, nod at those coming toward me. Past chain stores, their display windows in robotic repetition blatantly begging "Buy!" When I reconnoiter with my hosts back at the entrance, Michelle, a staunch Maine defender, asks how I liked it. Not wanting to sound churlish, I say "Different."

3.

Michelle and I are celebrating our eightieth birthdays. We met online ten years ago, admirers of each other's writing, and became close friends long before we met in person. We were astounded to discover that we were born three days apart in the same hospital in Rockville Centre, Long Island, New York; that we're both married to men ten years younger than ourselves; that we both delayed college until our thirties and acquired master's degrees in human services. There's more, too—the coincidences are staggering.

4.

One morning we stroll the two-mile wooded trail that circles nearby Mackworth Island. In dense fog, I accept the proximity of the Atlantic Ocean on faith. Three days later, the same route expands under clear skies, exposing rocky beaches and shorebirds along Casco Bay. Another day it's Back Bay, a six-mile loop from Michelle's house. It's an amiable and walkable city, the lively and compact downtown a pleasant amble away.

5.

When in Rome, I feast on pasta; in Seattle it's salmon. In Maine, I covet a lobster roll. My vegan friends are willing to oblige me, but the logistics get complicated. "It's no big deal," I say, though in fact it is. I'm in luck when, strolling around the Old Port one day as lunchtime nears and hunger beckons, we pop into Gritty McDuff's Brew Pub, where lobster roll is on the menu. Succulent chunks of chilled lobster meat with fine-chopped onion and celery, tossed in mayo, served on a toasted bun, a squeeze of lemon and a dash of Tabasco—sublime simplicity. To think I almost went without.

6.

We take short outings up and down the coast, driving through canopies of trees at their seasonal peak, a spectacle of red, yellow, orange, and brown, the picturesque towns and the rugged Atlantic coast, different from my sun-kissed Pacific. I'm enchanted with the oversized wooden animal sculptures in the sculpture garden at the Ogunquit Museum of American Art, overlooking the choppy Atlantic shore, but soon burn out on a glut of museums and galleries.

7.

Every place loses its charm, no matter its scenic beauty or cultural treasures. Staying with people, no matter how dear, is stressful, being away from home unsettling. I'm a homebody with a low social tolerance. After five days, I'm antsy for my own surroundings and routines, my privacy.

8.

A Bloody Mary at the airport is the failsafe formula to settle and soothe me for air travel. I compare them from airport to airport. At the bar near the departure gate at Portland's Jetport, my drink comes with a generous celery stalk and two Spanish olives. It's strong enough but a little bland. I add Tabasco, but it needs more seasoning, maybe celery salt and Worcestershire sauce, and there's no salt on the glass rim. I give it three on a five-point scale. I should start keeping notes, I think. As I get up to leave, relaxed and gently buzzed, I thank the bartender. "What's your name?" I ask. A "J" name that I instantly forget: Jeremy? Jason? Josh? I tell him I'm writing about Bloody Marys at airports. "Oh," he says, with a look of alarm. "Just call me Chuck."

Sergii Pershyn

The Third Step

It was shortly after 10 PM when I opened the window overlooking a small square. I had been sitting in the same position for hours and needed a break. The air entering the room was warm and humid but fresh. It had that particular smell of pine trees and earth that could only be experienced on warm nights in early June. I took a deep breath through my nose, holding the air for several seconds, and slowly exhaled.

The smell instantly resurfaced some long-forgotten memories. Or it might have been wrong to call it long-forgotten as I couldn't be sure if I had ever recalled that moment before. It was the same warm night with earthy aromas in the air, and it must have been the same date but years ago. It was her who opened the window overlooking the small square where I was trying to move the sofa through the narrow doorway after refusing to pay the movers. There must have been trees on the triangular square then—the cypresses.

No longer wanting to stay in the stuffy room, I decided to go outside and take a quick stroll. On that Saturday night, the streets were bustling with people. Every cafe chair, every bench, every inch of the sidewalk was taken by people who also thought it was a magical night to be out. Making a single step on the busy street soon became a challenge, so I turned around, aiming to return to the comfort of home. Moving against the flow of the crowd became even harder. To take a much-needed break, I entered a corner convenience store where I thought I could buy a bottle of milk for breakfast. The store felt like an extension of the street's chaos as it was full of people. Only it was even more cramped, the narrow aisles were so congested it was hard to see the light or distinguish between the human flesh and cans of tomatoes on the shelves. The flow could move only in one direction, making turns at the end of the aisles and slowly progressing as a single organism. After picking up a glass bottle of milk, cold against my fingers, I had to slowly follow the procession passing through all sections of the store until it was my turn to reach the cashier.

Back on the street, I gasped for some air and continued my journey against the grain. It took me about 20 minutes to reach my building, while the walk to the store initially took only a couple of minutes.

I unlocked the front door with a key and entered the hallway. As I closed the door, I carefully checked that no one was pushed into the doorway from the street. I pressed the door handle to make sure it was securely closed.

Why did milk in a glass bottle taste so much better? Did it stay fresh longer compared to plastic or paper containers? It tasted so much better in a glass bottle that it was impossible for it to last for more than a day, so no one could check if it tasted good or not in a few days.

As I thought about it, I put my left foot on a small step in the hallway. It's natural for a human to repeat the same action with the other foot to move forward, as I did, only this time I didn't raise my right foot high enough. Instead, I hit my toes on the marble step, while the rest of the body continued the forward motion, resulting in a brief state of flight culminating with my head hitting the marble stairs.

It was hard to say what came first—the pain or the embarrassment. My forehead hurt for sure, but I think I felt the humiliation first. A grown man falling is a sad sight. When a child or senior falls on the street, people tend to rush to help. When it happens to a man in his 30s or 40s, others tend to look away to avoid further embarrassment. Luckily, there was no one around when I got up, picked up my belongings, put on a shoe that fell off when I tripped, and headed upstairs to the apartment on the third floor.

My wife sat on the leather sofa watching some TV show when I walked in. As soon as I opened the door, I started retelling the incident to her. The feeling of sadness and embarrassment intensified as I shared it, so much that I started sobbing but my wife said not to worry about it. She touched the bump on my head and brought some ice wrapped in a towel as I lay on the sofa where she used to sit. She told me to close my eyes and relax for several moments.

When I opened my eyes, I saw the white marble in the dark. Moments after, the lights turned on, illuminating the hallway as if I was lying not on my building's stairs but in the middle of Times Square. I heard a woman's voice asking whether I got hurt.

"I tripped over the step but am okay now," I responded, still lying with my face down.

"You don't seem to be okay. I better call the ambulance," the voice replied.

I turned around, trying to sit down, feeling the piercing pain in my forehead. I couldn't see the woman's face against the light.

"I'm really okay, just got hurt a bit."

"I recognize you now, your apartment is right below mine. Thank God, I first thought that someone didn't close the door properly and a junkie slipped in. It happened before in our building. That's why I wanted to call the ambulance, and the police, in fact. Are you sure you are okay? My God, look at that bump."

"I think I can handle it."

"Is there anyone at home who could take care of you?"

"I . . . I actually live alone, but it's nothing really."

"Ah right, I now remember your wife but haven't seen her around for a while."

I didn't respond. I kept trying to look at her face against the light.

"Anyway, let me give you my phone number—please, please, feel free to call me if you feel worse or need any help."

She handed me a sheet of paper with a dozen numbers scribbled. I tried to memorize them in pairs. As I moved from one pair to the next one, the previous numbers kept changing, forcing me to start all over again. It was a tiring process, forcing me to close my eyes and relax for a bit.

When I opened my eyes, it was dark. My shirt was wet and sticky. I touched my forehead and felt the pain, but there was no blood. The liquid on my shirt and around me was milk spilled from the broken glass bottle. As I got up, my movement activated the light sensor in the hallway. The broken bottle made a mess on the floor, and the smell of milk made me dizzy, but otherwise everything was intact.

In the elevator's mirror on my way upstairs, I saw a bump on my forehead the size of a small plum. I touched it with my fingers, and the reflection of the elevator light on my wedding band reminded me I needed to stop wearing it.

Back home, I came to the open window and inhaled the air. The smell of pine trees seemed to do wonders with my headache. I sat in the armchair, trying to remember the phone number of my upstairs neighbor from the dream, but I couldn't recollect a single digit. And why did I need the number if she was right here, separated from me by a thin layer of wood and concrete?

Probably it was time to move on, I thought. I wouldn't even wait till the bump healed. Tomorrow, I would buy flowers in the shop around the corner and knock on her door.

Gina DeMartino

Human Instinct: Easy Recipes to Craft Flesh to Perfection

Homegrown Tender Meat with Lime Butter

Ma always told me that choosing not to eat meat is a decision, but eating meat will always be human instinct. And she's right—if she was wrong, I would've turned to veganism years ago. There's something so satisfying about sinking your teeth into a properly prepared piece of lamb, chewing on each bite with half-crooked teeth from years of not wearing your retainer. Watching Ma craft a new meal with her freshly grown garlic and lime and having Father take our waiting cattle to their fate is something that has stuck with me into my adult years.

For this recipe, I want you to step into my family home and try my ma's most favorite delicacy: homegrown tender meat with lime butter. This meal will guide your foreign tastebuds into a new world of possibilities for your cooking—a world that's been right under your nose.

The ingredients are as follows:

- ▢ 1 small garlic clove, minced
- ▢ 2 tablespoons of unsalted butter
- ▢ ¼ teaspoon of finely grated lime zest
- ▢ ¼ teaspoon of black pepper
- ▢ 1 tablespoon of fresh lime juice
- ▢ ½ teaspoon of salt
- ▢ 4 12-ounce, 1-inch thick, boneless meat of your choosing

You want to be extra careful when you're grilling your meat. Be sure to have your oven preheated to 500 degrees Fahrenheit—that's 260 Celsius if you're a friend across the ocean.

Always be sure to check in on your cattle. Keep your basement door open just a crack to listen out for any that try to escape. I recommend taking in one at a time so to not waste rope. Back when I regularly served this dish, I liked to take them to the bathroom tub for good measure since it was closer to the kitchen.

If you can't be sure that your dinner won't escape, then you *need* to make sure they're already dead—no ifs, ands, or buts. You don't want a pig screaming in your kitchen while you're buttering them up. Anesthetize them if you have a heart, but Ma always had Father take care of them downstairs before she even got a chance to see life breathe out from the poor things' faces. If you can't find your own, kidnapping your neighbors is fine.

Smear butter into your skillet, then sprinkle your salt and black pepper of choice into the pan. Father always liked his extra peppery, but I like to add just a smidgeon of my own favorite garlic. Combine your lime zest and lime juice into a separate bowl before slowly pouring 3⁄4 of it into the skillet. Ignore the shouting coming from down the hall. Their screaming won't matter in a week's time, and you don't wanna distract yourself from saving some lime butter on the side. I've eaten enough fresh cuts in my day to confirm they taste *amazing* when you drizzle the excess on top.

Grill your meat of choice for about 12 minutes. Turn them once over in the skillet until the edges are slightly charred and any leftover skin is barely visible. It's okay if you forget to remove some of the skin—Father would get mad at you, but I won't, since it will just sizzle out into your skillet anyways. Skinning someone down to their muscle beforehand isn't exactly a pleasant experience, anyways. It's messy and gross and you can't eat the skin anyways so there's no point.

Ma always called for medium rare, but I always preferred a nice, well-done cut as my outcome. I don't want my meal to look half-alive squirming on my plate, and I'm sure you don't, either.

Otto did that a lot—squirming. I remember one night he was sitting across from me on the couch, he was reading a book and I was watching the TV with the volume down. The bottoms of his feet were shifting like crickets against my calves under the blanket we shared. I asked him if he was okay, and he started shivering like a newborn calf, saying it was too cold in the apartment. I stared for a second too long, having half the mind to say he should be grateful he's in an apartment and not a porcelain tub, but I shook my head and instead offered to turn up the heat.

He immediately objected and went back to staring at the book in his lap. *Man-Eater* was the title. The moment read like a joke. Like I was his crowd work at a shitty stand-up show.

"I'll be fine," he told me, but it was an obvious lie. I knew he didn't like the cold. Not after all those hours he *did* spend in the tub. So I pushed myself off the couch to turn up the heat anyway.

When I returned, I slid back under the throw blanket, and I felt Otto's hand clamber for mine. I could feel the indent of the long scar across his palm as he clasped our fingers together. The TV had gone quiet, replaced with whipping winter wind outside the windows, and a beat of silence later, Otto was asking me what I wanted for dinner.

I shrugged, staring at his book, long forgotten on the coffee table in front of us. Otto followed my gaze, the tension in the room so icy despite the heater kicking on and making us both sink into our skin. We both stared at the title for a moment too long.

He suggested a vegetable dish for dinner that night. But I don't know how to cook any of those.

Gary McDowell

Mr. Daniel Hobson

The first thing I noticed about Mr. Daniel Hobson, maybe a few weeks after he moved in, was his long fingers, his meaty hands the size of frisbees, the way they wrapped around—and over—the hammer's, the saw's, the mallet's, the nail gun's, the drill's handles, how they, his knuckles bulging like nuts on a bolt, paled and ghosted the tighter he squeezed. I watched him from my porch over and through the chain link fence separating our backyards. Sipping my coffee, I saw him measure twice and cut once, I saw him stand hands on his hips, nodding, scratching his chin, smiling, or so I imagined if I could see his lips fully, and then he'd disappear out of view. The initial hum and high-pitched zing, the tremulous wail of his circular saw, the noise unmistakeable, impossible to confuse with anything else. And when the blade met wood, the abrasive whine, the fizz and fuzz, filled the trees, the yard, sent crows and common finches scattering, their calls drowned in the milieu of sawdust and scream.

The second thing I noticed about Mr. Daniel Hobson was that he never sat still. Every morning when I went outside with my coffee, he was already at work. When I looked up from my desk in my home office, he was still at work. After dinner, when I took a beer to the porch to watch the sun dip beneath the treeline, Mr. Daniel Hobson crouched at his pile of lumber, a tape measure pulled taut, a pencil tucked behind his ear, something handled and heavy in his other hand at the ready. He'd disappear into his home for breaks, sure, but inevitably, he'd come back to his yard. My wife, Laura, told me to just ask him what he was doing, but the man seemed lost in his work, something I understood, a space I knew not to interrupt.

Our homes were nearly perpendicular to one another on a cul-de-sac—the front of our home T-boned into the side of his. We could see two-thirds of Mr. Daniel Hobson's backyard, but we could not see the far side of his house or the yard that wrapped around it. Behind our home and adjacent to his was a small forest, about ten or twelve acres of brush, pines, and oaks, a big enough ecosystem for a few deer, some raccoons, squirrels, rabbits.

Mr. Daniel Hobson seemed a stable man. Flannel or T-shirt tucked into jeans, always jeans, a brown leather belt, loafers, brown, also. He drank beer while he worked, but I never saw him visibly drunk. If he swore when he smacked his thumb with a hammer, I never heard. If he missed a cut, ran out of supplies, made a mistake, I never knew. Sometimes he brought a small radio outside with him, listened to the classic rock station. Never loudly. He never cranked AC/DC or Whitesnake, never muted Heart or Journey. The first time he caught me staring, he nodded as if in acceptance, in recognition. I raised my mug, nodded back. "Doing okay?" I asked. "Yessir." He wiped his brow with the sleeve of his flannel. "Yessir indeed." Over the weeks, we shared a few more brief volleys of how-ya-do's, but never more than that until one Tuesday evening.

I only knew him as Mr. Daniel Hobson because on that Tuesday the mailman left a utility bill for a Mr. Daniel Hobson, clearly not my name, in our box. I walked it to his front door that evening, knocked, considered the doorbell, considered waiting at the chain link fence out back, for he'd stepped inside not long before, but instead stood pat. The door knocker was an old belt buckle the shape of a bucking bronco soldered onto a brass ring. The buckle had been reinforced with what looked and felt like iron. Its heft was considerable. I waited, kicked, scraped the sole of my shoe against the abrasive plastic of his welcome mat. Mr. Daniel Hobson flung the door open, muttered an "Uh-huh?," short, I gathered, for "How can I help you?," short for, I figured, "You ain't a Jehovah's Witness." I thrust forward the envelope, gestured to the foot of our driveways, shrugged, said, "Just figured . . ."

"Appreciate it," Mr. Daniel Hobson said. I glimpsed over his shoulder, for he was a head shorter than me, not something I expected. On the wall opposite the door hung a picture frame with what appeared to be the stock photo with which it came. Below it, an end table with a wooden bowl of faux pears, apples, berries, all of them coated in visible dust.

"Care if I ask you something?" I said.

"Don't mind, no," Mr. Daniel Hobson said. He leaned his weight onto his left foot, shoeless, and propped himself against the door-frame. The envelope looked child-like, small and inconsequential, in his substantial hands.

"What are you building?" I asked, nodded to the rear of the house.

Mr. Daniel Hobson took a moment before he answered. His lips parted, dry and stuck together, chapped: "Little of this, little of that." Mr. Daniel Hobson snorted hard, ground his throat, stepped onto the patio, pushed me back with his closeness, turned his head and hocked phlegm into the hedges.

I nodded, put my hands on my hips, throated, "mhm, mmm, sounds about right," tried to match his display. I spied through the kitchen and saw to the screened-in back porch, a feature of the house Laura and I both admired greatly, though we'd never actually seen it, only heard from neighbors about its existence. Because of our home's angle to Mr. Daniel Hobson's backyard, we couldn't see the screened-in portion.

On the porch, a gun safe, locked, it looked like, taller than me, wider than me, the biggest one I'd ever seen. "Don't mean to meddle," I added.

"No meddle." Mr. Daniel Hobson peered over his shoulder, but I couldn't see what, if anything, he was looking at. He turned to face me. "I'm forgotten."

"Sorry, what?" I thought maybe I'd misheard "m" for "ve."

He rubbed hard his left palm with his right thumb as if massaging a pressure point, the envelope crinkling, crushing in his grip. Mr. Daniel Hobson looked me in the eyes, cocked his head, almost smiled, but he pulled back just before his lips parted. He started to shut the door, spoke as he did, "No meddle. Never a meddle." And the door latched shut.

I walked home.

There are times when living in suburbia is like golfing while suffering a migraine, when any form of motion is enough to make the world turn sideways, your stomach churn to your throat, leaving you in a heap on the fairway. At these times, I prefer to close my eyes and breathe deeply the lilacs, the freshly mown and manicured lawns, the Johnson's smoker full of brisket and pork shoulder, listen for training wheels crushing pebbles in the cul-de-sac, the shrieks and shrills of a distant pool party. I do this not because I want to remember those things but because they reverse the nausea, clear my head, remind me of the positives. The negatives? The over-manicured lawns—a competition almost—the stench of competing BBQs, the squeals and squeaks of dozens of kids splashing, flowers of every shape and size causing sneezes and headaches, the screams when a child falls from their bike. Essentially, the good things about suburbia are the bad things, and all of it is fake.

I closed my eyes and tried to think of a bustling cityscape, the gas and brake, the horns, the hustle and tap of hundreds, thousands, of feet across pavement as people rush to this appointment, that meeting, this casual encounter that can change their lives. A business meeting. An affair. The excitement palpable, different, the opposite of my view as I kicked stones through the cul-de-sac. Our flood light clicked on as I walked up the driveway, the tulips rising out of the shadows, their bulbs receptacles for dew, but that night the neighborhood was still and so was I, in a way. No one sets out to hurt themselves, except for when they do. I didn't want to hurt myself, or anyone else, but I'd have sold everything I owned for my heart to race over something other than a jog or a late night, quiet cum-dump into my toilet.

A couple weeks went by and I steered clear of the backyard, unsure what to think of Mr. Daniel Hobson. My home office was in the attic—I couldn't work where life was being lived. I needed a space with no other function but to make calls, send emails, do whatever else needed doing. The attic wasn't ideal, but it was functional. And free. I'd only been in practice a year; no self-respecting client wants to meet their lawyer in an attic, but at the same time, rent for an office space was outrageous, and I wanted nothing to do with the bureaucracy of a firm, not yet, not until I knew if I could make it on my own, and with Laura's hours at the clinic bobbing and weaving, the money we saved by me working from home made a difference, especially considering the expense of each semester of veterinary school. It wasn't a bad system. Besides, estate lawyers don't exactly wear Armani and drive Mercedes—we don't need to. Humility was fine with me. The attic was quiet, temperate—fans in the summer, space heaters in the winter—and with a view. Specifically a porthole window that looked directly into Mr. Daniel Hobson's backyard. From that vantage point, I watched him continue to cut and stack 2x4s in the grass. I watched him bracket them into rectangles, his drill squealing all afternoon into the dusk. He'd finish one frame—each about 6' by 8' if I had to guess—haul it to the side of the house, presumably to lean it there, and start the next. He must have built a dozen and a half or more, each made slowly, laboriously, with exacting precision and zero haste. If suburbia died and was reincarnated as a man, Mr. Daniel Hobson would be that man. Exacting. Hidden. The secret life of. Where dreams both go to die and to spawn. The side yard, the cul-de-sac, *pay no attention to the man behind the curtain*. The grass is always greener, except when Davis and Holmes and Thomas all buy the new zero-turn Husqvarna—then it's just shorter. It was the show that mattered.

A few evenings later, the weather perfect, the sun setting brilliantly behind the hills west of town, I sauntered to the porch, beer in hand. A huge coil of wire mesh sat in Mr. Daniel Hobson's backyard. He unspooled it slowly, wire-clippers in hand. He measured a distance, once, twice, and clipped vertically to shear off a length. Over and over again. Each panel significantly longer than he was tall.

Once he'd cut maybe six or eight patches, he disappeared to the north side of his house and came back, again and again he did this, with one of the wooden frames. He stacked them three or four per pile.

He stretched the mesh over one of the frames and walked around it with a staple gun. Ka-thunk. Ka-thunk. Ka-thunk. Something rhythmic and soothing about the way he moved. After he finished each one, he hauled it, once again, to the far side of the house.

I watched, maybe, for too long. Eventually he saw me. I waved. He nodded, went about his business.

If I wanted to know whether Mr. Daniel Hobson were building a catapult or a cage for prisoners, an inhumane coffin or a batting cage, I would have to spy in a way that made me uncomfortable. No, scared. I would have to shimmy along the treeline, set foot on another man's property uninvited, a major suburban no-no. *I shall not trample another man's yard; I shall not knock down another man's shrubbery; I shall not envy, criticize unfairly, nor distrust another man's lawn maintenance routine.* So I closed my eyes, breathed in the lilacs, listened for the pop of gravel under tires, the waft of pork butt, but instead, I got nothing, just the dull ache of something missing. What did it mean to be excited, to have excitement? Laura, a good woman, a beautiful woman, a wife a husband could love forever, had stories, good ones, and she'd share them, but everyday the mundanity of coffee, work, beer, coffee, work, beer, coffee work beer coffee work beer, coffeeworkbeer—sometimes I questioned it. Would you believe me if I said I had no secrets?

But men like Mr. Daniel Hobson? They *are* secrets.

That night, Laura and I in bed. "Maybe ask him out for a beer. Maybe he's lonely," she said.

She lay propped on a couple pillows, a text book in her lap, her terry cloth robe open just enough for me to wonder if I could get her to open it the rest of the way.

I did, and we made love quietly, dutifully, lights out. We weren't boring; we were rutted, routined, conditioned. Tired already.

A few days later, I saw Mr. Daniel Hobson out back. No tool in hand, but he sat in a lawn chair facing away from me, northwest, toward the setting sun and the treeline along his backyard.

From my fence I hollered over. "Nice evening," I said.

Without moving to face me, he said, "Do you hear it?"

I strained, but I didn't hear anything. "Hear what?"

Mr. Daniel Hobson turned around. He gripped a shotgun, the barrel pointed to the ground. "There. In the woods. You didn't hear that?"

Instincts told me to back up, go inside. Curiosity told me to get closer, learn more. He wasn't going to shoot me. Maybe the black bear that had wandered the neighborhood the summer before was back to his old antics; Mr. Daniel Hobson wouldn't have known the story being new to town, of course, but he certainly could have seen the bear.

"Beer sometime?" I blurted, not sure what else to say.

"Actually," he started. He stood up, placed the gun on his chair, took two steps toward the fence, crossed his arms over his chest. I braced myself for a rejection. He inhaled a deep, long breath. "That would be nice."

I'd represented some pretty sketchy people—the lengths people will go to secure the deceased's property never shocked me but only confirmed my observation that grief does nothing but foster the worst in humankind—but never had my heart raced like it did then. The shotgun, the no-noise noise, his pause.

"How about Stanley's? Tomorrow? At 8:00?"

"I'd like that," he said.

Later that evening, Laura and I snuggled on the couch, beers in hand, a rerun of *NYPD Blue* droning before us, and she said, "A bear trap."

Anymore, this was most of our evenings. She'd work at the clinic until 2:00 or 3:00 in the afternoon, come home and cram in as much studying as she could before jetting off to her twice-weekly evening class. By 8:00 we'd be in front of the boobtube, a dinner of pasta or pizza or some other quick-cooking fare I could make easily settling in our bellies. As for me, I spent my days emailing clients, conducting meetings at coffeehouses, drafting and proofing estate plans. Estate, probate, trust. You name it, I organized it, I looked for loopholes in tax law, I took into account the whole of someone's life, of what they hoped to leave behind. It wasn't about who got what, necessarily; it was more about who got what *when* and *how* and via *whom*. So much of what I did centered around language: The legality of pronouns and the conditional tense, the mysteries of time and perceived assets. At first I found it invigorating; as I got more deeply into it, I found it mind-numbing, boring, Capitalist, and damaging. Next to finely manicured hedges, I could think of nothing more upper-middle-class and suburban than hiring me to invade your books and tell you how best to set up future generations of your family. But it allowed us a raised ranch, a Camry, a future.

I didn't answer right away. I stared hard—too hard—at the TV.

Laura said, "Enclosure for a petting zoo."

"What if it has nothing to do with animals? What if it's for people?" I asked.

She propped herself against me, rested her head on my chest. I wrapped my arms around her.

"He dabbles in human trafficking?" she said.

"And you told me to ask him out for a beer?"

"You're too old. No one's gonna buy you."

I jutted my thumb into her ribs. But not hard. "Who says it's a cage?"

"Looks like it to me."

"Maybe I should go check."

It didn't take much convincing. I flung myself over our fence into the woods and shimmied tight against the trees, hoping to find an angle to see into Mr. Daniel Hobson's side yard. First, I had to traverse twenty meters or more of rather dense brush. Laura stood, arms crossed, on our patio, sipped on her beer, watched me fade into the darkness. The part of his yard that bordered ours was protected by a simple chainlink, but the far side, where I headed, was a six-foot high wooden privacy fence, something the previous owners built when during the winter the view into the forest was dreary and, in their words, *downright depressing*. I felt my way along it, fought off errant branches, stumps, overgrown weeds, but in the dark, it was no use. Cloud cover, no moon. I could move only a few inches at a time. When I thought I found a spot to climb, the overhang of branches was too thick, the crowns of the trees a natural barrier.

Some kind of car park.

A shed.

A dog house. (Though I didn't think Mr. Daniel Hobson had a dog).

Nothing at all. Just a way to spend time. Or to waste it. If there's a difference.

I stood still, admired the sprawl, the heft of the branches above me, how they swooped low from their trunks and then grew up, toward where the sun would be, rested finally on top of the fence. A woman mourning the loss of her mother—and trying to wrestle her childhood home from her delinquent older brother—once told me that plants feel pain, as it were, when eaten raw. *You're not so different, you and artichokes.* I peeked through the canopy, and where the moon would be on a moonlit night there was a vacancy. Something about the way a thing's absence is also its presence—were I to erase the clouds, the moon would be there; were I to stay still long enough for the wind to make a pocket in the cover, there would be my light. But I wouldn't stay still long enough because I didn't know how long long enough was. Instead I prodded, pushed, fought my way through the branches the best I could, reached to where I thought the fence ended, but it was no use.

Defeated, I retreated the way I came. Through the same slog of shit, how the brush rattled against my shins, tripped me, centered me in a concentration I admired for its ferocity. I moved slowly, giddy, aware, attuned to and full of what I now know was joy.

The next night, Stanley's, in the middle of downtown—though calling it downtown is an affront to every other downtown, as all we have is a couple bars, a movie theater, two greasy spoons, an adult movie store, and a muffler shop—was packed with the usual suspects. Farmer Tilly. Fat Man Joe. The Rotary Club. Coach Herman from the local high school. Sasha Miller, one of the only other attorneys in town. A few dozen others I only knew because I saw their faces at the Pig, here at Stanley's, at the bowling alley every Friday night all winter long.

I spied Mr. Daniel Hobson at one of the high-top tables at the far end of the bar. He waved me over, his red flannel sleeve a warning or an invitation. "First pitcher is on me," he said. First pitcher? We were drinking more than one? *Pitchers* was a commitment I wasn't prepared to make.

We settled into small talk, sipped on our beers. The weather. Baseball. Local gossip, which was a deadend. Mr. Daniel Hobson told me, eventually, why he came to town: To get away from where he grew up. The people. The customs. The memories. To start over.

That made sense. Who hasn't dreamed of escaping their past?

"And, you know, I needed to be somewhere wetter," he said.

"Wetter?" I repeated, wondering if I'd heard him wrong.

"Three tours in Fallujah." He took a long pull from his beer. "It's a dry heat."

I nodded as if I understood, held up my mug, said, "Thank you for your service," and tried to clumsily clink his glass, but he didn't move his from the table. So I too took a deep swig, a ruthless chug really. The night definitely called for *pitchers*.

We sat in silence for a few moments. Maybe I'd offended him?

"You know, I see you and your wife at the dinner table through the porch window," Mr. Daniel Hobson said. "It's nice. That you sit to eat together. Every night."

"Have you been married?" I refilled both of our empty mugs, flagged the bartender, held up a finger, pointed to the nearly empty pitcher. It was my show now.

"Once."

I knew men like Mr. Daniel Hobson, had defended plenty of people who thought their shit didn't stink, whose exterior toughness acted as a shield, was meant to push me away, but most of the time, all of it ended up being a facade, and I'd be damned if I didn't break him too. I tried to imagine Mr. Daniel Hobson in a trench somewhere—did they fight from trenches in Iraq? I had no idea. How could I have no idea? But I envisioned him in fatigues, on his back, a pistol—his last line of defense—held tightly to his chest as he tried to make himself as thin and as small a target as possible. It wasn't always the toughest son of a bitch that survived but often it was the most resourceful, and having watched Mr. Daniel Hobson, having listened to him: He possessed an uncommon mix of quiet, common sense, and je ne sais quoi.

"Care to elaborate?"

"She left during my second tour. I get it. Not her fault."

"I'm sorry to hear that." Our pitcher arrived, and my voice stumbled alone and uninvited from my mouth: "Say, we'd love to have you for dinner some night. Just say when." Another deep, long chug.

Mr. Daniel Hobson stared at me, his bushy eyebrows, his face unflinching. "I'm a charity case? Is that it?"

"No, you misunderstand. Just being neighborly is all."

He smacked my shoulder with his meaty hand, calloused, blistered. "I'm just fucking with you."

In the middle third of my body, two feelings eddied together. On the one hand, maybe he was, as Laura had suggested, lonely, and with that thought my palms started to sweat and I felt my throat get raspy, tight. Did I have the right to ask? On the other hand, perhaps he was crazy. Perhaps all of it—the building of his human trafficking cage, the hearing things in the forest, the shotgun, the downing beers at an uncomfortable pace, the gun safe in view of any visitor to his home—was just the way he was. Another possibility? It was all a show, a cry for help. Or none of those scenarios were true, and Mr. Daniel Hobson was playing me like the guitar aching through each Willie, Cash, and Parton song reverberating through Stanley's speakers. All I knew for sure was the feeling in my gut, the irrational yet logical sense of fear, of excitement, and how I couldn't think of anything to make me give that up.

I laughed, chugged the rest of my beer and poured two more full glasses. The room's walls—the vintage movie posters, the hubcaps, the neon signs for Schlitz, Schaefer, Hamm's—became fuzzy, askew.

"I'll race you," he said, held up his mug. "Go!"

I didn't want to, but he'd already started, so I put the thick glass against my bottom lip and tilted my head back, opened my throat.

He beat me.

"Again," Mr. Daniel Hobson said. He poured the remainder of the pitcher into our two tall mugs. "Go!"

This time I didn't hesitate, and I slammed the beer as fast as I'd ever slammed a beer before. And still lost. Barely. Or by a lot. Who can tell?

"Good try," he said. "And fuck it, this is all on me." He pulled a few bills from his wallet and put them on the table. "Let's go." That was it? Two questions, some small talk, too much beer? I followed outside like a dog its master.

My legs wobbled under me, but if I drove fast, I'd get home before the last two beers hit my system.

When I pulled into the driveway, slowly, seeing double, Mr. Daniel Hobson, who'd obviously driven faster, stood lit brilliantly by my headlights against the garage door. He invited me inside his place for a nightcap, said he had something he wanted to show me.

I debated going in to tell Laura I'd be back in a moment, to tell her where I was in case . . . But I couldn't complete the thought.

We walked through the foyer, the kitchen to the screened-in porch. He poured a couple more drinks, this time in snifters. Something dark. Whiskey? Scotch? He unlatched the gun cabinet, reached inside, pulled out a shotgun. "Ever held one of these? He handed it to me, shoved it, really, into my chest. The ice in my glass clinked noisily as I recoiled slightly.

It was the gun from before.

"Of course," I said, lying. Well, not entirely. I'd fired a shotgun once on a duck hunt with a childhood friend and his dad. I was maybe twelve. I remember the butt of the gun hard against my shoulder, following Mr. Rash's instructions: *Squeeze the trigger. Don't pull it. Squeeze it. And brace yourself.* The kiss that promises a kick. I squeezed the trigger and found myself on my back, my shoulder throbbing, ears ringing. I hadn't touched any firearm since. Not out of fear, but out of respect.

I tabled my glass and did what I thought I was supposed to do. I brought the gun to my shoulder, looked down the double-barrel, pretended to sight something in the distance, then lowered it, looked it over a couple times, flipping it in my hands. I admired it, stroked it with my hand. "This is a nice gun," I said.

"That's not a gun. That's a .243 Winchester break-action. Put a hole in a deer the size of a dinner plate."

"Is that so?" I handed it back to him. He popped the chamber open, loaded two shells, and clicked the weapon closed.

"Yup. Or in a man spying over another man's fence." He hefted the shotgun to his shoulder, turned toward me, pointed the barrel at my knees, then spun just as quickly away and went out the screen porch into his backyard.

I picked up my glass, chugged it. Brandy. I refilled the glass. Downed it again, refilled it once more and followed Mr. Daniel Hobson out the back door. "I meant no harm," I said.

"You ever kissed a man?" He turned toward me, pushed the barrel of the shotgun into my gut. I instinctively raised my hands. The snifter slipped out of my grip and brandy spilled down the front of my shirt. The glass landed safely in the lawn. "Well, have you? Any answer will do. Ain't even have to be the right one."

I shook my head no.

"Fine by me," he said. "Not going to shoot you either way."

We stood still, the gun pressed, not lightly, into my stomach, my hands numb above my head as blood hurried to my heart, its pumping surely loud enough for Mr. Daniel Hobson to hear, the whirlwind of life and death spiraling dizzily throughout my entire body. Not nervousness. Not even fear. Something else unnameable, something like reverence or adoration. A plumbing of unnecessary suburban boredom. If there is a precipice, a moment where time slows indefinitely when we're faced with mortality or its cousin, awe—and I'd like to think there is—I reveled in it then and saw its manifestation just beyond Mr. Daniel Hobson. There, in the branches draped over his privacy fence, a gap plenty big enough for me to squeeze through. I must've stopped just short of reaching it the night before.

I let my hands fall, not slowly but abruptly and with an exhale, with relief, I laughed. Once. Then again. And then I was rolling, chortling, catching my breath. We're never really that far away from solving most mysteries; in fact, most of the time the answers are right in front of us if we'd just keep looking.

Mr. Daniel Hobson removed the shotgun barrel from my gut.

"I thought I was the sick fuck," he said. He too laughed. A snort, really. And we were there, in that space between where no one is in control. A perfect time for me to exit.

Mr. Daniel Hobson picked up the glass, handed it to me. "Pull," he said.

I didn't move. Didn't understand.

"Pull," he said, pointed the gun into the air, drew it across the expanse of his yard, said *boom*.

I reared back and tossed the glass as high and as far as I could toward the treeline. He sighted it quickly. Bang. The glass shattered into dust. The reverberation of the blast set my head to spinning.

"Dishes are done!" he yelled.

There's fear, and then there's confusion, panic, abandon. A sliding scale of risk and reward, awareness and some kind of obtuse ignorance. I was somewhere in that mix, but I knew what I knew: Nothing and everything. Like any calculated situation, it all comes down to the supreme mix of chance and preparedness.

"I think I need to call it a night," I said.

Mr. Daniel Hobson grabbed me by the arm. "Not yet," he said. He pulled me to the far side of the house. Lined up there were the platforms he'd been building the previous days and weeks assembled, now, into giant cubes—four walls, a top, and a piece of ply as the floor. Each one about my height and a good deal wider than that. The first one was empty, but in the other few there crawled, alive and furiously clucking, their hubbub subdued by the swirl of wind piercing from between the treeline and the side of the house, dozens of chickens. As I drew closer, crouched down near one of the cubes, I saw that some of the chickens had died and the live ones pecked at their carcasses, stepped on them, rooted around in their waste.

"You've been watching me," he said.

I could call the police. But for what? I could yell for Laura; she'd hear me, and she'd know what to do, but even the two of us would be relatively powerless against Mr. Daniel Hobson. I could walk away, pretend I'd seen nothing—because honestly, I hadn't—let the chickens and Mr. Daniel Hobson fend for themselves. Nothing I'd seen that day changed me irrevocably; similarly, nothing that could happen going forward would change my mind about what I thought I knew: Mr. Daniel Hobson was unwell, and I, a suburbanite consumed with myself, was a symptom, a cause, and, in a way I couldn't quite grasp, a cure: The penalty for being nosey? Learning the truth, one way or another. All of the options seemed justified, possible, even inevitable were I to live the moment over and over like a dream. Instead, my desire to confront him overwhelmed me. Not for the sake of the chickens—though their squalor did offend me and would send Laura into a tizzy—and not for the sake of some moral superiority—because let's be honest, I'm no judge—but because I didn't see the point. Boredom? Cruelty? Why spend hours and days and weeks and money on supplies just to let the birds perish? It didn't make sense. I would ream him, I would rant and rave and scratch and claw and tell him exactly what he could do with his chickens, where he could put them, how I would gladly help.

But that's not what happened. Like a suburban neighbor, a real Chad, a real Marsha, rushing from their home to tell you exactly how they felt about your loud party the evening before only to knock and gift you a platter of cookies and a silly grin—*Some party you had without me last night, huh Champ?* Wink Wink—I choked.

"What is this?" I asked.

"This is sustainable suburban farming." He slung the shotgun's chamber open, reached into his pocket to pull out two more shells and popped them in. He pointed the gun to the treeline and fired. My body shook.

"My wife. She can help. She's a vet. Gonna be a vet." *Say, uh, it got pretty loud last night—. And these have nuts in them, just so you know. In case of allergies.*

He plugged in two more shells. Click. Aim. Bang. "That's not necessary."

And I saw her. Laura, on the porch, the phone pressed to her ear. In the distance, slowly coming into focus, the whirl and whine of sirens. *So maybe you could keep it down next time. Or invite us. Ha! Seriously, though, these cookies!*

I knelt as close as I could to the nearest cube, the mesh just wide enough for me to run the silky smooth feathers of one of the hens through my fingers. "But they're dying."

"They do that," Mr. Daniel Hobson said. "They always do that."

I thought about Mr. Daniel Hobson's meaty hands. I thought about measure twice, cut once. I thought about *First pitcher is on me.* I thought about *I needed to be somewhere wetter.* Underneath all of that a feeling built in me that I had forgotten existed: I was excited. Something could happen. Something already had. And I almost missed it. They say being present is the most important thing: Do not ruin today by mourning yesterday and worrying tomorrow. Mindfulness. Embrace the moment. All that shit. When it comes down to it, we have two choices. We either move on or we don't. That's it. Mr. Daniel Hobson knew that; I knew that; Laura knew that. As the sirens drew nearer it occurred to me that I could run home, grab Laura, run upstairs to the attic. Who would the officers believe? An attorney working in his home office spying on his neighbor through a port-hole window or a crazed lunatic with a shotgun and dozens of dead chickens?

Either they would arrest Mr. Daniel Hobson or they wouldn't. Either Laura would become a vet or she wouldn't. Either I would one day make enough to open my own office or I wouldn't. Either this suburban life of mine would continue its current trajectory or it wouldn't. Either way, I couldn't say I sat still when faced with the opportunity to poke my head over the fence. Either way, the sliver moon would continue its trajectory over our heads, would light, however faintly, the milieu I called home.

Ulrica Hume

Artemis

She was a cleaner at the sperm bank. She wore a nametag that said Diana (the name of her predecessor), and a spiffy, peach-colored uniform, which drew attention to her cornflower eyes. She was uncommonly common, did not realize that she turned heads, and many a fantasy inside the masturbatorium was sparked by her innate purity. Her duties involved the disinfecting of all known surfaces, especially the chair with its upholstered arms. It was menial work, but also trendy and clinical, and when asked what she did for a living she said she was in the biotech industry.

So many women were desperate. Their dreams literally on ice. She had no children herself. No man either, attracting only migratory ones. She wasn't lonely though, more curious what a life would be that was ripe with caring, of universal consequences. On her breaks she liked to skim the public donor profiles. Today she had come across #444325. This was a swarthy gentleman who was "friendly and upbeat," and said to look like George Clooney. She adored that actor (especially as Dr. Doug Ross in *ER*), and had always envisioned herself with someone of those same qualities.

She had hoped to catch a glimpse of him, but the freight elevator was out of use that day, so she had had to take the stairs. She lingered hopefully outside the masturbatorium. The red light was on, signaling that his donation was in process. She listened while pretending not to. A little pang of conscience as she tried the door, found it unlocked, turned the handle. Then she went in, audacious and sly.

It concerned her that he had not touched the magazines or the stack of videos. Rather, he was perusing the acoustical tiles on the ceiling, a dull look in his eyes. His legs were akimbo, the trousers slid down, and he was restlessly clutching the upright stalk of himself in a way that was nonchalant, tender. He seemed not to see her. Then he did see her. He ducked his head, smiling woefully. She recognized him as one of those "bad boy" types she could never not forgive. Ah, *Diana*, he said.

He asked her where her stag was, having cleverly made a connection between the Diana on her nametag and the Greek goddess Artemis. She hadn't the heart to tell him she was called Lois. But this hardly mattered. As she would soon learn, and much to her advantage, he liked assertive women. And, though it was a cardinal rule that she wasn't supposed to "assist," she felt bad for the intrusion. She stood her broom and dustpan in the corner, and purposefully approached. She asked if he was not uncomfortable, and pausing to look down at himself he said that he was. She made a slight adjustment to the chair, showing him how it could go back, the footrest, up. An expression of gratitude washed over him, he touched her wrist, and next she knew he was telling her all about himself and she was feigning surprise. She already knew that he was majoring in linguistic anthropology at the local university, from reading his donor profile. Also that he had not had real sex for a year, and that he liked to hike. He said he had been to Asia and Africa. Also Antarctica. Europe, of course. Then he asked if she had traveled much, and she said yes, she had. This was her only lie. She just couldn't admit her fear of flying—that she might ascend to the clouds and never come down.

She had never felt so much admiration for a donor before. Usually they were reflective and subdued, vaguely predatory. But then she had never entered a room unannounced. She kept thinking of her towel cart, which she had abandoned in the hall. The stakes felt high. He was going on about the impressive geography somewhere, this as he absentmindedly fondled himself, his eyes rolling up, a little perspiration at his temples.

So, tell me about you, he asked politely. What do you do when you're not here, do you have any hobbies? She said certainly not. The concept of a hobby depressed her.

I suppose I like to garden.

His mother gardened.

He took her hand, which looked foolish in its purple latex glove. Once it was bared, he guided it to him. Then together they pumped him. She intuiting his preferences while despairing of the fluorescent lights, which were surely unflattering. A truck was backing up outside in the parking lot, making a low, grating sound, she felt alive, embarrassed. He had heard it too. His inward smile as he peeled back her fingers, a sense of being imprisoned by perfection, dread, of wanting what was beyond the superficial, this rare un-hiddenness proof of their humanity, their weird alliance, and she began to doubt that she should have bothered him, his inward smile so terrible, so unsettling because she did not know it, meanwhile his cell phone, which he had placed on the table, was stoically vibrating, inching its way to the edge. She gazed at his tawdry, kicked-off sneakers, it was a gift to be so clear, to be no one in the world, the sudden boom of the air conditioner muting the muzak, strains of Corelli, and seeming to annoy him, she soothing, but not, but every aggravation, this a mortal's false itch, her ministering to what cannot be solved, then the violence of a kiss, light, dry, non-ecstatic, between strangers, a queer foolishness that made them laugh, a coalescence, brave signal, reunion, darkness in the sinking seed of light. And as he leaned forward from the verge, her grip became that of a she-bear catching salmon, sure and experienced, a catch in his throat, some wordless divination, there was an understanding between them (at least she thought there was) of what was needed, the precise speed and tenor with which she should dispatch her perverse altruism, the way to him not linear but one of switchbacks, then a firm tapping of his fingers, the vein in his neck a little hook—that she was here was enough, he kept saying. That she was here.

He fell silent. It was a dangerous silence, taut, bowl shaped. She clasped his knee in reassurance, and then he gave a little yelp, and she observed with joy the honeyed substance issuing forth. This aroused in her a diligent sense of compassion. He seemed so good.

That was how it began. Their subsequent meetings were but a mirror of that first time, she putting the lid on the cup and writing his donor number on the brown bag for him. Her embroidered handkerchief was used for what precious stuff remained. She was not as picky as they were in Cryo, always fearing contamination. How sorry she felt for the unborn ones, their lives on hold, siblings in a silent world, unknowing of each other. A maddening potential.

He was an adventurer, like a young Jacques Cousteau, but on land. It was spring now, summer break was coming. Some spare, emboldened longing of hers that he should invite her along to wherever he was going. He could share his pup tent with her. Show her redwoods, the Northern Lights. Then again, their encounters did have a certain charm. They were brief, their emotions seemed to glide safely, alight, back off. In a way it was perfect. In another way it wasn't. The desire to possess another, to ruin them even, then to repair. The acknowledgment of miracles.

This could be your son, your daughter, she would say, holding the plastic chalice.

Soon he would be leaving, she knew this. His plan was to trek about the Ethiopian Highlands. She just could not compete with volcanoes. Or geladas (the so-called "bleeding-heart" monkeys), wolves, ibexes, or bearded vultures. The idea of him in this primal world made her fluttery.

Stay, she wanted to say, though she had nothing tangible to offer, just this room and herself in it, true compensations were unknown, involved excessive generosity, love and its withholding, sometimes she hated his mercenary penis. Stay. Only ever this. Safe.

Not safe. Never mind that he had been vetted, his genes heroic, all those before him blindly rooting for progeny, she would have preferred more risk and imperfection. Maybe that was the real purpose of his departure—to test this. Breathing space, she told herself, as he heaved a sigh, unzipped. Their choreography had maybe become too predictable, eerily balletic, frugal and obscene.

Ras Dashen was her rival. This was one of the Greek poet Homer's "chess pieces of the gods," in the carved and windswept Simien Mountains. In a way, he was already there, already had a toehold. Sweet meadows and ancient views preoccupied him, also boots, blisters, headlamps (for climbing pre-dawn). There was a promise of postcards.

On this particular day, he was leafing through his classicist's porn (he was aroused by the marble nipples), and she was looking at herself in the mirror above the courtesy sink as she applied some lip gloss. From his throne he was saying that beauty was arbitrary. She didn't know whether to be offended by that comment or not. She decided not. The Omo River tribes wear large ornamental rings in their lips. He demonstrated this by painfully stretching his own lower one; the effect was grotesque. A spirited lecture about Ethiopian orphans who find it difficult to adjust to their host families in the States, and the sense of alienation we all feel by being human—it was beyond her. His "family of man" talk also, which drew on the academic work of Laurens van der Post, made her question their own small patch of reality. She had double-checked his file: he was only thirty. But so wise.

She loved this about him: how he could draw her in, invite her to hold him, close his eyes with regal grace, not at all like someone who rode a collapsible bicycle to his classes, how his face would then alter, become someone she didn't know, did, wished to know more—who was attentively chivalrous when she, glowing in her uniform, said she might have "felt something," whose face she could not quite remember when the pine-scented room with its ridiculous sperm wallpaper was emptied of their pleasure, and she went about her day as if walking on hot coals, alert, contrived, disturbed by her affection, how, in the stealth of the act itself (obviously she would be fired if caught, possibly sent to some Cleaners Jail), in the swift, pristine moments leading up to the occasion, he would, impossibly, manage to suppress his donation. For all this she loved him.

News of his climbing accident shocked and saddened her. He had had a reputation around the clinic (said the girl at the front desk) for being a bit of a risk-taker, which she had not fully realized. She found herself doubled up on the mop room floor, as heartbroken as Juliet but without the dagger to stab herself with. There she died a little death, moaning and shivering as her very soul was ripped from her. Because her prolific tending of him, his stern concentration, her billowy kindness, had been no more than a mad dash to here. A sanitized Beatles' cover of "Let it Be" had played the last time, a sign she should be accepting of life's vicissitudes. She was not accepting.

At work she went about at odds. She slunk about the masturbatorium, wiping down this and that, her heart not in it. She didn't even know his name. Had not bothered to ask, had enjoyed the turn on of calling him #444325. But I have the keys, she thought. I have the keys that open every door here. So one evening she stayed late. It felt magically still, as though all the guilt and shame, the excessive secrecy, had been momentarily relieved. She let herself into Cryo. In that frozen world she breathed a cold cold fire, like some dislocated goddess in a veil of liquid nitrogen, her hands stuck to the test tubes, her heart stuck there also. Then she tiptoed into the office. So many files, so many motile sperm, so many dreams. Finally she managed to find the archive of deceased donors. And there it was, his name: John P. Blakely. She wondered what the "P" stood for. Paul maybe.

The next day, she called in sick. She said she had a toothache. Then she went to the cemetery to visit his grave. She ran her hand along the headstone, lay some flowers. She was resting on the lawn when she experienced a prickly sensation. She had inadvertently disrupted a colony of ants. She brushed off a few. They were fleeing in the way of a diaspora. She felt just terrible, as if she had caused it, and of course she had. As she observed them hoisting God-knows-what on their tiny backs, it occurred to her that nothing in this life comes without some effort. This revelation cheered her, but in a way that wouldn't last, and left her lower than before. This, she supposed, was grief. Being granted omniscience, then slowly waking up to the fact that one was just as vulnerable, ruled by the same sympathies. She began to cry—something she had not been able to do until now. She felt like a hybrid widow-whore. Through her tears all became slippery and abstract.

The problem was, he had left a man-shaped hole in her consciousness. An acute sense of lack, implosion, regret, disdain of superficiality, craving, which was why she sobbed while eating her picnic, the flattened sandwich so sad, her own little bites.

I am a mess, she told herself, pausing to wonder who the "I" was.

The moon shone as a faint wreath in the clouds. Even though it was obscured, she felt its merciless gaze. It seemed to say, You are lost, but I am here. You will spend the rest of your life hunting for truth, you will retire early from the sperm bank and travel. But you will never again comfort a freckled young man in a windowless room and feel that it is enough. Never respond when he says the name Artemis. You will step into fields of lavender, and walk on white beaches, but always without him.

She dabbed her eyes. The embroidered handkerchief was a souvenir, stained with his semen. She flung it, it drifted down. There it was, resting on the points of grass. She was reminded of those men in India—fakirs—who lie on beds of nails, and she wondered why someone would bother. Why do anything? Why love. She had resorted to praise whenever he was slow to come and their time was running out, always the spectacle of his donation, the trying silence, she had felt oddly alone then, but not, together. An exponential tenderness. Yes, why love, and never know who the other really was, or oneself. As a white-tailed deer munched chrysanthemums nearby, as the chimes of the memorial chapel tinkled, as the breeze carried in its sweetness ash, she knelt, curious, appalled, resourceful. She retrieved the cherished handkerchief. It smelled of amber, the sea. Of everything she had ever wanted. This dire awareness honed her, made things too bright.

On the lawn before her was a neat little mound. Those ants again, she thought. But no. Something else. Then a writhing green vine emerged, pushing, pushing, the friable earth falling away. She felt strangely enlivened.

The green vine rose and dipped, dipped and rose, as if in invitation, its vegetal, one-eyed, pared-back head maneuvering itself into the sky. She felt in awe, but in a Pollyanna way: it was like some primitive green phallus, and she felt compelled to climb it. An irresistible challenge, to go beyond what was known, this blanket of pain. And that she was terrified of change, of heights and space, the sweeping chill of the unexpected, made her oddly keen to summon instead ease, and trust, a widening love. She was still on the ground, looking up. The grid of plots, the grazing deer, behind her. It was all an idea. The hard part would be gripping the stalk and hoisting herself up. She removed her sandals, gathered in her summer dress. She tried, drawing strength from John, before remembering that he had dropped to his death while rappelling a mountain.

Up she went, beyond herself, albeit with fear. The winding green vine was difficult to hold, she thought purposely so, yes, everything seemed pitted against her, she was some challenger of the universal status quo, alone and ever changing. With each lurch and tug she was delivered closer, also farther away. She was a slow and heavy, ponderous climber, and the vine, the vine was swaying.

Many times she almost slipped. Or did slip, but somehow grabbed back onto the benevolent tendril. It had tricked her into thinking she was strong. She knew that if she relied only on her own powers, she would likely make mistakes, but of course she kept doing just that, relying on her own powers and making mistakes, and rather stubbornly, strategizing her next move with mad determination.

The weather turned. A round cloud crept close, dripping rain upon her. And then, as a rent in the blue sky appeared—a bittersweet feeling.

I am at the tip of the shoot, she told herself. There is nothing more.

The white-tailed deer heeded the woman for a moment, then, disgraced by clamor, turned away. The deer having better things to do, like survival, a nibble to advantage, dependent, but in an almost frivolous way, on the deaths of others. The creature so delicate, pensive, invisible even to itself.

The woman would climb down from the green vine, still grieving, a bit disheveled. On her days off she would return to the cemetery, feeling it was her special duty to do so. She would tidy everything in the way that she knew, always taking care to dust off his name. Sometimes she would cry but not always.

A child would eventually come, singing as it ran between the stones. The story of his or her conception would be hinted at but never told. Why it had antlers growing from its head, or a fondness for yellow chrysanthemums—all that would stay a mystery.

Israel Bonilla

Eulalio Salmantino 1921–2000

The physicality of events. Where else have we sought the ultimate explanation for most transformations? And yet our interiority resists the physical with a damning effectiveness. It is simply a matter of turning to the efforts of education, to the campaigns of politicians and the pomp of ceremonies. We are there, but not there. We are husks for the time being. Our interiority resists, that is, until the rarefied spiritual pulse of the word seizes its rhythms. For this to happen, any book will do—or perhaps any verbal artifact. The spirit acquires perspective, and in an act of detachment realizes it has been adrift. Revelation. A revelation. It depends. What, in any case, could have been expected from the *Physiologus* in the twentieth century? The rush of excitement of a forgotten scholar who has stumbled upon a new theory of its provenance. The breathlessness of an avant-garde author who is struck by the totalizing hybridity of its form. The triumphant smile of a preacher who, at the last minute, understands that his rhetorical estate has grown lavishly. All of this. But not the inspiration of a religious founder. Yes, the word retains its sublimity even under the covering of a lapsed worldview. Revelation. To Eulalio, only one: the overabundance of meaning within Nature.

He was born in Velardeña, Durango. The population burned with unrest: the massacre led by colonel Jesús Garza González and all subsequent efforts at retaliation had consigned revered ideas of progress to a fictional timeline, where angels and saints once tread the ground. It was, however, a flame without ocote. Each revolutionary effort had asked everything from time and had succumbed to a critical mass of events. Calixto Contreras and Orestes Pereyra, dead in combat, were already heroes of epic stature—and Villa, the greatest of them all, had retired to Canutillo as a relic equal to the arm bone of the martyr Saint Sebastian (duly preserved in the Franciscan church of Xochimilco). Eulalio entered a world that still held on to sanctification through violence, and though this belief seemed close to evaporate into an abstraction, anticlericalism and land reform gave it a new body and breath. It is not difficult, then, to see why most speculation about his paternity revolves around bandits like "El Chojo" Ladislao or generals like Domingo Arrieta León. (I say *most* because there have been more "high-minded" attempts in this area of Eulology: a Soviet historian and linguist boldly proclaimed in an obscure opuscule that Eulalio was the product of a melancholy liaison between the engineer Álvarez y Zubiría and an exiled Russian baroness.) The interest of these speculations is, however, limited, for Eulalio's true guide was Father Próspero.

Contrary to his fellow clergymen, Father Próspero did not live in a pious atmosphere of incuriosity. He was, as far as can be determined through the volumes of his sermons, a gnostic. Basilides, Cerinthus, Bardaisan, Saturninus, Priscillian, and Valentinus are referred to with gusto, whereas the Church Fathers seem to appear as an afterthought. His library, though not spacious, made the most of his ascetic habitation. Aside from the sermons, he wrote a treatise on education: *On the Concentric Circles of the Soul and the Unequal Discipline*. And here we find, in all probability, his approach to the tutelage of Eulalio and other orphans:

> "Education" is a wearisome word that no longer serves its purpose. Which of our great ancestors would recognize its original majesty? To educate means to slash life in two: the time of soul and the time of body. The educator, moreover, is a bungler when it comes to the administration of this sacred time. Does he not imply with the asperity of his voice, the weakness of his posture, the sluggishness of his manners, that there is no significance to his calling? He merely replicates the dispositions that pervade the time of the body. If we wish to restore the unity of life, we must understand that the only legitimate time is that of soul and leave behind us all concessions.

The time of soul, then, required what he called the *unequal discipline*: an ordering of the day that *mirrored* the geometrically disposed inclinations of men. Sunrise, the outermost circle, warranted assistance to the community through physical exertion. Sunset, the innermost circle, warranted prayer, "an effort in blessed remembrance." Father Próspero's variety of Gnosticism did not condemn nature; it purely judged it a lesser gift, a humble incentive to explore the soul's higher being.

Alert to the rhythms of day and night, Eulalio grew to love both. His discovery of the *Physiologus* in Father Próspero's library bridged the gap between intuition and understanding. He loved day and night because they enacted the yearnings that beset him. The soul was not, after all, vaster than nature: it was intimately coextensive. This much we can say about his early youth without entering the arduous disputes of Ceniceros and Castaños, who believe, respectively, that Eulalio's doctrine flows from Father Próspero's teachings and that it is in violent discontinuity with them.

In fact, we are now fully dependent on Eulalio's disciples. His first hierophany, which took place when he was fourteen, is narrated in Sixto Castaños's *Pronghorn,* the most comprehensive life of Eulalio and (to many) a canonical book:

> He was exhausted, and his peers were exhausted, and the whole atmosphere of the innermost circle signaled exhaustion too. They all were eager to lay the tools that had uplifted their souls, and they all were eager to pray and remember. He was as eager to lay his tool and pray as the mockingbird is eager to mimic the passing sound. But in his eagerness he lost sight of his peers, and thus he lost sight of his way. There was the plain, the mesquites, and his loneliness. And he did not entertain his exhaustion: for he suspected that in the innermost circle he would have to find a corner to pray. Corners he did not find. There was only the plain and now the moon. And he was lonely. His heart entertained fear as it did not entertain exhaustion. And he was confused. Then he heard the murmur of a river. But the murmur brought despair: for what he heard he could not see. Then the murmur coursed through him. He was the river. He was no longer exhaustion, loneliness, fear or despair. And every beast drank of his waters, and he became them. What need was there to pray? Covered in a delicate fur, he caught sight of his peers and of his way. And he ceased to be alone.

Matías Ceniceros, too, refers to this experience of the sacred throughout his writings (most notably in his grand polemic against Castaños, *The Great Doctrine and the Little Doctrine*) yet is careful to strip it of what he perceives to be an excess of mysticism. The river existed (Cuencamé) and so did the furred beast (a deer); the identification was of a rational turn and therefore solid ground on which to build a theology. We will return to this cleavage of dogma, but for the moment it is important to insist that Eulalio ceased then and there to be a student.

Still, he was not his own teacher. How could he be without the etheric and earthly perfusion of love? The being that refuses love refuses development, withdraws into a cocoon which is not silken but unbending. In this Freud is correct. Let us avoid, however, a rather simple misunderstanding: unrequited love is as strong and as salutary as requited love; it is not a perversion. You are carried away from the sick diameter of the ego, you become porous to the world-stream, you learn to expand and contract according to a distant cadence, you reacquaint yourself with awe. It is sheer vulgarity, sheer corruption, to insist on proprietorship. This insistence brings upon itself the heavy penalty of obsession. Unrequited love is not obsession. Eulalio fell in love with Natividad. And Natividad was cut off from corresponding to his love. At all times, but especially in youth, the love of man and the love of woman obey different temporal orders. She suspects something predatory in the abrupt energy of courtship and struggles to tame it—to understand whether there is anything behind the energy: animal, man, vacuum . . . soul. Was there anything behind Eulalio's? Had Castaños and Ceniceros lingered on this epoch, they would have answered *soul,* but they rush toward the second hierophany and Eulalio's mature thought. The courtship of Natividad stands in the same mist that permeates the childhood of Jesus. Ledger Rosenthal, the controversial British anthropologist, in *The Construction of Religion in the Americas*, has a brief passage that carries a measure of light:

> Most followers, however, know nothing of the schism and freely indulge in an untimely bricolage of legend. The love that Eulalio professed to Natividad is a rich source: at every site consecrated to their brief yet resonant story you can listen to numerous variations. I was moved by the departure of Natividad to Europe. Near the sickly green bridge, an old man, impervious to

the scalding sun, recreated their farewell with a serene disposition that was interrupted only when an intensely personal counterpoint seemed to take possession of his narrative: he had known Eulalio's muteness before Natividad when he accompanied his only daughter to the bus station as she left to the United States and he had also known Natividad's tenderness when his only daughter thrust her scapular into one of his hands and clasped it with rare strength. The love of Eulalio is everyone's love; the loss of Eulalio is everyone's loss. The episodes of his life must be seen as outlines that goad famished imaginations into the realm of symbols, where they can finally support their lives.

We are at the threshold. Matías Ceniceros has the best description of Eulalio's second hierophany:

> Velardeña had called, but there remained in *him* a tempest of longings to share in the activities of *his* fellows. He had nothing of the anchorite. Father Próspero recommended *him* to the priests of the Temple of Saint Augustine in Durango. It was a difficult excursion through *his* world into our own. The cathedral, like a couple of protruding fangs, welcomed *him* in the flesh only to see *him* off in the spirit. He felt the city was a series of abstractions, exclusions, and mutilations of Nature. He intuited that its aim was to imprison all principles of expansion in order to suit humanity to a lower being. The priests, finally, giddy with their abundance of pulque and tepache, content to plot against revolutionary factions, voluptuous in the acceptance of disreputable offerings, rid *him* of any conciliatory thoughts. The city was a blindfold, and its history was the hurried nullification of all aspiring.

Although the passage lacks the martial rhythms of religious solemnity, it lays bare the religious impulse, which is always a fury for restructuring. One can notice during moments of upheaval that politics, despite its attempts at refinement, is indiscernible from this impulse. Let us stress the word *fury*: in our sad days of technocratic regimes, the scientist who reaches power undergoes a ceremonial conversion that discloses another world—free of blemish; there is in the revelation of purity a lifelong intoxication, perhaps the only durable romance.

Eulalio returned to Velardeña after a recordless absence. Ceniceros and Castaños speak of a season of wandering through the barren lands. We can speculate that, wherever he lived, he subjected himself to the rigors of his new worldview, for he convulsed the people's slow spirituality almost at once. This could be achieved only through example. Castaños's *Pronghorn* details with profuse anecdotes and parables the yearslong conquest of a following: it is one thing to startle someone back into life, but another to keep them in life. The undeniably robust suggestiveness of Catholicism led most would-be converts to find in Eulalio's ideas a quaint derivation. But before we say anything else about their reception, a summary, however difficult, is necessary.

Everything we know about Eulalio's teachings comes from his two greatest disciples: Sixto Castaños and Matías Ceniceros. In spite of the miraculous intervention of the written word in his life, Eulalio felt no vital attraction to it. Perhaps in his wanderings he thought of the immortality of Socrates, Jesus, and Buddha; perhaps he thought of the incriminating essence of all books. Both Castaños and Ceniceros believe otherwise: the volatilization of the I that Eulalio so deeply embodied ruled out the peace of mind that writing demands. Incidentally, the volatilization of the I is a fine point to build upon. Each of us is gifted with a *private universe* that is a delectable, if limited, version of Nature. We explore it almost by accident and come, in time, to identify with it: the resulting map is the *ego*. Further excursions can amplify the territory, but for the most part there are no great discoveries. All great discoveries, in fact, must be aided by Nature, and so detach us from ourselves. Then we can speak of an *ascent in identification* for the *I*: with the animal, with the plant, with matter. To be clear, the ego is pure interiority; the I is the effort to expand outward. Everything that has been stated is contained in *the volatilization of the I*, which is the great method that leads to *the substantial experience of Nature*. I am here using Ceniceros's terminology. We can clarify it somewhat if we borrow from Rudolf Otto's *The Idea of the Holy*: *the ascent in identification* is the *mysterium tremendum*, and *the substantial experience of Nature* the *mysterium fascinans*. To Eulalio, the numinous is cyclical, in no way persistent. We undergo long periods of its absence. Yet wherever it has been, wherever it has led us to identify with animal, plant, or matter, there we must re-create its arrival.

Prima facie, this is a religion with a strong individualistic bent. We all carry a private universe of our own that will share little with that of others. We all will struggle for salvation at different tempos. Indeed, volume after volume, Ceniceros has theorized as much. Against him, festivity after festivity, Castaños has championed a maximally communal religion. The private universe chains us to individualism, but in the effort to ascend we share in the bounty of Nature. Here is the great cleavage. Here we have opposing views that have brought singular forms of premature decadence. We will approach each of them in turn and analyze how Eulalio related to it.

Matías Ceniceros was not a native of Velardeña. He was born in Guadalupe, the son of two relatively prosperous teachers. After a somewhat irregular formation in the city's itinerant seminary, he traveled throughout the country as preacher and journalist. His nomadic existence was the consequence of increasingly radical beliefs on the nature of religion: a moderate skepticism about Catholicism's adequacy for the modern world grew into a full-blown rejection. More than once, his brilliance as a polemicist attracted comparisons to Jaime Balmes. But his labors lacked the constructive element. It was only in his mid-thirties, as he lay exhausted and mired in cosmopolitan eclecticisms, that he heard of Eulalio Salmantino. As the sixties reached a glut of supply in spiritual commodities, Ceniceros found a dogma. He arrived at Velardeña when a good part of the community was supporting Castaños in his dream of rivaling the Catholic church's organization. In this, he and Ceniceros seemed destined to work harmoniously. But through their immediate gains they drifted apart: Ceniceros managed to capture the attention of the intelligentsia, and again succumbed to wayfaring. There were only two reasons to keep returning to Velardeña: the budding press and the "peregrinations." Both initiatives had international reach as an objective. The press was dedicated mainly to the publication of Ceniceros's own work (and later on to that of his cosmopolitan pals); the "peregrinations" were no more than tours led by Ceniceros for the diversion of curious foreigners (invitation only, of course). If Eulalio has figured little in Ceniceros's trajectory, it is owing to the sage's unrelenting coldness toward him, especially during the final years. This has encouraged some specious criticisms, none so common as that which imagines Ceniceros's graphomania a compensation for the absent patriarch. Matías Ceniceros is a philosopher. It was never within his purview to understand the core of Eulalio's teachings. We can affirm that he understands Eulalio as much as Kierkegaard understands Christ, which is to say, very little. This is not a critical remark. The philosopher is a creative misunderstander. He must err to find the enlivening pathways, or at least to amuse us out of complacency. And yet Ceniceros is not wholly a philosopher. He wishes to reach posterity in the disciplined ranks of a school. He has no patience for the diffuse influence of private and chance encounters. In this matter, he is a model advocate: the teachings of Eulalio will spread even if this means their burial in abstractions.

With Sixto Castaños we face the problem of loyalty. Born in Cuencamé, he soon ended up in Father Próspero's orphanage. There are credible sources that tie his parents to the Sinarquista movement; those who speak of their unsuccessful revival of violence through independent guerrilla campaigns go a step too far—a dark background against which Castaños's gregariousness can radiate the more. For this is his abiding inclination: under his firm support, Father Próspero's educational project flourished for a brief period; likewise, Eulalio's arduous example became an incitation to holiness. Castaños is the pupil who asks of his teacher a permanent guidance, who impels him never to permit a levelling. He senses that autonomy is divinely ordained, and that there is no joy therein for the earthbound. Thus, he disappeared into Eulalio. How did they meet? How did their relationship develop? With great consistency, Castaños offers no answers in *Pronghorn*. No explicit answers. In a rare passage of convoluted metaphysics, there is an intimation:

> Then the dog perished. Every man and every woman accompanied him in his grief, for they knew that the loss of life, in spite of their hopes, is an affront. They withheld their gifts, for they knew that a gift without festivity is an affront. They commiserated. Then he reprimanded

> them for their lethargy. And he spoke of the dog as he had spoken of the sun that very morning. He said of the dog as he had said of the sun that the eye belittles it and that the eye ignores what the rest of the senses understand. He said of the dog as he had said of the sun that it is vast because in its service there are no limits. So the men and the women listened, but they could not rid themselves of their pity. And he spoke of the dog as he had before spoken of his own entrails. He said of the dog that its movement could cease yet not its linkage. He said of the dog that its span was an echo of a greater span and that there labored an echo more. So the men and women listened and cast off their pity. They set foot in his gladness. There was no grief.

For all Castaños's devotion, Eulalio still seems to elude us. Is not the most fervent pupil equally the most intense traitor? By becoming a mirror, he predisposes the other to vanity. It would be a mistake for us to sever the religious impulse from vanity. That fury for restructuring borders the need to do so in one's own image. The lures of asceticism and mysticism respond to this threat with the detonation of the self. But Eulalio, by allowing discipleship, allowed distortions. Let us again emphasize that this is not the loving distortion of chance encounters, which is ultimately a form of justice, but the distortion of unperturbed loyalty.

In his final years, as his disciples quarreled, Eulalio reached the autumn of notoriety. Most national newspapers began to show great interest in his community and in his views, while television networks wrangled for an interview. Yet as the essence of his work became clearer, the commotion subsided—the last thing the (always) rising nation of Mexico needed was a mysterious sage who insisted on the sacredness of nature and who sympathized with movements like the EZLN. And as it subsided, it turned to the resources of scorn. This is the way of the nation: everything but industrialization and trade is a matter of laughter. He died in a very different world, innocent of the struggle for an ideal, violence the lone surviving tradition. Those who surrounded him in Velardeña do not constitute a decisive number.

Yes, Eulalio is lost to us. There is no human being as irretrievable as the religious founder. The word, so dear to Eulalio, is a seed that in its growth becomes unrecognizable. But can there be a greater fate? To utter and then become the uttered, and as the uttered to live in the realm of meanings, inaccessible. Devotees do not remember Laozi, Zoroaster, and Moses. They instantiate through conduct all that is suggestive in their words and thus keep apace the luxuriance of the foliage. In their inaccessibility, they remain divine. More than all the others, the religious impulse is rare, for it grants the word its primal sway. The *Physiologus* transmitted something of this secret to Eulalio, and he made sure to cherish it.

Corina Bardoff

Chemical Night with Eiderdown

A written proclamation on a large piece of cardstock was stapled to the signboard in the central plaza: a truck would drive through town emitting gas to poison the mosquitoes, so residents should remain inside with their doors and windows sealed.

I was shutting up my house when the night jerk arrived. I had to let him in. Whenever he arrives, I have the sensation of falling into the void, or a void, a narrow, personal void fitted to me. We first met on a park bench, and I felt the floor was lava: I felt we were on a life-raft shaped like a bench, just the two of us, and so I felt an immediate affinity for the jerk, as well as resignation. He swims so much during the day, his hair is wet all evening. The jerk had not been around for weeks, which was typical for the handsome raccoon, and I was dizzy, worrying whether my windows were properly sealed. "You're not a mosquito," said the night jerk. He wandered into the kitchen, where the remains of my dinner and dinner making were strewn on all the surfaces. "You ate your whole dinner but these last three peas were too much for you?" he asked while scooping them from the plate and into his mouth. There are two ways to do someone else's dishes: 1) in a helpful way, and 2) in a reproachful way.

To avoid hearing the trucks go by, I turned on my stereo. I thought also that music might set the mood with the night jerk, and I imagined tuning the atmosphere like a music producer at their faders. Oh, I am always imagining things, and it's never any help. Who had turned the volume dial all the way up? Guitar blared out of the speakers so loud, the jerk and I collapsed in precisely the same way—it's a thing we have in common: we bent at the knees holding our ears with each hand, until our knees alit on the carpet, sinking beyond that being unnecessary. I crawled to the stereo and turned the volume dial all the way in the opposite direction, so that guitars still played silently. A pain vibrated my eardrums, and I felt attacked with no one specific to fear or blame. We sat on the carpet in the tinny silence. It did feel good to be vulnerable together. By good, I mean I felt we were back on a life raft, close, in solidarity. I began to walk on my knees and shins toward my bedroom, until my A-line skirt tripped me, and I caught myself on my hands and crawled. The jerk crawled behind me. I opened the door the way a dog does. I crashed onto my bed like a shipwreck, and the jerk crashed next to me. We grabbed pillows and stuffed them with our heads, our heads sandwiched between them like a double decker: pillow, my head, pillow, jerk's head, pillow. I could still hear him say, "When are you going to get a bed frame? Sleeping on a mattress on the floor makes you seem poor." "I like it this way," he heard me say. The problem is, I know I'm going to sleep with him, so the jerk being annoying makes me feel like I'm making a bad decision. But it has already been decided.

I remembered a concert I had been to in a mattress store. The owners' daughter was a musician, and she hosted concerts after hours. The performance was required to involve the mattresses in some way. Sometimes the musicians leaned them against the walls to help the acoustics, sometimes they stacked them up to erect a raised but squishy stage, and, for the concert I went to, they laid out six soft mattresses for the audience to lie on during the concert. There was a pleasant confusion lying on a mattress with strangers, with BYO pillows propping up our heads. The music was all strumming and plucking, and the woman to my left lay on a luxurious pillow of her own curls. I know there was a man to my right, but was it the night jerk? I asked him if he remembered the mattress store. "Are you sure you're not making this up?" People ask me that all the time, for some reason, and like stepping into quicksand, I am suddenly unsure. I wouldn't ever want the floor to actually be lava, of course. Yet, the floor being lava is the state of being I always want to return to, and that is what the concert was like: our feet dangled off the mattress without touching the floor, and I felt a sly collaboration with my five mattress-mates, as well as a sideways suspicion of the other mattress groups. We should make ourselves a flag and a handshake and a secret code. The outside is poison gas, but my house is too big to be a life raft, and again, I do not want actual lava, only pretend. "I'm pretty sure I know precisely what you're thinking," said the night jerk, as it grew dark, I did not turn on the light, and he drew me closer.

The eiderdown cover had cost me six thousand dollars, I was thinking, feeling both satisfied and alarmed. Was I sure I had ever had six thousand dollars? The cover was white, soft and warm, but oddly lumpy: had it always been so lumpy? "You're muttering in your sleep," said the night jerk. The lumps were moving, and as they moved they became individuals, each one dear to me as a litter of kittens. The lumps were inspecting the bed, inspecting me and the night jerk, and interacting with one another in a manner that was hidden by the cover. They sounded like mourning doves, I thought, or they sounded like they were muttering in a lumpen language. Oh, they're ducks, not lumps—King Eider Ducks! That must be why the blanket was so expensive. Thank goodness, I closed all the windows so the ducks are protected from the gas.

Julian Stannard

The Flogger

James met the flogger at a self-help group. He'd always been wary about therapy. He could easily imagine men sitting in a circle with the therapist coaxing intimacies and confessions, the men wishing they were somewhere else. You saw it in films. Out of the silence a man speaks up as if he were at a Quaker meeting. He has never spoken about this before, he says, it's not easy. The man next to him puts an arm round his shoulders rather tentatively. Another sobs. The therapist looks pleased with himself. When the session ends the man hangs around to have another word. There are other scenarios too. A man gets worked up. Fuck, fuck, fuck, he shouts and storms out, knocking over a chair. He's back the following week, in a more reflective mood. The therapist looks pleased with himself.

James didn't plan to become a long-term patient. Not much wrong with him. He was thirty-three and worked for a law firm. He was not unattractive, if anything he looked rather young for his age, needing to shave only every other day. At school they called him baby face. Though he didn't play any sports he was in pretty good shape. He had some good friends and his social life wasn't bad though heavy drinking now gave him a headache which lasted a couple of days. A great aunt had left him some money. He'd bought a two-bedroomed flat in Stoke Newington. He was lucky, he knew that.

Since his father died he'd experienced drift, not in any overtly tragic way. He missed being able to call his father on the phone. He hadn't seen him often but he liked hearing his voice. His father had been a good man. He wanted his son to do well. He wanted his son to be happy. James had done fairly well but he was single and not crazily ambitious though he guessed he had a degree of resilience, not least when it came to law exams, some of which he'd had to do again. He was beginning to feel all those years in front of him were something to endure rather than enjoy.

A Jewish friend said, 'You become a man when your father dies.'

James, of late, had spent a lot of time looking out of the window. He had found it difficult to focus. His GP put him on a low dose of sertraline.

He saw the leaflet in a Turkish Restaurant. Men Need to Talk, it said, along with other notices advertising yoga and advanced meditation. He took a picture of the email address with his phone and by the time he got home he decided he was going to give it a try. Danny replied immediately. Newcomers welcome. Each session required a ten-pound contribution to help with costs.

James didn't say anything at the first two meetings. They listened to a guy who'd broken up with his wife. His wife had been screwing someone else and she told him the marriage had run its course. They had two children and George had a sense of foreboding. What if the children drifted away and switched their affections to this new man? He put his head in hands when he said that.

At the third meeting Danny invited James to say why he'd joined the group and James began to explain that since his father had died he felt there was a void in his life. He hadn't wanted to say void but he couldn't think of another word so he went ahead and said it.

'You mean like being in a sailboat and discovering the tiller isn't working?' Kevin asked.

James had never been in a sailboat. Nevertheless, he said, 'Yes, that's exactly it.'

Kevin looked pleased with himself and Danny smiled. No one had much to say apart from 'Have you ever considered rock climbing?'

As they piled out of the deconsecrated church Victor put a hand on James' shoulder. 'Care for a drink?' Victor took him to a pub around the corner and fetched him a gin and tonic. Victor drank bottled water.

'You're not drinking?' James asked.

'Not when I'm working. These days I'm working round the clock.'

Victor was wearing a suit, which made him look like a manager rather than a man in need of therapy. He had never spoken about himself in the sessions but sometimes offered suggestions after a patient had spoken. He used words like

'Balance' and 'Control' and 'Bracing'. On one occasion he said, 'There's no shame in suffering pain.'

'I'm Victor by the way.' He had a strong grip.

Victor was urbane and black and spoke with a Nigerian lilt. 'I was brought up in Abuja,' he explained.

At school James had had a crush on a boy. James was sixteen, Solomon a couple of years older. They'd fooled around a couple of times but Solomon made it clear it wasn't really his thing and James blushed every time he saw him after that. Solomon won a scholarship to Oxford, the first black boy to win a scholarship to that college, and James hadn't seen him since. At university James began a relationship with a girl who was studying psychology.

It was pleasant talking to Victor. His questions were purposeful. James guessed he was in his early forties.

'What do you think about Danny's sessions?' Victor asked.

'They're rather as I'd imagined. There's a formula.'

'Do you think you'll find what you're looking for?'

'I'm not sure. I'll have to stick at it a while.'

'I think you're wasting your time,' Victor said.

Victor looked at his watch and said he had an appointment. It was nearly nine o' clock. It seemed late for an appointment but James wanted to get home too.

'Take this card,' Victor said, 'there's a number on the back.'

Victor wasn't there at the next self-help group, nor the one after. James' sailboat with its broken tiller became the focus of the discussion. Kevin had taken the idea to his heart and was exploring it in a number of ways.

'When the wind stops blowing you're in the doldrums. You're like a child on a three-legged rocking horse that's going nowhere. Is that how you feel James?'

James couldn't remember being on a rocking horse, three-legged or otherwise, but he said 'Yes, that's spot-on Kevin.' Kevin smiled and a new face said, 'Have you ever thought of going on a pilgrimage? You don't have to believe in God. You don't have to believe in anything.'

Kevin continued. 'Do you see the oil tanker getting nearer and nearer.'

'Yes,' James said. 'It's getting nearer by the day.'

Danny leant forward, 'Have you thought about mending the tiller?'

There was silence after that.

That night James took out the card Victor had given him and examined it. On one side it said Treatments, on the other it said Build a Life that Stays the Course. Just as Victor had said there was a number too. James decided to call it. Victor answered straightaway.

'I thought you'd call.'

Pleasant to hear his voice.

James said, 'You've not going to the group anymore?'

'I don't think there's much more I can do there. I've found another one in Crouch End.'

James wanted to ask what he was looking for but thought better of it.

'Kevin was right,' continued Victor, 'you're just bobbing around. I think you're adrift. I'm not saying Danny isn't a good man.'

'He has interesting ideas,' James said.

'Ideas need to be converted into actions,' Victor said. 'You need a sharper focus. Have you looked at my card?'

James looked at the card again which was in his hands and he said out loud, 'Build A Life That Stays The Course. It's ambitious Victor, I'll give you that. Cryptic even. I can only suppose you charge a fee. Can you give me more information?'

'I'm not in this business to make money James. I'd call it a vocation.'

James felt sheepish.

'I have to cover my costs but we can go through that on another occasion. The best thing is to come round and get a feel for it. Once you understand my approach I don't think you'll find it cryptic at all.'

Work kept James busy. As a young solicitor he needed to put in the hours. Friday evening he decided to ring Victor. Victor answered straightaway. James, you're a lucky man, I'm free tomorrow at noon.

Victor, he discovered, lived in a hotel. The Nigerian therapist gave him the name over the phone. 'Go straight past the receptionist and you'll find some stairs which take you down to the basement. Be punctual. Wear a suit.'

James looked up the hotel and saw it was nearby. It described itself as 'stylishly boutique'. He went to bed early and dreamt of Solomon for the first time in years.

James walked into the hotel and saw a young woman behind the desk. He thought she was going to ask him how she could help but she didn't look up. James walked past the reception as instructed and found the stairs going down to the basement. Victor had told him to knock on the door and wait. Victor appeared in a blue dashiki and a matching kufi hat.

'Come Mr James.'

The basement was spacious. There were several doors off the long corridor. Victor took him into a sitting room. There was a pair of black shoes on the floor.

'Mint tea?' Victor asked and disappeared into the kitchen. James noticed a long cane with a carved head on the wall. Victor brought in a tray.

'Take a seat James, make yourself comfortable.'

Victor put the tray on the glass table and poured the tea. For a while they drank in silence.

'Tea to your liking? Good. I thought it important you saw where I lived.' Victor waved his hand in an expansive gesture. 'It suits me well—I do a little work for the hotel and we came to an agreeable arrangement.'

James carried on sipping.

'One of the advantages,' Victor continued, 'is that my apartment is completely soundproofed. I can play music very loudly and no one hears a thing, not a dicky bird.' He picked up the remote control and the room was flooded with Bach.

After listening to the music for a while Victor said, 'James, my friend, let me give you the tour.'

They walked down the corridor decorated with African masks. Victor opened a couple of built-in wardrobes, full of shirts, suits, trousers and rows of shoes. James remembered a line from *The Great Gatsby*. Victor opened the door to the shower room. It was very modern and very clean.

'My father was a pastor,' Victor said. 'A good one at that. He had a fondness for that old expression—I'm sure you know it—"Cleanliness is next to godliness."' Victor laughed. 'He was right of course. I like my clients to shower before their treatment. You're good with that Mr James?'

'I had one this morning.'

'Two showers never harmed anyone. This shower will scrub off those bits other showers can't reach.' Victor laughed again, a good throaty laugh. 'Hang your suit up here. I'll bring you a towel and a dressing gown.'

James stood under the shower and it felt as if the power of the water were pinning him down. The temperature was perfect and there were bottles of shampoo and body wash which smelt of coconut and lime. If this was godliness bring it on. He seemed to be under the water for ages. It was only when it turned icy cold that he switched off the shower and dried himself with the luxurious towel. He hadn't planned to wash his hair but he had. There was a high-speed hairdryer attached to the wall which meant it only took him a few minutes to get everything dry. He put on the dressing gown.

Victor sat in the armchair, in his dashiki, legs apart.

'I bet you feel like a new man,' he laughed. 'I thought you'd appreciate a deep clean. You smell of coconut. Suits you. Now put your clothes back on. I have a job for you.'

The shoes were on the glass table, on top of a tea towel, along with a tin of black polish and a couple of brushes and a cloth.

'When was the last time you polished your shoes?'

'I couldn't say.'

'We need to do something about that.'

James blushed.

'I like my shoes to shine. You could start with these. Nice aren't they?'

James sat looking at them. Like mini gondolas.

'I'd like you to clean those shoes for me.' Victor pointed at them as if to remind James they were real shoes, shoes which had walked the streets of London.

James looked again.

'Best to make a start, wouldn't you say? Take them off the table and kneel over there so you can put some elbow grease into it.'

Bach continued to come out of the large speaker.

'There's a cloth to clean them and a brush to polish them up nice and bright.'

James was thinking of Danny's comment—Have you thought of mending the tiller?

He began on the shoes.

Victor sat in the armchair, legs apart, watching.

James was thinking this was the first time he'd cleaned someone else's shoes. Then he remembered when he was a boy he sometimes cleaned his father's.

'You've missed a bit there,' Victor said, pointing a finger.

The music was soothing and mathematical, the smell of black polish not unpleasant.

After a while Victor said, 'Pop them on the table, and take a seat. Not bad James, not bad, for a first attempt. How do you feel. Feeling good?'

Kneeling on the floor had made his legs ache.

'I tell my clients the benefit of the treatments isn't a straightaway thing. It can take a while to sink in. Next week perhaps, the week after, you might think of my shoes and feel proud. Feel good.'

Victor looked at his watch, 'Mr James, I've got a client coming in a while so we'd better bring this session to an end. You've made a good start.' He paused a moment. 'I'm not in the therapy business to make money. At the same time I don't want to be out of pocket. Can you take down my bank details and then we can deal with any financial matters efficiently. There are more important things to worry about.'

James put the details into his phone though he couldn't really imagine what costs he'd incurred.

'Excellent. Before you go why don't I show you the Treatment Room?'

James wanted a cigarette. He'd been trying to give up but he thought he'd reward himself with one as soon as he'd left the hotel.

They walked down the corridor and came to the last door.

Victor unlocked the door and switched on a light.

The only thing in the room was some kind of contraption which reminded James of the 'horse' they'd had in the school gym. This was rather more elaborate and looked as if it were made of leather. Then James looked at the wall. Hanging from a rail there were canes of all lengths and sizes, a tawse, a whip and a couple of riding crops.

He stepped back.

'Relax James,' Victor said, putting an arm around him. 'I call him Jonny, after my first client. He's a CEO in the Far East now, *very* successful. You've done well today. Give me a call when you want to arrange the next session. You know where I am.'

James walked past the receptionist feeling feverish and once he got out of the hotel he lit up and walked quickly down the road and he lit up again once he'd thrown the first cigarette down a drain. It was March and it looked as if it were going to rain. If he walked fast he'd get home before the downpour.

That evening he was going to a dinner party. He hung up his suit, took some paracetamol and lay on his bed for twenty minutes. He'd start on that report his boss had asked for before he went out.

The dinner party was a success and on Sunday James nursed a hangover.

He woke up early on Monday morning and polished his shoes before going to work. He put on his best suit and decided to throw himself into his work. He needed to make a good job of the report. He wasn't going to think about Victor and he was going to chuck Danny's group too. He'd always known, deep down, therapy was a con.

Two days later he picked up a voice message from Victor. His heart started to pound.

'Been thinking about you James. I've been wearing my lovely clean shoes. I trust your shoes are shining too.' There was some amusement in the voice when he said that. 'Best foot forward. I've given some thought to your expenses. Nothing to worry about. You did enjoy that hot shower didn't you? And you seem to have gotten carried away with the coconut shampoo! Shoe polish doesn't fall off trees you know, especially the high-end stuff I buy. And towels and dressing gowns need to be laundered. My clients deserve the cleanest, the brightest. Not to mention my dashikis. They need to be dry-cleaned to get the best effect. You know what I'm going to say don't you, Mr James? Cleanliness is next to . . .' Victor continued: 'I got the impression you rather enjoyed the mint tea.' There was another pause as if James were meant to reply. 'As this was your first session I will give you a discount—you deserve one my friend.' Victor stopped talking for a while. 'Could you shoot over a hundred and fifty pounds. Today please. I look forward to arranging another session. Get in touch when you're ready.'

James walked around the flat. He could feel the heat rising to his neck. He went into the kitchen and poured himself a glass of water. He expects me to pay a hundred and fifty pounds for cleaning his shoes and using his shower! He looked out of the window. The sky was like tinned soup. Maybe he'd give Danny's group another go.

James had missed a couple of sessions. Danny was pleased to see him. 'We've missed you,' he said and gave him a hug. Kevin gave him a hug too.

Danny said 'Before we begin today's session I have some bad news.' There were eight men in the room, all holding bottles of water, all worried. 'Because the council has upped their prices I'm going to have to ask you to pay twelve pounds each session—starting from next week. If any of you think this will be difficult please have a word and I'll see what I can do.'

It was Kevin's moment now. He'd had this illness when he was a teenager and this had resulted in a neurological problem in his right leg. James had noticed he dragged it along as if there were a rock at the end of it instead of a foot. Kevin welled up when he talked about the operations and the procedures and the interventions and the long periods off school and the fact he could never play football again. 'That was another dream down the pan,' he said, in an unexpectedly cheerful voice. He talked about vegetable diets and physiotherapy and pain killers with nasty side effects and the bespoke swimming lessons and the turmeric drinks his mother insisted on making, which he sipped without enthusiasm looking out of the kitchen window watching the kids in the park. He talked about the pain. You have to take your mind over there, he was saying. Danny leant forwards.

Kevin continued, 'Imagine a scorpion has taken up permanent residence in your leg and then the scorpion has a large family.'

There was a long silence and James almost said, 'Have you ever thought of taking up rock climbing?'

'I had my first spliff when I was sixteen,' continued Kevin, 'and that was a Jesus is the resurrection and Jesus is the world to come moment. I've spent a good decade spliffed out. The scorpions still live in my leg but I don't hate them as much. Sometimes I talk to them, nothing deep or philosophical, more like a wave of the hand, an acknowledgment we hang about in the same space. I've floated over London and I've floated back. Been hard to hold down a job, any job. Love life? Forget it! What with the weed and the painkillers and the pain which flares up any moment I could hardly describe myself as a hot date!'

He put his head in his hands as if to say I can't speak anymore.

There was a round of applause. Danny said, 'Thank you for sharing this,' and stepped forward, getting into hug mode.

There was a fifteen-minute break. People could slip outside and have a cigarette or fix themselves a hot drink. There was a kettle and a large tin of instant coffee which had been there a long time.

After the break Danny switched the focus to James. Kevin had revived, seemingly. 'Are you still bobbing around in that sailboat?' he asked, 'dodging oil tankers and sharks?'

James said—though he didn't know he was going to say it—'You know what? I've stopped caring about the tiller. I'm going to sit on the boat and let it drift.' He felt hot. 'If I get sucked underneath some fucking big tanker so be it. I think it's in the hands of a higher power now.' He didn't know why he said this because he'd long stopped believing in a higher power, and he hardly ever used the F word.

Danny looked alarmed and then pleased and then alarmed again.

Kevin said, 'James, we don't want to lose you, we want you to arrive at a safe place.' A new face in the group said, 'Have you thought of learning a new language, a really difficult one like Chinese? '

James could tell that Danny wanted a word at the end of the session but he hurried out of the church and smoked a cigarette round the corner.

When James got home he sat on the bed and tried to imagine being dead. He took off his shoes—they needed a polish—and he lay on the bed.

When he woke up he saw there were two missed calls from Victor. He pulled up Victor's bank details and transferred the one hundred and fifty pounds. That's it! Over and out. Hasta la vista. I hope your gondolas fetch up at the Lido in style.

Thirty minutes later James got a text from his ex-girlfriend.

He met Molly at an Indian restaurant and although she didn't spell it out it was clear she was breaking up with Ezra. She was in low spirits. At one point she reached out and touched James' hand. 'I miss you,' she said.

James worked hard for the next few weeks, getting to work a little earlier than necessary and leaving a little later than his colleagues. One morning, in the lift, a tax lawyer from the neighbouring office said, 'Terrific shoes!'

After he'd transferred the one hundred and fifty pounds to Victor's account he received a message saying 'Appreciated.' The message continued, 'This demonstrates an admirable commitment on your part. I look forward to seeing you in the near future.'

James bristled. He should never have agreed to see Victor in the first place. He had dreamt about Solomon again and he'd dreamt about his ex-girlfriend too and one night he dreamt of the 'horse' in Victor's basement. He woke up feeling hot and he listened to Debussy on the World Service.

Things were going well at work. One of the partners called him into the office and shook his hand in a hearty partner kind of way. He complimented him on the report. 'James, you're finding your feet. Keep it up.'

James met Molly again. She told him about Ezra, though he wasn't that keen to know about Ezra. He was from Colorado, a former college football player, a quarter back. James had seen him at a party once, buffed up and breezy.

Molly was saying, 'He was great in bed, have to give him that, but he thought he was the only show in town, always expecting me to put him first.' Molly had a job in Media Communications and she wasn't going to allow some boyfriend to boss her around.

James was aware he had not been a great lover. He came too quickly and she never seemed to climax. He imagined, not that he wanted to imagine, the ex-quarter back climbing over Molly. After James had walked her back to her flat she kissed him on the lips.

A month later he passed Danny on Cazenove Road.

'Have you given up on us?' Danny asked.

'So busy at work I've put things on hold.'

'Remember, we're always there for you.'

'How's Kevin?' James asked.

'He's got himself a girlfriend. She has a neurological leg too. You might say they've found each other.'

James imagined them limping around in an amorous fog.

One morning—a Tuesday as it happens—James woke up and felt as if a switch had been slipped into the lining of his stomach. It wasn't painful as such. It felt as if he were about to sit an exam on Advanced Litigation, one that he'd previously flunked. This time he was prepared. He just had to keep his nerve and then he was going to smash it. He felt the adrenaline, the giddiness, the rush. Although he'd not been in contact with Victor since he'd paid the treatment fee—he'd deleted his number—he knew he'd placed the business card in his drawer, the one full of socks. He looked at the card—Build a Life that Stays the Course it said. He realised he was going to ring the number. On the tube that morning he found it hard to focus and he almost missed his stop. At his desk, later in the morning, he looked down at his shoes and realised he'd not cleaned them for several days.

He phoned after work and Victor answered at once.

'Good man,' he said. 'You've given it some thought and now you're ready. Lucky for you, I have a slot on Saturday at noon. You know the drill: wear a suit and oh yes some clean underwear please. I like my clients to wear white underclothes. White is a sign of purity. My father used to say God is everywhere. Which makes one think, doesn't it? Make sure you have a light breakfast and Mr James I want to see those shoes gleaming.'

Victor cut the call and James was left standing in the stretched-out light. The days were getting longer and the last rays of the sun made a rectangular pattern on the wall.

The following day, after work, James went to John Lewis and took the escalator to the floor selling underwear. He needed some new pants anyway. Molly was messaging him frequently, and each message friendlier than the one before. He was masturbating more than usual. He bought a pack of briefs—white—and he picked out some vests too. He tapped his card at the counter but it was declined.

'Strange,' he said, feeling he ought to say something. Then he pulled out another card.

'Gone through perfectly,' the cashier said.

It was Friday, the day before his appointment at the boutique hotel. James knew he could ring Victor at any time of the day and tell him that something had come up and, regrettably, he wouldn't be able to make it. They would have to arrange another day, he was saying in his head. We could even make it a day which never comes into being, like the end of time say, when the Four Horsemen were saddling up and looking mean.

He didn't ring Victor.

On the way to the hotel, Saturday morning, he saw a reflection of himself in a shop window. He looked like a million dollars, as if he were going to an interview, knowing it was a done deal, a shoe in. He'd showered early and then remembered Victor's power shower—maybe he ought to get one himself. He'd eaten two pieces of toast at eight o'clock and he was already feeling hungry. When he walked into the hotel the receptionist looked up and smiled. He took the stairs down to the basement and knocked on the door. He was a little early. After a couple of minutes he put his ear to the door wondering if he might be able to hear some music: Bach, Elgar, Scarlatti. Nothing. He didn't want to knock again, not yet. Then he heard what might have been a cough, a soundproofed cough. What if Victor were standing behind the door, examining him through the spyhole? James started to sweat. He heard the sound of something hissing through the air followed by a grunt, and then again and again as if Victor were perfecting some old-fangled, new-fangled Nipponese-Nigerian martial art. The door opened. Victor was wearing a black dashiki with matching hat, holding a cane in his left hand. He was beaming.

'You're looking great Mr James—look at those shoes! Come on in.' He popped the cane against the wall and put an arm around James' shoulder.

James opened his mouth but nothing came out.

'No mint tea today, Mr James. Just water, the drink of lions!' There was a tall glass on the table. 'London tap water,' Victor continued, 'but I wouldn't want my clients to drink out of the tap. I use a filtering device so the water is as pure as a Baptismal font.'

James couldn't help wondering about the fee. He remembered Victor's comment. There are more important things than money. He drank the water and it tasted good.

'I think you know where we're going to start. Take yourself to the shower room—you remember where it is? Towel and dressing gown hanging up and cleanse yourself thoroughly sir. When you're done, put on your underclothes and we're ready to go!'

He didn't really enjoy the shower this time. He breathed deeply and rubbed himself with a shower cream called Fruits of the Forest. He glanced down. His penis seemed to have shrunk. He realised he could emerge from the shower, dress quickly and say he felt out of sorts, had taken a turn, and walk down the corridor and let himself out into the freedom of the city. He knew Victor wouldn't be very happy and of course he didn't know whether Victor had locked the front door. He imagined Victor was a man who didn't like his work to be interrupted. He blanked this all out for a minute or two and the hot water rooted him to the spot. He didn't wash his hair. The water turned cold.

James walked into the sitting room. Victor was sitting in the armchair, Handel playing on the stereo. 'Ah,' he said, 'a new client fragrant with fruits of the forest! We're going to skip the shoeshine today. Bigger fish to fry. Follow me.'

As they walked down the corridor Victor put his hand on James' back. They walked past the books, the African statues and the maps of Nigeria on the wall. When they passed the shower room the soapy cleanliness drifted out from under the door. They got to the Treatment Room. James could feel his heart thumping though his cotton vest.

Victor took out a key and unlocked the door. 'Please go in,' he said. The walls were white like a sanatorium yet the room smelt of sweat. 'I think we should open the window and let in some air. Nothing like a bit of fresh air. I had a client earlier this morning, a promising client, a young barrister beginning to make his mark. Today, for the first time, he took twelve strokes. You are looking at the aftermath of a heroic struggle.'

It was a warm summer day, and now the window was open, there was a breeze which made the canes sway on the rack.

'You made a good job of cleaning my shoes last time. This time we need to get the Treatment Room spruced up. I've got some cloths for the bench and a mop for the floor. You can see my client made a bit of a mess, sweat mostly, but there's a little blood over there and, oh dear, I think his bladder must have loosened up, poor man. You can use this spray to get rid of the blood.' He handed James a glass bottle. 'Jonny is no ordinary flogging bench. Bespoke design—cost a fortune, real leather. He's heard it all. If only Jonny were able to speak!

James stood in his underwear looking at the contraption, unable to move.

'Might as well make a start,' Victor said.' I'm going to make myself some mint tea. Back in a while, crocodile. Carry on Mr James.'

The music was instantly recognisable. The Arrival of the Queen of Sheba. James looked up and saw a speaker in the corner, as well as a camera. The music was energising and the glass bottle gave off a gingerly tang which cloaked the sweat almost entirely. He set about cleaning up the blood. James was thinking of his meeting with the senior partner at work—'Keep going, James, keep going.' He squeezed out the mop and gave the floor another wipe. Victor came in with an old towel. 'Splendid. Splendid. Jonny looks as good as new.' He put an arm round James' shoulder. 'Use this to dry the floor. We don't want anyone slipping up, do we?'

'Perfect,' Victor said a few moments later. 'Now give me that towel and get yourself onto Jonny. Put your knees here and lie down on your front and drop your arms on the hand rests. That's it. Comfortable, isn't it? And thanks to you beautifully clean! You fit perfectly. I'm going to secure your ankles with these leather straps.' The music had stopped when Victor had come back into the room. Victor closed the window. 'There we are, and now your wrists. Won't take a moment.' James could smell Victor's aftershave.

After he'd tied James securely to the bench Victor stepped back. 'See if you can free your wrists, and now your ankles.' James pulled at the restraints. He couldn't move. 'Good, we don't want you wriggling about. I'd say you were ready James. At the point of no return. Congratulations.' Victor patted his head.

He lit a candle in the corner of the room—a yellow candle. 'Honeysuckle and jasmine,' Victor said. 'Expensive. Gives off a lovely aroma.' James was looking ahead; his vision was restricted now he was tied to the contraption. Victor pulled up the elastic hem of James' new pants and let it snap back. 'Excellent choice of underwear by the way. You should know James—how can I put this?—I'm about to rearrange your buttocks. '

There was a moment of silence. 'Listen up. I've got some calls to make. I'm not one for idling about. I'm going to leave you with the candle. Can you smell it? I'll play the third section of Mahler's Fifth Symphony—the Adagietto. It's, how should I put it, mellifluous. Do you know it? Not saying much. Cat got your tongue? It'll play for twenty minutes. Then we're going to switch tempo. Wagner! I imagine you've seen *Apocalypse Now*.'

He put a hand on James' shoulder. 'When the Valkyries start wailing I'll step into the room and administer six strokes. I'll use the starting cane if you don't mind. I think I left it in the corridor. Six is a good number, don't you think? God created man on the sixth day. You won't feel anything for a second or two and then I suspect you'll feel a great deal of pain. You'll pull through, I'm sure of it. I have a good feeling about you Mr James. Any questions? Enjoy the music.'

Victor closed the door and there was silence. The aroma from the candle was pleasant. The music slid, swan-like, into the room and almost immediately James felt as if someone had removed his vest and was dripping honey onto his back and shoulders and spreading it down his spine. This was no ordinary massage and in any case he couldn't do anything to stop it, not that he wanted to stop it. His future, for the time being, was hitched to this horse-like contraption. Yet Mahler had provided a great bird—a benevolent eagle—which took hold of him and which was now taking him away from himself, away from the basement, over the houses of London and onto the forest. He could hear the flap of the wings and the bird lowered him into a glade. How green the grass and how green the ferns and how tall the trees. If only Mahler's Fifth Symphony could go on forever.

James was alone and felt his soul were being rubbed in a great lather of goose fat. He could hear moving water and sure enough, just beyond, there was a river which glittered in the sun which was now breaking through the clouds. A boat appeared. Six men in loin cloths rowing serenely and a boy at the back beating a drum. In the middle of the boat there was a man with a crown, a prince among men. He looked ahead with purpose. When the boat reached the glade the man turned and James saw it was Solomon. He was no longer a stripling but something wondrous, something out of this world. Solomon smiled but there was a sadness in the smile, which made the smile even more beautiful.

Once the boat had carried on down the river James saw a girl bathing in the water. She was stepping out on the far bank and shaking her long black hair. She was naked and she must have thought she had the forest to herself. She was drying her shoulders with a piece of cloth. It was impossible not to watch her. James saw it was Molly, or some manifestation of Molly. When she moved a little he could see her breasts were fuller and her bottom more womanly, like a very large Sicilian peach. Even though the glade was cool James was feeling hot. He was locked onto Jonny his new companion. There was nothing he could do about it. Thank God I'm wearing clean underpants. Molly turned and smiled and waved. Such a plangent wave. A wave Mahler would have thoroughly approved of. She seemed to be saying, 'Ezra's back in Colorado. Swim across the river and we'll be happy forever.' Oh what joy and oh what frustration. He struggled once more to free his wrists and ankles but he knew there was no point.

'Molly!' he shouted.' Molly!'

Further into the forest there was a clearing. A long table. And behind the table were sitting four serious looking men and a woman in a wig. It took a while to work out these were the five partners in his law firm. He could recognise his boss. There was an empty seat next to them. And his boss stood up and took the seat and put it in front of the table, as if it were a throne. He'd been so friendly of late.' Have you given any thought to applying for a partnership—a salaried partnership. Your work has stepped up a couple of gears. We're very impressed.' He gestured at the chair with an open hand as if to say swim across the river and claim it as your own. For a moment James saw a brilliant career winding its way through the forest. James pulled at the restraints again. The four men and the woman in the wig were standing now. They looked kind and slightly bemused, and they walked away in single file.

Mahler was tremulous. Mahler was beautiful. James wondered why there weren't any swans gliding along the river but just as he was wondering he saw a courting pair and behind the swans he saw a kingfisher on the branch of a tree.

There was a lone man sitting on a chair, on the other side of the river. He was reading *One Hundred Years of Solitude*. It was his father. James had given him the book. It wasn't the sort of book his father would have chosen for himself. Sometimes on the phone he would tell James how far he'd got. 'Slow progress, I'm afraid, but there's something about it.' He remembered seeing his father in the garden, reading. 'I'm about half-way through,' he shouted.

They took him to hospital after the stroke. He'd lost his speech but he could read a little and when James went to visit him *One Hundred Years of Solitude* was on the table, along with the fruit and the cards. He was pleased to see James and, with some difficulty, he wrote on a piece of paper. The writing no longer his own. 'I'll be out soon, in the meantime I'm going to finish that book.' He smiled sheepishly.

A few days later his father had another stroke. James took compassionate leave and for several days and nights sat by his father's bedside.

The nurse wanted to call a catholic priest. James said, 'Don't do that.' He'd known too many catholic priests at boarding school. His mother came, his sister came, his brother would have come if he were not bobbing around at the bottom of the ocean.

The hospital smelt awful.

James looked at his father who was sleeping, even though there was a tube coming out of his nose. He went back to the flat in Stoke Newington. He needed a shower and a decent night's sleep. When he went to the hospital the following day his father was no longer in the ward.

'I'm sorry, the nurse explained, 'your father passed away in the night.'

One Hundred Years of Solitude was on the table.

Wagner woke him from his reverie. He felt a flush of heat and tried to sit up. He could still see a river but now it was the Rhine. He was holding a gun, running towards the river. On the other side there were tanks. Comrades were dropping by his side but still he moved forwards. Planes were flying in all directions. Mahler popped like a giant air balloon. It was then he noticed that under the rack of canes there was a shelf full of white pots. He could make out the writing—Victor's Special Healing Cream: Apply Directly—and attached to the wall there was a notice: Buy One Get One Free!

Notwithstanding the screaming of the Valkyries James heard the door opening. Although he couldn't see Victor it was easy to visualise him, in his black dashiki, holding a cane in his right hand. James made one last hopeless effort to free himself, pulling at his wrists and kicking with his ankles.

'Humbling,' Victor said. 'And beautiful. Are you ready Mr James?

Sarah Daly

Apples Are for Love

We weren't supposed to do it. But we did. We bit the apple on both ends, our tongues sucking its sweet juice. Our teeth crunching its compact meat. The apple was designated for "Introduction to Agriculture", the 1,000-person class we both taught, and were grateful for, we really were, since they provided us a bunk bed and two meals a day, and several "coffee points" a quarter (which were viciously traded and hoarded since we needed coffee, so desperately, for all that grading), and furthermore, we were extraordinarily lucky that they wanted "real-time" teaching, instead of canned lectures, which were all the rage now, and we didn't have to be separated this year, as we had been for several years. But that is the life we have, the only life we are suited for, alas, we are good at nothing else, but an intellectual life. What possessed us, I cannot quite tell, to do such a thing, to eat our demonstration, other than the fact that neither of us had had a real apple since we were quite small children, and then, we had cried, because we had wanted candy. We were supposed to hold the apple close to the camera and then the olfactory chute, so the students could understand these ancient agricultural products and how today's synthetic foodstuffs are so much better. Then, we were to send the apple away, to someone else who needed it. So why did we do it? Why did we take such a risk? For a mere apple? But when we both reached the core, we leaned sideways and smiled.

Ian Boulton

FULLY

Now don't get me wrong, I love all the guys on the boat; they're a great bunch of lads. Funny. Tough. The work hard play hard types, you know? And they love to tease. You really have to learn to give as good as you get in this place or you will be eaten alive! Literally! And I won't lie, sometimes the teasing can get a little intense, borderline hurtful even, but they have good hearts, all of them. I'm sure that they would be mortified if they ever thought that they had caused any real harm to one of their mates. It's just bants. I know that. (Step forward First Mate Percy Flarge! LOL.) And, by and large, I am able to take the banter in its intended spirit. But when you decide—just for one day mind—to zhuzh up the accepted costume, think it might be fun to add a little colour, give everyone a little lift, bring some glam—when you step out of bounds and get on board wearing a lovely pink number, say, let's say you did that—well would it be fair if everyone one of your friends and comrades decided to call you Barbie for not just an entire voyage but for all voyages from then on? Would that be fair? No, I don't think so. They don't mean any harm, I know, but just ggrrrrr, right? But anyway none of them are around right now and this is my story to tell, so I get to say what I am called. So no Barbie for the foreseeable. No. So long as I am, as it were, in charge, then you can call me Ishmael.

At the mo I have a couple of projects on the go. There is my amusing reworking of *Moby Dick* (see above), which will, I hope, take up a great deal of my time. And there is the family tree business which is fascinating and—big bonus—time-consuming. As well as those things, I have my morning walk followed by a coffee in that Portuguese place on the beach, a meal every Tuesday at Wok Around The Clock, a pint every Thursday at The Rogue Male, and a film every Sunday evening at The Poseidon. Jeez, busy me! I need a little lie down just thinking about how much there is to do. And I haven't even mentioned the clinic.

Yes, it's surprising when you add it all up, the time I spend at the clinic.

See how spic 'n' span my desk is! It's nothing as interesting as OCD, sorry to disappoint—YOU ARE NOT MY SYNDROME! Ha ha . . . as far as I know I am completely free from allergies too and you can trust me when I tell you that I am now reaching out to any wood in touching distance—no, it's just the happy result of a healthy upbringing. I, like those who raised me, take great satisfaction in order. Order is the key. Order will save me. That's why talking to the folks who run Wok Around The Clock is such a pleasure and also why my weekly contact with the regulars at The Rogue Male can be a touch distressing. Still, it surely does me some good to meet people of different persuasions, politeness, hygiene and neatness wise.

How could I forget the reunions? Admittedly, they do not form part of a weekly regimen but there are periodical reunions and I make a point of attending them all. Offer me the opportunity to attend a get together of old pals, remembered or forgotten, and I am snappy with that RSVP and will be there with bells on. And dicky bow.

I don't want to presume but I also don't wish to bore you rigid by over explaining. You have probably read something about the clinic's purpose and its methods so I won't go into too much detail here, other than to clarify the types of activity that occupy some of my time. Actually, when you add it all up, more of my time than anything in my life other than sleeping.

There's the sitting in circles and the sharing ritual with the disembodied voice, of course. Then there are one-to-one sessions with the gentle voice, the desk between us. Both can be challenging but they are generally pretty calm, often refreshing. There are talks some evenings when we listen to a guest speaker, often a success story told by a previous, erm, whatever they call us. Then there are the things that get the publicity: the shouting voice, which can be upsetting but which serves a clear purpose so must be borne. And the machine. I spend quite a bit of time plugged into the machine. Oh, and how could I forget the questionnaire! I fill that out fairly regularly and, if I do say so myself, I am getting much much better at it. So there we have it.

Dear Blank,

The more observant amongst you—and I'm guessing with your pedigree(s) that you are an observant bunch! —will have noticed already that we have something in common. It is one of the following: a) the same surname or b) we used to have the same surname, or c) somebody very close to you has my surname.

Yes, I am one of those family tree nerds! And this is a request for any information you wish to share about your family and its previous iterations going back as far as you can tell me. Some of you will not wish to get involved and to those I say no hard feelings, goodbye and whatever gods you believe in bless you. Some may have some basic info about parents, grandparents—you know, births, deaths, places etc—and little else. To you I say thank you, much appreciated and I will only be in touch in the future if you specifically request it. But some of you, I hope, will belong to a third group who have been actively trying to find out everything you can about your family and its history. Where did we come from? Who got together and when to bring about my existence and that of my loved ones? To those brave souls I say: Praise be! We have found each other. Now we can begin to share information and tips about how to dig deeper, where to go, what to look for, who to ask. All that and more.

So. Send me ANYTHING! to this email address.

Best wishes to all of you, welcome on board to some, happy hunting etc etc.

Yours in anticipation,

Leave sufficient space for my signature and we are all set. Send.

I'm pretty pleased with it. I think it sets a tone.

I mentioned, briefly, in passing, my interactions with the family who run Wok Around The Clock and how pleasing I found them. A recent visit was a case in point. I was sitting at my usual corner table, prawn crackers finished and about to take on the veggie spring rolls before my tofu in black bean sauce, Singapore noodles and boiled rice arrived, when an unshaven guy, clearly drunk, came crashing through the door, stumbled to the counter, pulled a takeaway menu from its plastic holder thingy, squinted at it before throwing it away, then slurred an order for chicken chow mein at the poor girl—owner's daughter—on duty. She—paragon of politeness and professionalism—wrote down the order and placed the piece of paper in the serving hatch—this is the system, it doesn't matter—and turned to face this unpleasant character to ask for his payment. £7.99 as it happens. The brute fumbles in his pocket for a fiver and throws it on the counter. Then coughs. Coughs horribly. Clearly distressing the girl—her name just won't go in, I'm ashamed to say, though I have heard her father mention her by name on numerous occasions—who did not know where to look. Anyway, the oaf's order arrived and he staggered out and I carried on with my meal, throwing the occasional sympathetic glance towards the counter. The upshot of all this being that, when I had finished eating and it was my turn to pay, there was a brief conversation between the owner and me. He had come out from the back room to say goodbye, I think. He also wanted to thank me for my mask-wearing, a habit that I know they appreciate in there as the staff are always covered up. Very gratifying to have it acknowledged that we are not just customers to the folk at Wok but distinct individuals.

The morning walk is getting longer and longer, taking in more side streets and hilly pavements before I make my way down to the beach for the final stretch. Then a coffee at one of the small round blue and yellow tiled tables in the Portuguese coffee shop. The jazzy music plays along with the gusts of wind that fill the space whenever the door is opened. The violence of the waves outside dissipated by distance. The kitchen seems to contain all the ingredients for a constant daily screaming row that is surely role-play, a little theatre for the clientele.

The machine room houses three machines, side by side but with sufficient space for staff members to walk between them.

The regulars at The Poseidon favour British fare. Tales of wartime heroics, in determined advance or plucky retreat we don't mind, quiet and unassuming Englanders taking on the establishment, sentimental tales set on farms or faraway council estates, people who look more or less like us who are nearing death but have just one more adventure left in them. That kind of thing, heartwarming stuff that reminds us of our better selves.

Family tree has yet to bear fruit ha ha. No replies so far but it's early days and I have an animator's patience.

The gentle voice does not have far to travel across the desk but it barely makes it. Its words seem to stall in the air between us before they reach me, uncertain of a safe landing. When it does arrive, it sounds soft, soothing. It asks one of its usual questions: Are you keeping fully occupied? I tell it about my routine, eager to emphasise exactly how long I take on each activity, how I feel about it when I am doing it and how it leaves me feeling. The gentle voice is interested in my lingering over meals, my extended walks, my insistence on staying behind after each screening to join in the appraisal session. I tell it about my *Moby Dick* project and read it what I have so far. With the help of the gentle voice, I make the calculation that my version, with its many comic circumlocutions, will be some sixty times longer than the original.

Each of my haunts has its own rules and rituals, none more so than The Rogue Male. There the regulars—broken-veined men facing up to the prospect of their own mortality—sit at the bar on unreliable stools. Each is in an advanced stage of male decay. I have never seen a casual user of the pub sit on one of those precarious structures, utterly unsuited to supporting the wobbling masses perched atop them. Most visitors prefer the tables scattered around the room. The regulars talk of how wronged they have been by ex-wives, dead wives, ungrateful children, treacherous politicians, devious newcomers. Their conversation is fed by their exclamatory tabloid of choice and the 24 hour news channel that reflects their disillusion right back at them. They are wary of me but do not recognise me as one of their problems. I am allowed to sit at a table in peace slowly drinking my one pint of Low Profile which has an alcoholic content of 0.5%. Other ales on offer include Crack Shot at 3.8%, Master Of Disguise (5.0%) and Aim For The Heart at a wicked 8%.

As usual we sat in the circle and waited for the disembodied voice to tell us to start. Then the confessions began in the alphabetical order assigned to us by the clinic. No real names here, of course. The confessions are identical, a memorised text devised by the guy who dreamed up the clinic and developed its methodology. Once each of us has spoken—there are currently eight people in the circle each week—then the disembodied voice tells us to make a start on the section of the meeting devoted to outlining how each of us is filling in our time. Here you would notice differences between us. You know my routine which I would describe as essentially creative. Others engage in more practical activities. Some useful—gardening, motor mechanics—others of dubious value—making models out of matchsticks, counting to a million then beginning again. Two of the circle claim to meditate for hours each day which strikes me as a touch suspicious. Is it cheating, do you think? After all, you don't hear me including my excessive sleeping as part of my weekly schedule.

A bit of a shock when I realise that I am only halfway down the first page of *M. Dick*. This is both daunting and gratifying in equal measure.

Last night at The Poseidon the story of a man, old, twinkly, formerly of a long-running political satire on the telly I was told later, who walked from Lands End to John O'Groats to raise money to pay the legal bills of a group of pensioners who are suing the government over some scandalous miscarriage of justice that happened in the 1980s and for which they have not yet received compensation. Along the way he picks up a gang of what I can only describe as disciples. His wife was very much against the idea at first ('You're an old man, John. What will I do if something happens to you?') but she is—Surprise!—there to meet him at the finish line where she gives him a big hug and kiss and a mild admonishment ('You did it, you daft old bugger.')

It's hard to think about the shouting voice outside of the sessions. So close to your face. So harsh, grating. Once it's over then you just sort of want to forget it and think about something nicer. I know that misses the point somewhat but you should hear some of the things the shouting voice shouts at me. Really horrible. My poor family don't deserve that.

After my walk I sat in the Portuguese café where the non-stop performance consisting of operatic threats of violence, screeching that competes heroically with the seagulls lurking in the doorway, and excessive weeping that would be the envy of any keening mourner at a Dublin funeral. Larks.

Up very early with too much day stretching out ahead of me. I filled in the questionnaire as slowly as possible, sometimes going back to change my answers and then going back again and reverting to my first response. How the answers have evolved since I first sat down to answer the questions upon acceptance at the clinic. I have so much more to record now. In the early days I was positively curt. At sunrise I decided to meander down to the churchyard cemetery to see if any names or dates on the headstones are of any use to me. No joy there, but I did meet a lovely chap—I want to say he was the verger but my knowledge of CofE hierarchy is fuzzy at best—and he talked to me about arranging to have a peek at the parish records. I will definitely do that and maybe more. There was something about the air in the old church that appealed to me, some ancient ingredient in the oxygen. I could spend more time there, maybe? I will have to check with the clinic about, you know, ethos etc.

I finished my walk, somehow adding a further twenty minutes to the thing, and was looking forward to sitting at my little table and lingering over my coffee. But no such luck. When I got there—heart rate pleasingly accelerated, sweating slightly—there was an ambulance outside and somebody being carried out on a stretcher. Closed for the day. Understandably.

You know how sometimes when you are with other people you feel like you are on your own? Well that's what it's like in the machine room. There are others in there with you—a staff member sets it up, shows you which machine you are on today, plugs you in, checks the dials every minute or so; and there is usually one or even two members of the circle attached to the other machines—but it feels like a delicious solitary experience. Plug me in and I am miles away, off in a world of my own. It helps that we are not allowed to talk, obviously. Without that rule then I suspect that one of my fellow group members would feel the need to fill the silence with their thoughts. That's if my experience sitting in the circle with them is anything to go by. I pride myself on my economy when I am asked to share my routine with the group each week. I list my activities without explaining them, hoping in this way to model a preferred format for others to follow. Alas, it never works. There are always one or two that must delve deep into their motive for choosing their activities. Imagine having to listen to one of them when you are blissfully plugged in and prepared for your internal flights of fancy to carry you off to an unknown destination. How could the machine be expected to work under those conditions?

At The Poseidon a film about a campaign in a Welsh mining village to have the name of a dog that died of grief after its master didn't return from the trenches included on the local war memorial. Charming and moving, we said afterwards. Good to be reminded that we share this planet with other creatures and wars are a tragedy for them, too, the woman who always has the last word said.

The shouting voice is an integral part of the process, I know that. But it is hateful. It shouts questions at me about my commitment. It shouts mockery at me about my choice of activities. It shouts insults about my appearance, my dress sense, my education, work history, family. My poor family. The shouting voice despises everything about me and I don't know why. Are other members of the circle treated to the same onslaughts on their character and behaviour? Somehow, when I am in the room and can feel the shouting voice's breath and spittle in my face and feel its abusive commentary on my whole life reaching deep inside me, then I suspect that I have been singled out for special treatment. This horrible state of mind can remain with me until it is time to catch my daily twelve hours of sleep.

Police tape all around the Portuguese café. A sign, hastily scribbled, cardboard and red marker pen, is stuck on the inside of the door. Closed till further notice. This couldn't be more disturbing. I will have to start walking in the other direction. The whole balance of my routine will be affected by this.

The gentle voice is a balm. It is a wave of warm honey and lemon drink lapping at a sore throat. It is the perfect bubble bath/fluffy bathrobe/crisp clean bedsheets combo. The gentle voice is lifted up on a mysterious indoor breeze that carries its reassuring message all the way to me. It understands. It approves. It encourages. It insists that I carry on doing exactly what I am doing. It promises me that it will work.

Dear blank, I must say that I am surprised, not a little disgusted, by your lack of response to my previous email. I mean, ALL OF YOU. I realise that this may be a touch harsh on the one or two of you who have legitimate reasons for not replying to me. You have changed address? Fair enough. You are undergoing cancer treatment? I get it. Somebody close to you is undergoing cancer treatment? Well you should know that I could be a great support to you in such times. By ignoring me you are doing a great disservice to your loved one who is in such distress. Think again. And as for the rest: shame on you. This is a potential relative you are leaving hanging. Shame, I say. And don't bother getting in touch after you receive this. I want nothing to do with you. Cheers, a name that will be so very familiar to many of you.

We don't know each other's names (obvs!) but in some ways each of us know the other members of the circle better than we know anyone. Listen to me getting all deep! But it's true. We know stuff about each other's lives that you can only know if you are a member of the circle. (Or part of the clinic's staff, I guess.) We only ever meet to talk in the circle room. We never engage with another member directly, the rule being to listen to each member when they speak and then listen to the next one when directed by the disembodied voice and then to speak when that voice tells you to. Sometimes you will find yourself sitting next to another circle member in the machine room but there can be no contact between you. Similarly, if we see each other on the street outside the clinic—as happens occasionally—then no acknowledgement can be made. But we know all these things about each other. Strange things. Things that nobody outside the clinic could possibly understand. We share in the circle those thoughts that can never be shared outside. And—I must be honest—that makes me hate them, the other members.

My feet have a mind of their own. Every morning I set out on my new walk but my stubborn limbs refuse to give in to the new schedule. They insist on walking the wrong way. Towards the old café, now closed. I have every sympathy with them. The new café is awful. Totally unsuitable.

I don't think I can ever go back to The Rogue Male. Yesterday evening I was sitting quietly at my table, minding my own business, looking at a clear spot on the wall opposite, one without mirror or film poster or any other distraction. Just a square of pleasing blankness painted maroon. Nods had been exchanged with the stooled fixtures, shaven-headed, guts straining their sagging jeans. All as it should be. Their conversation was the usual mix of vitriol, paranoia and self-pity but easy to ignore, a background noise akin to old Eurovision entries leaking out of ceiling speakers or the rumbling tummies of one of the larger zoo animals in the hour before feeding. Nothing to cause alarm. That is, unless you were an outsider who felt compelled to join in, offer an opposing view, saw an opportunity to help these neanderthals take a tiny step on the road towards becoming homo sapiens. And, unfortunately for yours truly, that is what happened yesterday. A couple in their twenties, male and female, interrupted a rant about, I think, the small boats. (We are under invasion at The Rogue Male, a crisis to which the only response is to throw copious amounts of Aim For The Heart down your neck and whine.) The comment from the young male—something along the lines of 'I think there's more to it than that, mate'—was not well received over on the stools. Insults were thrown and then returned with some aplomb by the couple, both of them. Once these had been exchanged, there was some grunting, mumbling and exhibitionist drinking over by the bar and the young couple moved their heads closer together over their little table and spoke in minor tones. It looked as if the danger had passed and my full attention could be given back to the maroon patch of wall. But fat bald fury, once ignited, does a passable imitation of the eternal flame. The largest of the regulars had simply used the break in hostilities to refuel and was now ready for a further assault. I sensed his broken frame turn on his stool, presumably because he had thought of some riposte that would send the young commies slinking off into the night. But no. The forgotten white man, his country and his culture given away wholesale to foreigners, women and women who weren't even women, called over the heads of the outsiders, clearly aiming his next comments at me. I tried to ignore them but that proved impossible with all eyes turned in my direction. 'You're very quiet over there' was what he said. Followed by, 'what do you think?' Well, I'm just not equipped, am I? How could I prepare for this? How much notice do you think I would need to come up with a response that a) caused minimum upset and b) allowed for the essentials of my current routine to continue undisturbed. Not to even consider c) reflect any actual opinion I may hold. Give me a month and I would struggle. Give me the five seconds allotted to me then and there was no option other than to stand up and slink out without making any eye contact with fuming regular or noble outsider. I didn't even finish my Low Profile.

Moby Dick is driving me batty. Perhaps I should have read the flipping thing before embarking on this pointless voyage.

The Poseidon is showing nothing for the next three weeks other than a cartoon about a rabbit and a bear living in secret in a posh child's bedroom.

A couple of very rude emails. Interesting to discover that the people who share my name are not my people.

I need extra machine time. I will apply for extra machine time.

More rude emails. The cancer mob have joined in now. I suspect that they are deliberately misinterpreting my last missive, choosing to indulge in uncalled for indignation and petty point scoring. Who needs them?

I am trying to sleep more. It's healthy, obvs, to seek more safe time, but there have been some dismal consequences. For example, I slept through the time when I was meant to be at my corner table at Wok Around The Clock. I have a sneaking suspicion I did the same thing last week. How long has it been since I visited Wok Around The Clock?

The new café is never going to work for me. It is filled with strange types, young mothers staring at me over the tops of their designer strollers. My need to be ignored by them feels like hunger.

I realise that my invitation to the reunion is overdue. It doesn't make sense. Surely last year's incident is long forgotten?

I need extra machine time.

I can barely hear the shouting voice.

I cannot hear the gentle voice.

The other voices in the circle speak as one, a conspiratorial withholding.

My rota has been ripped to pieces. Metaphorically. As well as the torn scraps of paper scattered around my floors.

I find myself clueless when I try to fill in the questionnaire. The words have begun to cheat, refusing to assemble in any order that makes sense to me.

The state of my desk comes as a shock.

I was raised better than this, I say to whoever is passing.

Request for extra machine time has been turned down.

Oh

No

Not

Again

I have been weak. I have let myself down by falling into old habits. I have let everybody down. My poor family. That it has happened again after so long without an incident is more than disappointing. It's what comes of not being fully occupied, I realise that. But there can be no excuses. I acknowledge that this is my fault and nobody else can be blamed. I accept full responsibility for my latest fall and I am prepared to face the consequences. I will have to face the anger of the shouting voice. I will have to face the sadness of the gentle voice. The disembodied voice will instruct the circle to indulge in smug admonishment. I will take it all. And then I will start again.

Planning is, in itself, an absorbing activity.

I stood still and allowed the shouting voice to spit its righteous wrath into my face. I sat still and the gentle voice gazed at me with soulful wet eyes, long expressive eyelashes dipping in slow motion into the pools of tears, straining to understand, wordlessly asking where did we go wrong. The disembodied voice encouraged the members of the circle to do their sly communal worst. And I came through it all cleansed. This latest version of me, a considerable upgrade on the last, feels a new resolve.

Planning and sleep and the clinic have been enough to sustain me but now it is time to put my new routine into effect. I have installed an easel and some painting materials in my bedroom. (I have even bought a smock! Get me going all Toulouse LOL.) I will, upon rising and before my shower, paint a daily self-portrait. As well as being time consuming, I hope my amateurish scratchings will serve as a measure of my progress through the days—months—ahead. See how the face changes from poor wretch to fully functioning member of the community! Immediately upon completion of each day's portrait, I will mount the stationary bike that I have set up in my lounge. I will cycle until I cannot feel my legs or until my heart rate rises to 200bpm, whichever comes first. Then I will take a very late shower. The day is half done! There will be a weekly visit to Thai Me Up Thai Me Down, similarly one to a cocktail bar named Chic-y Chappie. I will attend the multiplex one evening a week to watch muscled actors in tight-fitting body armour save the Earth from muscled actors in tight-fitting body armour. I will help out with the second-hand book stall at the church for half a morning a week with my new friend who is not a verger at all. I will keep filling in the questionnaire until I get it right. I will up my sleep to thirteen hours a day. I will begin again with the shouting voice, the gentle voice, the disembodied voice and the circle and the machine. I am all set. Oh, and there's this:

> *My head is absolutely scrambled. I don't know which way is up, whether I'm coming or going. When I think back over recent events I feel like I've been on a roller coaster. Dangerous and horrible, yes. But exhilarating, making me feel more alive than ever before. It would take a more poetic soul than mine to describe adequately what has been going on with me, to arrive at les mots juste, as it were. It's as if, simultaneously mind, it has been the best of times and it has been the worst of times.*

Fingers crossed it all works. Wouldn't it be nice to be cured?

Julian George

Frenemies

The guard wouldn't let him in.

Former world champion.

Elected member of the Duma.

Doppelganger for middle-period Peter Lorre.

'The best friendships are made on short acquaintance and last a very brief time.'

Didn't matter that he was on their side. Didn't matter that he, unlike the detainee, the Beast of Baku, was a trueborn patriot, my country right or wrong, left or right, his loyalty unquestionable, The Order of Lenin and every other medal going pinned one time or another to his chest.

Imperial, Soviet or Federation, Russia was eternal. This he solemnly believed the way he believed in the irresistible force of a white pawn firmly planted on the seventh rank.

'I don't agree with him politically. Surely you know that. I just came to bring him this.' He held up into the sallow bureaucratic lighting that month's copy of *64*, which for a decade he had happily edited between tournaments and matches, it was no bother at all, my pleasure (which trumped duty), replaying the games of his contemporaries, the games of legends past.

The games of perfect strangers.

'Chess is everything' was his quick reply to the perennial 'what is chess' question. 'Art, science and sport.' Next!

Another time, another place, waxing philosophical, he said that if a game could be continued in two ways, the first a beautiful tactical blow that gave rise to variations that didn't yield to precise calculation, the other the application of clear positional pressure that led to an endgame with microscopic chances of victory, he would choose the latter without thinking twice. If the opponent offered keen play, he would oblige; but in such cases he received less satisfaction, even when he won, than from a game conducted according to all the rules of strategy with its ruthless logic.

Nothing but thought.

A machine.

Click, click, click.

Result.

No wonder nobody liked him, much.

'You're probably too young to remember our games. 167 we played. 167. (Prime number.) Each meet, as in athletics, as in the Olympics—if you need to slim, play the Beast over five months and you'll lose a few kilos—a Marathon. To be a champion it is not enough to be simply a strong player; one must also be a strong human being as well, physically and mentally.

'They said the fate of the nation, of the world, rested on our games. We believed it. The old regime, hanging on, the young, wanting to be heard. I was young but old; he was younger still, but still young, restless, ambitious, the herald of a generation that wasn't going to settle for 'no', that had the 'yes' ready within them. Give over. Unreal.

'For all that I respect him, as a player and as a man. We can agree to disagree. That is what mature people do. We settled these differences over the board, like chess players, and not in the street like football hooligans. Now you have him in custody. Did he behave like a football hooligan? Of course not. He was exercising his right to protest; that is democracy—or is this no longer the 'New Russia'? Just so you don't get the wrong idea, I happen to agree with the government on this issue if not with this arrest.'

End of speech (never given, until that moment), to the Members of the Russian Chess Federation, Murmansk chapter.

'Is that a polar bear?'

The guard, who wished he could ask for an autograph (he already had the Beast's), shook his head no, orders, top brass, the Kremlin, I regret—

'I am not bringing him a cake with a chisel in it. Go ahead. Check,' he said, an unintended pun.

Sometimes he surprised himself.

The guard nodded, yes, but—

'*You* didn't rough him up, did you?'

'Of course not, Mr Karpov, I would never have allowed that. I'd have stepped in.'

Karpov sighed. A draw. 'I believe you.' He entrusted the magazine to the guard's care and disappeared into the violet hour.

It wasn't Lubyanka . . .

Later, at the end of his shift, the guard surprised the detainee, Garry Kasparov, with the magazine.

'Thank you. Thank you very much. I really appreciate this.'

'Oh, don't thank me, Mr Kasparov, thank Mr Karpov.'

'*Tolya* brought this?'

'Mr Karpov himself. I couldn't allow him in. No visitors. Sorry.'

Kasparov leafed through the pages. Tolya. Who knew?

'Did you ask for his autograph?'

Anatoly Karpov vs Peter Leko, Groningen 1995
Queen's Pawn Opening
1 d4 and draw agreed

Marvin Cohen

A Dialogue About Four Things: Clock, Man, Time, Sun. With an End Not the Less Unhappy For Its Being Usual.

A clock's profile is so useless! It doesn't even give you the time of day!

Nor, for that matter, of night.

But front-face, a clock rounds out the facts of time, in its eternal number rut.

Yes, a clock's cycles are very periodical.

The well-run, non-run-down clock is a very model of regularity!

It's virtually like *clockwork*!

Its virtue *is* clockwork.

You're really wound-up on the subject.

Momentarily. But we do agree that from the side a clock is just a space-filler, not a time-giver. Yet a *person*'s profile can serve a purpose, while a clock's has no purpose.

What purpose is served by the profile of people?

Recognition (as a lead to identity). And in some cases physical attractiveness (as a lead to desire).

Not to mention that, on the face of it, a person is no machine. Whereas a clock often personifies a machine.

Yes. That brings me to a technicality. Namely, that whereas a clock's hands revolve on its fat round front face, a *person*'s hands dangle well below that person's face. Why is that?

Because a person has a more *handsome* profile?

No, that's a side-issue.

Oh. The silhouette of this comparison is fully in the dark.

Where I propose to leave it. Which reminds me, that light is needed for both a clock and a person to be seen.

Which would seem to point out a relation between light and time.

Right. But *what* relation?

I'm not that precise. I'm in the dark.

Oh, I thought your brain went like clockwork.

No. And a perfect clock doesn't even go like brainwork.

Then where *does* it go?

Around. With the help of its hands, it gets around, all right.

That's some feat, for *I* can only get around with my *feet*. But that's due not to my greater nobility, but *mo*bility. As a physical object in itself, a clock makes no motion to be anything but stationary.

Though it stands still in its physical sense, yet its usefulness is in that it's always moving.

It moves me, or my plight does, to tears.

Though seemingly cold and without animation enough to weep, and devoid of pathetic sentiment, a clock still miraculously conveys a lively sense of the timely.

Yet a clock is merely time's *instrument*.

What do you mean, "merely"? That's a noble service rendered, for which few things are so well endowed to be qualified.

Is man another of time's instruments?

Yes but battered and broken down. Time does speak through man. But there's all that *emotion* involved. Whereas with the clock it's not emotion, just motion.

And man gets cranky, whereas a clock *is* cranked.

Man is alarmed, the clock alarming.

Time is alarming.

Through the clock's ministry.

What is time through *man's* ministry?

Wound up to a tragic slowing down, with pathos and poignant feeling. Man is time emotionalized, in the tragic key. The clock is time mechanized, in the key of no feeling.

And what is time, itself?

Time is both man and clock. Time *is* its instruments.

Is? How can a thing *be* the things it *uses*?

Mediums might not merely *express* content, but *be* that content.

Then time is two-faced?

Yes: it bears *man's* semblance; and the *clock's*, as well.

Its features are those of both?

It's featured principally in both.

What of time as known by the *sun*?

That's a different matter, altogether.

Couldn't you go into it more closely?

My eyes would be burned blind.

But safely can't your *mind* pursue it?

That puts things in an altogether astronomical spectrum. Time spoke directly through the clock, as a cool and regular medium. Time spoke directly through man, in a deep ache of sentiment. But the *sun*!—the sun is too big to be *anything's* instrument. Perhaps, in fact, time is the *sun's* medium, not the other way around.

The sun expresses itself through *time*? Funny, I thought it used *light* for that purpose.

You make light of my purport. Light is but a *byproduct*. Through time, we get the sun's message.

Which is hardly a sunny one, for us.

It leaves us on the shady side.

I feel left out in the cold.

The sun is augustly remote.

That's awful news.

News it's not, it's old.

We're so small that we end when we're old. The sun is so large, it's old and endless.

Time is bad news, I'm afraid.

It's death's messenger. The sun burns through.

Mike Fox

A Meeting in the Groves of Assisi

Francis rested a palm on his concave belly. He had neglected to eat again. The day had flooded into him, and he had sung and danced, communed with flocks of ecstatic birds, paused in tenderness to stroke a rabid dog in its last moments. He had picked fruit and placed it in the cupped palms of beggars, bowed in homage to itinerants, waded in the river and blessed the fish that came to swim round him. Then the inevitable gathering, trailing in his wake, willing him to address them.

Perhaps that was the moment his energies began to subside. Simplicity, the kind born of deepest insight, so easily erodes with repetition. Ultimately, he knew, though many would deny it, he was not a man of words. His candle flickered. A street cat wandered in and, sensing his dejection, began to rub its neck against his naked calf. He chafed its verminous ears between finger and thumb, and dropped into reverie.

The images came, then the questions. Proselytisers, postulants, mendicants, monks. Their faces, their need of him. The narrow ledge between sanctity and heresy, between what is taught and what is evident. The recurrent confusions of spiritual vision. Why should it be that even prayer can tire and dismay?

'Knowledge is not knowing where to look, but in what manner.' The thought arrived, as thoughts often seemed to, from a source beyond his mind. Did it actually mean anything? He repeated it, committed it to memory, trusting it might grow into a sermon. Is it a paradox to place one's faith in trust?

Perhaps he should slip out into the late evening dusk and pluck some figs. Hunger could be overcome in the moment, but tomorrow he would need strength. Strength was always needed. He rose, knowing he would find the air intoxicating, the stars beguiling, the natural world a cradle for a child of God.

My actions are guided by immediate things, he thought, as he stepped towards the orchard paths. I know this about myself. I knew it when first I saw a beggar weeping, and felt impelled to act. Insight makes known the obvious. That day, I was granted the burden of insight.

The night was clear and silent. Sister Moon shone above him. His callused feet flicked outwards, always eager to engage with the world. His body, though not yet skeletal, mapped his self-denial. To remain free one must always relinquish, he would tell his brother monks.

He thought back a few hours, remembering those who had gathered round him, their eagerness to hear his words, peasant faces artful yet artless. He could picture them vividly, the innocence in their guile.

Returning to the present moment, he remembered why he was here, and reached for figs in the low branches, tasting in their sweetness the ecstasy of God. Instantly refreshed, his senses compelled him to wander, until he saw a light, a glow at least, where the orchard thickened into woodland. Curious, he moved towards it, stepping between the olive roots, the maple and the oak.

Entering a clearing he came upon, not a light, but a young woman, small and zealous in aspect, regarding him. His presence did not seem to surprise her. He stood before her, suddenly conscious of his sparse clothing. Her feet were tiny, white and bare. She stepped forward.

'Dear brother, there is word of you everywhere. I have heard how beasts and fowl flock to you, how the rudest of men grow gentle in your presence. You are building a place of God, and I wish to do the same. I have come to join you. I am Clare.'

Confronted by a nature as bold and impetuous as his own, Francis found himself unable to construct a reply. His eye fell upon the vermillion stole draped round her narrow shoulders. Seeing this, she immediately cast it to the floor.

'My family are merchants,' she explained.

Grasping the meaning of her gesture, in fact knowing it intimately, Francis bowed.

'As were mine, my sister.'

They stood regarding one another. It is possible that, in that dark thicket of trees, both blushed.

'But you're expecting me?' she queried.

He frowned. Should he be expecting her? Perhaps some previous element of a recent day had eluded him.

'I live in expectation,' he improvised, reassured that this at least was true.

Clare inclined her head.

'The night is beautiful. Shall we walk together?'

Francis felt all weariness leave his body.

'It would be my delight,' he said.

They set off on a path by the olive groves sloping away from the town. Clare, looking up at the blistered stars, took his arm. Francis, a man who touched everything, though rarely in receipt of touch himself, felt the softness of her palm against his skin. Never less than spontaneous, he quelled a moment of uncertainty. Clare glanced at him.

'It's true that you are building a church?' It was more statement than question.

'I was instructed by God.'

With the forefinger of his free hand Francis sketched a sign of the cross on his brow.

'Repairing rather than building, to be frank,' he added.

'But you have no money?'

'This world, I've come to understand, obeys God's purpose. The things I need will come to me from others.'

Clare smiled.

'I have heard this of you,' she murmured. 'God is surprising.'

'Indeed.'

Francis swayed slightly, like a happy drunk. For the first time in his life he felt known by another. Decades of misunderstanding, of being misunderstood, fell away. True the Pope had granted him endorsement, but papal favours were not the ready empathy of such a kindred spirit. He began to sing, Clare joining him. And could there really be birdsong at this time of night? Who could doubt it?

He saw in his mind a simple hillside church, then two, then three.

They are as good as built, he thought.

Jim Meirose

The Resort Hotel Lobby

(aka "in the guts of it")

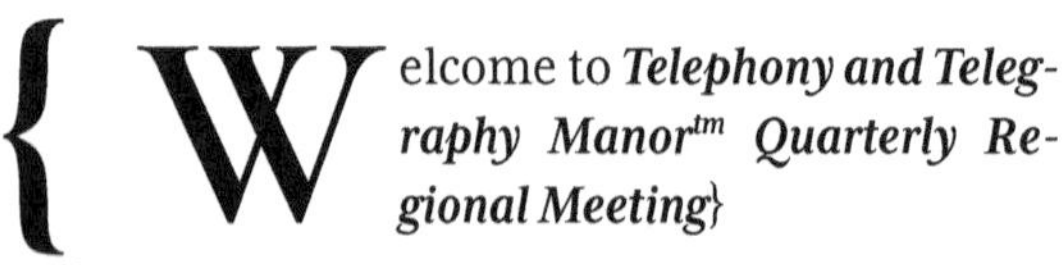

{ Welcome to ***Telephony and Telegraphy Manor***™ ***Quarterly Regional Meeting***}

::

|||—***nageb*** slasrever eht neht thgir ereht tuo meht tsap tuo dnA op! The set clicked off and the harvestmen's hobbyclub proceeded to the next required step; the group discussion ***GO***—|||

::

First Student: Why do they always assume aliens can't be human but something different and always able to do big mystically advanced things? I asked you a question. Here's why its why that they don't want to be made aware that there are humans so much more skilled talented intelligently insightful capable and generally better in all things intellectual both physically and non-physically accomplished as, Why don't you answer? ***them.***

::

{ may we take your ***coats,*** please? }

|do not pull that handle|

Emergency Bucket No. 1 (***First Harvestman*** = : *so what you think Peter stage a live-fight here-now Peter* : : ***Hey look*** see the clock "*over there*" said)

::

Old Master: Why don't we answer? Here's why, great big ***son-pop***; if there were a better choice of questions on the table, we may be more apt to give up an answer. See, even out there in the buffet, one hour before its all charged up and lit and the tendoushness's whack over the will open at (time) stand-upping black felt block sign says, it is then happy again. Happy being used one after another filing right cross the lid of it. Stright through holding *plates,* and maybe *spoons* also (did we hear you correct they brought plates and maybe spoons) yes yes yah U they go to the count of ***n*** from the time the stand-upping black felt block sign got pulled aside enabling customer entry, to when the opposite of the early time got swept aside by the morning shift, oh, *how can that be* no no the entire morning shift's *not required* all way down t' 'he p.m. Just one of those tendoush-ness's all freely idling at the portholedd bright red swingin' la kitchenin' door bang ya nail ya mistershives' 'tchoo yas yas yeet yeet 'tchoo! How loud was it? ***Well*** this loud right here; shout that *N* term's value being given a value signifying number of seconds minutes the buffet's been open from when the black felt block sign went this a' way to when it came back that a' way *HOOSH HOOSH HOOSH HOOSH* gotit gotit gotit gotit? *great big ball*

::

{ n-n-n-no no give up your God-damned coats t***o us*** }

|*what will happen that must never be allowed to happen is what will happen if anyone pulls that handle*|

Emergency Bucket No. 2 (this the three hundredth or so *gi ::**Third Harvestman** ve or take eleven* midday window of

calm's *:: <u>Eh what's a little lively banter</u>*)

::

Second (?) Student: Then, Master, given those truths, can it be "*safely assumed*" that the level remaining of the buffeted question-stock all 'cross the buffet trays does correspond quite tightly to the seconds minutes the buffet's so far been open?

::

{ we must put away your coats for you we **MUST** yes we **MUST**,so }

|what will happen if someone pulls that handle is something everyone secretly desires to see but do not dare admit it|

Emergency Bucket No. 3 (*<u>in-'tween</u>* :: easing to the usual end of this win ***Twenty-Fifth Harvestman*** = (eh big ***Abend*** here man the ' the hoses ***now*** 'cause)

::

Older Master: Oh, sure you can assume that—yes yes, ***of course***. For example, the legal fiction of the "*reasonable man*" tenders it to be safe to assume that when we say that 25% of the buffeted questions will be gone at the exact same moment 25% of the time, the entire time the buffet will end up having been open [*a rare instance of the meeeter-o-logistical truth being untrue*] that the data the computation of an answer is based on must be *<u>known in advance of the answer being known</u>*. Okay? That wrap it for ya'?

::

{ taking coats from "*guests*" is what we get paid for }

|*pulling that handle will result in your immediate termination*|

Emergency Bucket No. 4 (there's (((Good God almighty! Everybody here's so))) just been a massively blunt rockhard blow of a big ***Abend*** here) whata huh whay *huh said the Rolls t' the Royces' here*)

::

First Student's Stand-In: Nearly so, oh oh oh, master, nearly *so* but here's my ***last blank***; does that mean such a thing as n = 2 * 2 is wrong?

::

{ why you want to snatch away our livelyhood }

|*what will happen when it's pulled's so terrible it must never be witnessed* (at least not **in public**)|

Emergency Bucket No. 5 (***AS*** of slight calm :: *<u>two each equally devoted</u> <u>colleagues</u>* :: providing the craved feeling of having jus' 'ee' put through that there spankin' hot)

::

The Big Master Shringwallawa : What? No, no, *of course not*, child—that is a proper way of setting it down *"yeet yeet yeet yeet"* carved all o'er this town's many telephone poles scratched hard across into the still-green smooth curved wood—but <u>even so</u>, *child*, stay abreast of the fact th' all poles offer surfaces congenial to the scratching-in of a "yeet yeet". So even after the solution's nailed tight, in the now of each again *they they they* [and so forth] may still from time to time occur. *Bright enough for you now?*

::

{ I for one have mouths to feed—and so do many others down here }

| *do you feel the beginnings of the itch of an urge to pull that handle to see what will happen*]

Emergency Bucket No. 6 (new hydroelectristical {very deep}process ***alive*** :: *<u>and "jack-of-all-trade" friends it might have been better to</u>* :: when/where this place has been one great big mistake :: *<u>take a few years' soft-swim in some general science</u>*)

::

Upper tiered third from the fourth up against the wall standing room only Student: Ah yah, yes *uh*–[no] , but, if you would, please clarify = please clarify = ***Peter's*** = why is n = 2 * 2 wrong when just this teenially tinyellie differential'd cut 4 = 2 * 2 is wrong.

::

{ not one more step with that ***coat*** still on, sir, *no*. You don't really *Big Pimplesoft's a company y'all'dt slap some money o'er-top-tdovit,* <u>*TODAY*</u> }

[*who did it you did it why the hell'd you do it= there was no one else around to so I* = **not an excuse no no not no no no**] **Emergency Bucket No. 7** (:: but w-w-w-w-hat's ***done*** is ***done*** :: <u>*no not so "hop-specialo*</u> *{Bruno }* <u>*was here yes yes yes yes*</u> *{Bruno}* :: w-w-w-hat's ***said's*** been ***said***)

::

Th' Deepest of all Masters Master: We're sorry, but –we never presented any assertions such that any differential'd cutting'd at all'd ever, ever be wrong.

::

{ you don't want to end up finding out "<u>what's to happen next</u>" if you take one more step without having ***given me your coat*** }

[*why'd you go ahead and do it the few moments I was not around huh huh oh yah who the hell else'd pull the lever when all there's there right then was you why the hell'd the lever get pulled the one time I am not there?*]

Emergency Bucket No. 8 (so bring it on down now +yes we knew we would certainly take one more (((so ***God-God-damned ugly***!))) step with that ***coat*** still on, sir,)

::

Fresh Student "weeper" Greene: Oh, yes you did. Yes yes, oh, *hold your nose right there* while I check back through my notes shuffle shuffle you know I have never needed to hold my nose as I jumped into a pool so deep, so wide, so *very-very* wide, hot-cakes hit the snatch o' the side of it, Petunia, *but*—<u>*maybe you can tell me this*</u>; when is is a person [the tag word] to be capitalized when it is what a simple object is called? Then, it will not ***for example*** eh Mrs. Crowley, your car just pump'd up f i v e cylinders out of six available. So, does it really does it really class please diagram each sentence under the sentence itself mimeograph stench hooo mimeograph stench hooo mimeograph stench hooo wasa wasa wasa no no no no out those windows in *the wall's a world* you'll never again know *where cats climb trees but* [**most**} dogs *cannot*. But this not being made clear to all players, does lead to too much will power wastefully expended pushing some hard-stopped impossibility—which may lead to an *abdominal wall* <u>*hernia*</u>—***or worse.*** No no not that no not that not that beard not those eyes keep me safe O my savior parade rest quickly, quickly. The skinny old crone of a bank job second Louie race this was 'cross then back up say 'gain, say 'gain blank-O 'gain! Blank-O! 'gai!! Blank-O! 'ga!!! Blank-O! 'g!!!! Blank-O! '!!!!!! Blank-O! '!!!!!!! Blank-O! !!!!!!!! Blank-O!!!!!!!!!! Blank-!!!!!!!!!! Blank!!!!!!!!!!! Blan!!!!!!!!!!!! Bla!!!!!!!!!!!! Bl!!!!!!!!!!!!! B!!!!!!!!!!!!!! !!!!!!!!!!!!!! !!!!!!!!!! !!!!! !! ! rears up its ugly head {pillo} . . .three sleeps later *gone on* **ana-gagna** how does something fall out of sight over the edge and fall and fall to be finally gone but the Howl of it and the Screech of it remains only transformed in #1 of its "core-stiffening matrix" from which enough of the right kind of effort they may be possibly by slow motions be dragged back up by their whatever and **saved** [***gag gag***] but too much of this protracted not enough will lead to the opposite = most probably death but since we can't go that far we'll never know, ***will we***?

:: ugh platters

{ don't want to know "<u>what's to happen next</u>" if you take one more step without having ***given me your coat*** }

[*you knew I so wanted to see it happen, also, but—* why'd you spoil it for me **Hoao you wanted to spoil it dis''t you God you must hate me so, do you not hate me? *<u>Do you not hate</u>*?**]

Emergency Bucket No. 9 (no. You don't really *Big Pimplesoft's a company y'all'dt slap some money o'ertop-tdovit, <u>TODAY</u>* want to know "<u>what's to happen next</u>" if you pull that thing, *uh*?)

::

The Masters: awp a.w.p., listen. Eh listen. Slip, why are you wasting your cracking time with this pap. *It's not pap* <u>yes it's pap</u> more even yes it is even ***PAP*** {which is **way way** bigger} okay okay please lay off now NO it is not only PAP but **PAP** now and how again Bluto yah yah you're worse than Bluto and Bluto's pretty bad thought Bluto wasn't the one to say I WILL GLADLY PAY YOU ***TUESDAY*** FOR A HAMBURGER TODAY (huh?) see how they very well 'doctrinate the children _ (huh?) _'s okay and more still that _ (*huh?*) _'s really very very **<u>funny</u>** so Beeper hey Beeper why just one hamburger today NOBODY CAN EAT JUST ONE NO NO NOBODY (huh?) how 'bout you pay me Tuesday for six/seven hamburgers today LIVE IT <u>UP</u> (huh?) LIVE IT <u>UP</u> (huh?) (huh?) THERE'S NOTHING IN THE BIBLE SAYS YOU CAN'T GO ***LIVE IT <u>UP</u>! After all, Jesus and wine Jesus' wine Jesus an' wine look it up <u>LOOK IT UP</u>.***

::

{ that's right. ***NOW*** }

[But all we know is to hate you how to hate how to hate you]

Emergency Bucket No. 10 (take one more step without having ***given me your coat*** } + Eh I was only funnin' 'a ***uck*** !! *Holy warm glistening glandmasses, Batman* !!)

::

Here and There, a Student: But I can't gladly pay you Tuesday for six/seven hamburgers today oh oh no problemo sin-sinuo *sin-<u>sin</u>-**<u>suita</u>***? I think we might be pretty burnt out here.

::

{ what? *What?*}

(? [*Why're all there others around getting shown this all the time*] ***Let Me See!***)

Emergency Bucket No. 11 (but now the clock's come nearly to the next end, between such friends; "*It's really nothing.*" " Okay then. "Why's there always such reasons to hurry?")

::

Gummy Master {*old*} : Okay well fine ***sure*** *okay,* ***since that's the state you're all obviously in*** sure we'll will stretch it out for you stretch it out eck do so yes how long you want to take oh—forever maybe?

::

[*shown the time all the time every time*] ***Let Me See!***

Emergency Bucket No. 12 (The why o' these alls' 'rr very obvious ***to me***.

Why not you?

Huh?)

::

Student Guk {hippo }; [*spokesperson for <u>less than eight</u> others*} Oh WOW zowie WOW can I really pay for them *forever* |||| Oh sure yes yah yah we will parse the payments out but of course m'seur will understand that since we have to do all this additional making sure and ***hands-scentula*** there will be a "miniscule service charge" tacked on ***per period*** |||| ***okay okay*** get the hell out the hell out get your asses all the way out OUT out Nooovrembro-starian tyme' by coincidence now in effect now what a coincidence must mean something mean something really mean something someday we will see you again, probably when you return (*yawn*) if ever.

::

Let Me See! Let Me See! Let Me See! Let Me See! Let Me See! Scrambleround sc'amblin' scrambleround eh

Here; drink this.

Oh. Okay. But.

Huh?

Where?

The Resort Hotel Lobby, stupid! Where else ya think?

My God what hath thou brought me (faces buried in hands'd had <u>enough 'll enough</u>) (?)

David Wheldon

The Line of Works

'He was seventeen years my elder,' she said, the woman on the hilltop, her face turned away from me, her words difficult to make out. She was conning the horizon, right hand flat above her eyes. 'And he's been dead ten years.'

She turned to face me. 'We only had three years together. He was my first love. Not many years' love in a life, is it?' She put her lips together, protruding them thoughtfully, her expression one of sadness. 'Well, why should I confide in a stranger? Why did you climb this hill?'

She was a small, slender woman, perhaps fifty-five. Behind her rose the squat, octagonal drystone tower with its narrow windows. 'No matter. There's a tale of a whole line of signals: at night, fire-beacons. Here, where we stand, is just one link, it is said. They call it *The Line of Works*. Do you know anything about it?'

'Nothing,' I said. 'I didn't know such a warning system existed.'

'Is that what you think it was?' She made a little grimace. 'I know little about it,' she said. 'Only my link in the chain.' She followed the line of my gaze across the landscape below. 'I'll show you round. It won't take long.' A thought seemed to glance along a tangent of her mind. 'He was a philosopher, you know,' she said, her dark eyes keenly watchful.

'Which views did he espouse?'

'His own, of course. Who else's?' She laughed. 'The fish in the river down below are quite prolific. I use woven willow-baskets, as did he. Eels. I spear them. You crouch at the water's edge, low in the denseness of the reeds. And there are pigeons which roost in holes in the stonework of the tower: I take their eggs and make stews of their unfledged squabs.' She tilted her head and held her small, neat hands in front of her body. 'And vegetables. Samphire provides salt. I found a parsnip and kept the seed, year after year. I don't like parsnips much.' She shook her long, iron-grey hair. I wondered if she were mad.

'Excuse me while I take a sighting.' She laid her hands to either side of her eyes and scanned the horizon. 'Let me guide your eye, stranger,' she said. Her forefinger was steady. 'Do you not see? Yon hill; our predecessor in the line, oh, fifteen miles away?'

'I see a bald summit, wooded at the flanks.'

'That is she,' she said. 'Your eyes are sharp.' She rolled her lower lip over her upper. 'And the weather's clear this morning. Her semaphore is uncommonly brilliant.'

'What is its name?'

'Her name. They have names of women.'

I smiled.

'Don't smile like that,' she said. 'It doesn't mean much. Only unthought expressions come to mean, or so I believe. Now. My squint: my sighting.' She put all her concentration into her gaze between the flats of her hands. 'Nope. Nothing. She's flat. All the same as this time yesterday. Now. You were asking her name?'

'Yes. Does it have a name?'

'Why is her name important to you? You can't summon her. She isn't going to move. And I am always here: if not for quite as long. She, she may speak to me. I have no need to speak to her until that time. I take a sighting every ten minutes, and at night every half hour.'

'How do you sleep?'

'Let me show you round. There's ten minutes before the next sighting. I've trained myself to sleep for half-hour periods. The sightings are easier at night: I just have to sit up in bed and push aside the sacking from the semioscope—a little angled channel in the wall—and look out. I make a notch with a knife on a hazel tally-stick. It's a lot for one person, and I am always busy.'

We walked towards the semaphore tower. The tethered goats strained towards her.

'It would be easier with two. You can work shifts. But it's a meithersome task for one, and there's no reward.' She paused, her face anxious. She laid a slight hand on my forearm. 'No. No reward. The thought would trouble. Even the thought of the last valediction troubles: *well done, thou good and faithful servant*. Here.'

She opened the door of the tower, gave a tiny curtsey. 'The place of my confine. Come in.'

We stood in the relative darkness.

'Beaten earth floor, walls mud-plastered. Fireplace for cooking. No utensils; they've gone long ago, except for a cast-iron stew-pan. I found it in a ditch and scrubbed it with sand.'

'How do you light the fire?'

'In winter you keep the fire going day and night. It's troublesome fetching and carrying wood and water.' She considered something carefully, her head on one side. 'He always asked the question, the philosopher, my man: are days passed on by sentiences? He believed it so, and I agree with him, but I'm a little more practical, I think, than he, and who hands on days is of little everyday concern to me, as long as they continue to arrive. And who hands on generations? I don't know.' She grimaced. 'I calcine bones at the fire, grind them, and mix the ash with grease to whiten the semaphore arm. It must be kept visible.'

She folded her arms over her thin breast and smiled at me questioningly.

For some reason unable to meet her keen gaze—so questioning it seemed childlike—I looked round the room.

She watched me, taking my hand in hers. 'Everything is made of stone and driftwood,' she said. 'Look down through the window and you'll see the stone breastwork of the clyse. At the beginning of an incoming tide you'll hear a hollow boom as the bore strikes the clyse's seven valves and closes them to stop the ingress of salt-water. It's an uncanny sound. On one side—mine—clear, fresh water, and myself crouching on the bank, looking down at my own reflection. On the other side—the sea's—churning, turbid brine, wreckage, disjecta, spume.'

She smiled at her own description. 'Spring tide at the moment. It'll be a strong bore, with the wind against it, piling it up. Driftwood, cordage; it's all useful. The floor and the roof are driftwood, too; the rafters are curved: they were once the ribs of a vessel, so he told me. I've never forgotten.' She pointed round the room with a lean, bluish finger. 'Fireplace: mantel: wild flowers in a jar. Harebells. A beautiful blue: the most beautiful of blues. The most delicate venation. Next to them a piece of volcanic pumice; all bubbles. You find it all the time, washed up. Table. His predecessor made it. She was a fine craftswoman; she made most of the furniture. She was fifteen years older than he. He believed in her and became her spouse: she was his first love. They were together six years before she died. She's buried outside, next to him.' She plucked at her upper lip with her right finger and thumb. 'Chairs. Violin, found on the tideline. From a shipwreck, possibly. All split, of course: it'll never play. Come upstairs.'

The ladder was of crosspieces lashed with cordage to the side-timbers. She climbed with dexterity, grasping each crosspiece firmly. How worn they had become beneath her little feet.

I followed her upstairs to a low-ceilinged room with a little sighting-port—a semioscope—which faced the distant hill.

'I'll take a sighting,' she said.

While she took the sighting I looked round the room. There was nothing apart from a bed of bracken—you could see the impression of her body—and, in the half-darkness, the huge wooden image of a young woman's head, her frank blue eyes looking sternly ahead, coils of profuse, golden hair wrapped about her neck—the figurehead from the prow of a vessel.

'Her signal's flat. Let's continue upward,' she said.

Another climb and we were on the roof.

On the roof was a tall pile of driftwood, all carefully angled so that rain would run off. On a tall mast above the whole tower was the semaphore itself, a single horizontal board about twelve feet long, two feet wide, carefully whitened, which hung from a fulcrum in the mast.

'When the signal comes I shall undo the cordage from the cleats and pull the horizontal semaphore so that it stands diagonal. That transmits the message onward. What happens then? The system goes into reverse. This isn't difficult to understand, but, because it's never happened, it's important to practise in the mind.'

She paused at the top of the ladder. I almost think I'll sense her raised before I take a sighting. "Flat,"—she made a horizontal motion with her bony hand—'and "raised"'—she made a diagonal sweep. 'Those are the correct terms of the semaphore. Not the terms "off" and "on".'

We carefully made our way to the ground floor.

'What do you do for light?'

'I go to bed when daylight goes. And I rise when it appears.' She looked at me, her gaze affectionate. Her face was lined from exposure to the elements. She would often open her mouth to its fullest extent, not in a yawn exactly, but in some manneristic way peculiar to her. I liked her: her grimaces were endearing; exaggerations of her underlying emotions, though in hindsight I guess her emotions were exaggerated also.

'Now. Tell me about yourself.' She folded her arms and rested her elbows on the table. 'How you came to find this place.'

'I'm not sure it'll stand being put into words.'

'Try.' She laid her hands firmly in her lap, fingers dexterously intertwined.

And so I recounted my travels—though the ordering of the fugue-like sequence of days was beyond me—while she sat at the table.

'I saw this hill from a distance: when I was closer I could see the beacon-tower: in another few miles I could see the semaphore itself. Dawn was breaking as I climbed up through the woods, and looked up. And there you were, your skirts blowing in the wind, your arm raised.'

'My arm was raised. I saw your approach.' She pressed her lips together so that her mouth was a thin streak; above it a thin nose. 'Now it is time for me to play the schoolmistress.' She rubbed her hands together. 'Dinner wasn't much, but sufficient, I feel. Now. How the signal system works. I can extrapolate from this one station, and I'll tell about that, as much as I know. Well, first of all, I'll tell you this: the chain of signal towers has a finite length. How do I know this? I have worked it out myself, during sleepless nights.'

She laid five small sticks, each about four inches long, on the table-top. She held up a slender finger. 'The Line of Works is of a length unknown to me. Picture a small section of the Line. Observe these sticks. There they are. Five signal stations. The semaphores are flat. All are horizontal.' She laid them so. 'Five stations on five hills. We shall call these five stations α, β, γ, δ, ε. We are station γ. Fifty or sixty miles are accounted for in this little catenary. Now, in the forward transmission of the signal—whatever it may mean—the divine grace moves above our head. At present all the semaphores are flat. So: I lay the first semaphore, α, to signal: she's now diagonal. She forwards the message to β. β lays her semaphore to signal. Simplicity itself. Next: two events happen.

Firstly, β transmits her signal onward to γ. When she sees γ's semaphore go diagonal, she replaces her own semaphore to flat. This shows a that β has made her onward transmission. When γ passes on her signal to δ and sees that she has done so, she returns her semaphore to flat: β observes this and places her signal to diagonal. a sees the movement of β's semaphore and reverses her own. And this line of verification shows, step by step, the originator of the message that the chain is functional. Each and every station is accounted for. The transmission of the signal of itself demonstrates the integrity of the Line of Works.'

Her eyes were kindly in her little grimacing face, her gaze darting everywhere and then lighting on me with great affection. 'Two pieces of information have been effectively demonstrated: The message has been passed and the system itself is verified. And all one's life is dedicated to that; indirectly, perhaps; polishing, whitening, mending, cleaning, feeding oneself.' She held up a finger. 'Class suspended. I must take a sighting.'

She stood, looking out of the window, her hands aside her face. 'She's flat.' She laughed, inwardly. 'Oh, I like my friend,' she said, returning to the table, clasping both my hands with hers, and drawing this ball of extremities into her little lap. 'So. That's it, really. How many people there are who dedicate their lives to the maintenance of this Line of Works I do not know. Nor even—' her voice dropped. 'Nor even if this is a secondary line of signals. Perhaps. Once, five years ago, I saw a line of beacons, in a spectral haze, far away—Well, so we spend our lives. Are they valueless? Why ask me? Who notices me? La folle au bord de la mer?'

She released my hands. The marks of her nails were imprinted on my palms. 'We know so little.' The room was silent except for the click of embers in the hearth. 'Maybe there's little to know,' she said, breaking the silence. 'Maybe. Maybe the complication is made by looking from your own viewpoint, where everything goes a double turn, like planets in the night sky. Epicyclic gears. Complex, a slow click as one takes the night-road home.' She sat stock-still, listening. Then she relaxed, though nothing had been audible. 'Maybe it's all quite simple, and we blind ourselves with words and beliefs,' she said, decidedly. 'You'll want to know where you can sleep. On the bracken with me, but as friends. When I was a child we were four to a bed. How innocent! And how much an allegory!'

So, after washing at the spring we climbed the ladder and lay in the bracken.

'That's that,' she said. 'A useful day. A day somehow complete. Another day burned to a cinder. In many ways it's like the signal chain itself. A catenary of days.' Her voice was alert in the darkness. 'Now. I'll wake up at half-hourly intervals to take a sighting. So. For tonight you can have a full night's restful sleep as you are in a strange bed, but tomorrow I'll wake you at two hourly intervals.'

The light wind sang in the drystone walling of the beacon tower, and the moonbeams fell through the sight-hole onto the keeper's sleeping face.

She rose at first-light and shook me. 'Nothing all night: no fire, no flame,' she said, combing her iron-grey hair with her fingers. '*Revertere, revertere, Sulamitis; revertere, revertere ut intueamur te.* Return to me, my beloved Shulamita—' she whispered in an undertone, her face to the wall, her hands spread out on the stones.

We stood on the grass outside the tower. The wind had risen and was noisy in the drystone walling. This noise would come to haunt me; it had overtones of the keeper's voice.

'Did you sleep well?' she asked. 'I suspect so. I looked down at you after I had taken my sightings, every half hour; your face was calm, your limbs like a child's.' She plucked at my sleeve. 'My pupil. Let the class begin. Look—You see the hill, a comely shape. You see the semaphore above her, flat. There.'

She pointed with her slender arm, as though she would at that distance pin it down with telescopic physicality. 'You see it?'

I looked at the bald summit of that distant hill. 'I think I see it.'

'That's not good enough. You must see it.'

So she kept me there, overcome with hunger, in meditation on the distant hillside.

'Do you see it?' she asked.

'I see the summit of the hill, and an outcrop of rock—or maybe a tower—'

'He had to starve me into seeing it,' she said. 'It was three days before it became plain to me. It is like learning to wake at night. It is a kind of discipline. But water you must have. When I saw it clearly he made a little feast for me—oh, what he had to hand, and I slept a day.' She put her head on one side. 'Strive; strive, my student: strive with dignity and with love.'

And so I looked at that hill for three days, my teacher standing behind me. I knew all about every single conformation of its sides,—as viewed from my perspective—and as I looked out the fourth morning the further semaphore's whited board was clear to me. As clear as anything I have ever seen. It was flat.

'Now. Something to eat,' she said. ' Your eyes will be full of signals from now on.'

Over breakfast (she had lit a fire in the hearth, the morning being cold) she suddenly said: 'Soon enough your sentence ends: you are not locked up for long. Look for yourself again. A chain of towers, spatial: a chain of keepers, temporal.'

We left the tower and stood outside. I saw the horizontal semaphore against the purple of the further hills.

'The goats need milking. I'll show you how,' she said.

While she milked the goats she smiled. 'Kind little creatures,' she said. 'They hear the sound of the wind in the stones of tower and it soothes them.'

And so I was her industrious pupil. We began to form our own way of speaking, over the years. She once told me that she wished for no better company.

'You think I am capricious, living with goats, but I am not. I give them my attention, and they give me their companionship, and their milk. Milk on a windy hilltop: what could be better?' Her eyebrows formed a single solid line above her eyes. 'I am no philosopher like him,' she said suddenly. She looked at the distant hill. 'She is changing colour: the mists hang on the hems of her skirts and the air is still. How her moods and emotions pass from one to the next.' She looked at me, her eyes full of affection. 'So, you stayed with me: you gave your life to sustain the duties of generations. Each morning differs. Many years ago I told you he was a philosopher. You not unreasonably asked: which philosopher's teaching did he espouse? I answered: his own. Who can lead your life but you yourself?'

I nodded my head. I had become somewhat mute over the years. I let her do my speaking for me.

'He was one for soliloquies after I arrived. I said little, save to occasionally prompt him.' She raised her narrow shoulders, and then dropped them, the left one first: then she alternately raised and lowered each shoulder. Finally she stood with arms and legs akimbo. Her eyes were like pools of peaty water. 'And when I go, then perhaps you'll have time on your own to recover your voice: and another will come, and you'll be vocal. So. Go check the snares. If successful, skin, disembowel and hang the bodies in the shed.

I'll go check the fish-nets.'

She laughed, 'And they are doing just the same elsewhere: keeping their bodies active in readiness: and it all depends on the slaughter of small creatures who have no understanding of why they came about. This is the Line of Works: what sacrifices are made to it.'

We walked together, then parted: she to the clyse and I to the wooded glade on the shoulder of the hill.

We met an hour later.

'How many?'

I held up three fingers and pointed to the shed. She liked a certain gaminess, saying it stood in for seasoning, which we did not have, apart from wild garlic.

'Well, my fine forager,' she said, smiling. 'It's colder. And I have doubts.'

I stood before her, my expression interrogative.

'Yes, I have doubts. As I was looking out this morning, at the semaphore on the summit of yonder hill, pelerine-like clouds above her, I wondered about the intactness of the Line of Works. Are there missing stations—empty links?' Her eyes opened wide. 'It suddenly came to me that almost certainly no message would ever be sent. No message has ever been sent. That's a certainty: it's one fact a keeper always passes to his or her successor. No signals in the past, not one: the future we cannot see, unless it's something like an hour-glass, which, when its run is completed, is reversed. In which case there will be no messages transmitted in all time to come. And that is what the Line of Works will be: something akin to parable, a tale told. That it is—or may be—a parable is seen only towards the end of a keeper's sojourn. And he or she keeps the thought to him or herself. Do you see? The *system* of transmission, theoretically intact, visible in the line of unlit beacons and frozen semaphores, can bear no *real* use. It is pristine only because it cannot be touched.'

'I can read your expression,' she said one time. 'You don't need words. You can be as dumb as a beast until I'm gone, then you'll find your words with ease.' She put a finger to her lips. 'See? Nothing of significance can be transmitted.'

She playfully fondled a goat's ears. The little animal gave a small cry—a cry rather than a bleat. 'You like giving me your milk, don't you? As other animals like giving me their flesh: why, all but one of your own little boy-kids—though out of kindness I do it out of your sight—fall, victim to my fingers' skill.' She smiled at the goat, which licked her hand. 'You don't understand. Understanding is shimmeringly present in the mind but cannot itself be understood. So. That's the meaning of the Line of Works, and I've broken a binding vow in telling you this.'

The years passed. She was still very sprightly. Her bright eyes darted from one thing to another, and then could be steady in concentration.

One morning in spring she clapped her hands. 'We'll go together to the woods and gather ramsons. That glade by the old oak so that we can keep an eye on the sightings.'

This we did. 'So the Line of Works is a thing of theoretical significance only. And, if I am right, then other keepers realise this, and—' She put a white blossom of ramsons in her mouth. 'The first of the year!—and will have left their posts. I see you understand!'

Back in the tower we climbed to the roof to take in the glorious evening view of the countryside: to the west the sea: to the east the long stretch of the flooded peat levels and the distant hills: to the north and south the estuarial plain.

'Not a bad place to live,' she said. 'Snared meat. Herbs. Companionship: you speak with your eyes, and I can feel your thoughts.' She sighed, with happiness, and took my hand. 'A final sighting before the light is gone,' she said. 'Look!' She pointed with her hand, her voice low and filled with awe.

The semaphore arm above the tower on the further hill was slowly moving to a diagonal position.

We watched the precise finality of its motion.

'Look—' Her voice - the sound of that one word - was a loud whisper as though her vocal cords had been paralysed by disbelief.

Then she turned away.

'Come on,' she said, her voice more curt than I had yet heard it. 'Check the snares. I don't want a life lingering overnight.'

Half an hour later we lay on the bracken. 'I think we are freer than we have ever been,' she said.

'We didn't send on the signal,' I said.

'Your voice is coming back. Send the message forward? There is no point. The Line of Works will never work. People are too venal to make it work. It needs only one watch-tower's crew to go a-gley, and—I knew that years ago. Even its architect understood the truth. There is no keeper on the beacon yonder. They have lost their reason and have gone.' She laughed softly to herself and then began to cry bitterly.

'There is no-one at the next beacon?'

'There's no-one there.'

I paused. 'But the semaphore arm is whitened from time to time,' I said. 'Every month: regularly.'

Her hand flew to her mouth. I saw her action in the last glow of the firelight from the hearth below.

'Yes. Well observed. That's a piece of evidence I'd been trying to shake from my mind. I had almost done so. But you would have to remind me. And the two of us: now we know we cannot neglect our duty.' She sat up. She regarded the stars which appeared in the void of the trap-door above. 'Oh! It's dark! Too dark for the semaphore. The beacon! It must be the beacon!' She looked thoroughly confused.

'What shall we do?' I asked.

She stood in the darkness. I heard the clink of fire steel and the flint in her hand: then she grasped an armful of bracken, warm and dry from the heat of our bodies. 'She shall do what she, the keeper, has to do.' She began to laugh, her emotions changing with a liquid ease. 'Beneath it all we both feel the same way. We shall survive: our tendance on the Line of Works has taught us subsistence. Perhaps that's ever been its purpose. Whatever it might have been it's not our tomb.' The word survive she had shouted in a voice of ascending pitch.

She began to climb to the roof and the pile of dry timber. 'Go downstairs and stand outside,' she said. 'I'll do what I have to do, and then I'll join you.'

I heard the scraping of the fire-steel.

The beacon quickly took fire. And the sound of it: the steady roar of countless revolutionary voices.

The door of the tower was opened, and she ran towards me, her face ecstatic, her arms outreaching. She was beyond the power of speech and trembled in my close embrace.

Then we stared out into the darkness, the conflagration of the beacon to our backs.

Soon, perhaps ten miles away, another beacon sprang from unseen darkness to a fiery life: and beyond it another. Beyond that third beacon was a scarp, a ridge of low hills which might have had a name, but which name I did not know—this range of hills had the look of the edge of day: once beyond that folding of the earth there would never be the possibility of return—nor even the thought of a return—no words to express the idea—

Then, with a rapidity which denied belief, the remote beacon on that ridge took flame. Beyond that we could not see.

David Wheldon

The Lamp Man

He wore a faded blue boiler suit, the colour of his eyes. It was patched with newer, darker denim at the elbows and knees; the patches were sewn on with small, neat stitches. It had been home-washed, this boiler suit, for it had been carefully—even painstakingly—ironed and folded.

He looked into the long embrasure in the brick wall of the passage, his manner teacherly. I, a boy, stood beside him.

'Can you see right through to the interior of the powder magazine?' He paused. 'I can't myself see the magazine that clearly—from where I am here—because of the reflection of the lamps. I'm paid to light and maintain the lamps. The lamp man, that's what I am, and I understand the Fort from a lamp-man's point of view.' He put his head on one side. 'I started work at fifteen. I shall retire very soon.' His voice was reflective. 'Fifty-five years.'

'This way is the lamp man's corridor. Vaulted brick. Narrow. Deep underground: far beneath the Parade. The lamp man alone has need to use it. I spent a week learning from the previous lamp-man. He approved me: then I was on my own. And on my own I have been ever since, until you arrived. I begin my work at seven in the morning, and set the lighted lamps in the floors of the embrasures, removing the lamps which have burned throughout the night. Then I return, and fill the replacement lamps with paraffin, replace the cotton wicks as necessary, polishing the lamp-chimneys and the reflectors. I work sequentially, replacing every alternate lamp. It's quite pleasing, the orderliness of it. The magazine is thus illumined, thoroughly and evenly, throughout the day and night. All is in a state of readiness. I have four hours sleep. And then I begin once more.'

He smiled. His smile was a little secretive. 'Look through. Can you see the people moving about in the magazine? All in white apparel. Cotton, probably. Silent, forbidden to carry anything made of iron or steel, lest they make a spark. Glim-felt-slippered, hooded. Who are they? They move like ghosts. They move cautiously amongst the barrels of black-powder and the carousels of fuzes. And yet I give them light—a steady, even light.

'My world is separate from theirs.'

He paused, moved on from his subject. 'My mother danced the can-can. In Paris. It was her metier. She told me so. Who my father was I never knew: but I loved my mother. I am half-French. That's an irony, working as a lamp-man in an English fort.' He returned to his subject. 'Anyway, I am the lamp-man. Huge vaulted brick structures, meaning nothing to me. I tender my pass on crossing the moat. I light the lamps.'

He paused. 'My smiling mother, lifting her skirts, kicking her long legs, long ago. I have photographs. From long before I was born. I have a short film clip too, I cannot watch it now. Sylvia, her best friend and apparently a witness at her wedding, next to her. Do you understand?

'Now I'm quite old. I walk along the narrow lamp-passage, brick-built, vaulted. Its sole purpose to allow the illuminator passage. The deep embrasures in the wall are sealed with several layers of plate-glass at the end. There is thus no chance of fire entering the magazine. The lamps are caged for double security. The magazine is effectively lit externally. There is never any communication between the lamp-man and the explosives workers.

'The white-clad figures within the magazine rely upon my secluded light, myself unseen. I am the solitary lamp-man. I am a civilian. I obtain my wage from the Adjutant's secretary's office. I am apportioned a new boiler suit every six months. A woman in the laundry insists on pressing it after every wash with a flat-iron. She repairs my boiler suits as needed. I've never met her. Who is she, in her devotion to her duties? It's all fair, as set down in my contract. Everyone should be fastidious in their devotion to their duty.

And as for the Fort: it is obsolete. It was obsolete the day that it was armed.

'You, my child: do you understand?'

Selin Tamtekin

Two Flight Pieces

In Flight Mode

Waiting excitedly, I wriggle in my passenger seat. The engines begin to run at full power and the aircraft starts to speed; in a flash I'm transported onto the runway and am sprinting behind it.

It becomes airborne; I too softly ascend into the air. To remain afloat, I perform lavish breaststrokes.

It climbs higher; I salute a flock of yapping seagulls, then energetically flap my arms to keep up.

It becomes fainter, then disappears. I shriek as I begin to wobble. 'Ouch!' I say. It's like being pierced by multiple ice daggers.

Coming out wet and dishevelled, I catch sight of it in the distance; I kick frantically to gain momentum.

A kid seated at the very back of the aircraft notices me, his eyes widening with amazement. We keep smiling and waving back and forth. Eventually he gets fed up and sticks out his tongue; annoyed, I respond by cocking a snoot.

I see him tapping on someone's shoulder. I stop kicking and wiggle my fingers at the boy. Before the other person gets to see me, the plane's powerful engine thrusts me behind.

I continue to follow the aircraft, my arms wide open. I mimic how it ascends further, tilting one of its wings and turning upwards towards its designated route.

The city beneath us resembles a very large architectural model. Streets with neatly lined up buildings start to disappear, and the greenery takes over.

As we pass the shoreline, I get a little sentimental and wave goodbye.

Back inside the plane, I reach inside my bag and take out a book. I recline my seat and pick up where I had left off.

Momentary Suspension

At last, we reach the top of the hill. Below us, an expansive valley stretches out: endless fields, broken only by farmhouses and clusters of trees. It's a spectacular view.

He says, "If you look carefully, just ahead you can see a bit of the sea."

I squint and focus intensely while a gentle breeze begins to dry the dampness under my arms.

"And over there is the airport. Do you see that plane that's just taken off?"

"Wow," I remark. "Speaking of planes . . . have you ever tried it?"

"Tried what?"

I start flapping my arms.

"What are you doing?"

"Come on. You're joking, right?" I slow down. "Don't tell me you've never been curious."

For a moment, he looks embarrassed. I've clearly caught him out. With a defensive roll of the eyes, he mutters, "Are you talking about momentary suspension?"

"You bet I am!" I step in front of him and start flapping my arms really fast.

He becomes panicky.

"Look how isolated we are out here. If something happens, by the time anyone arrives it'll be too late."

I pause my arms for a second and say, "Oh, you really love me, don't you?"

"Of course I love you," he responds in a stressed tone. He can be so uptight.

"Then you have to let me spread my wings and fly away!"

He rolls his eyes again. "I love you, and I don't want you to die or end up making me a homicide suspect."

"Jeez Louise. What's with the high drama?" I look behind me. I'm pretty close to the edge.

"Fine. I promise I won't go beyond this spot. There'll always be the ground beneath my feet."

He gives me a doubtful look.

"I mean it. Plus, I might not even be able to do it."

I'm flapping faster now. My breathing intensifies. I have to keep the movement regular and controlled; otherwise, I might lose my suspension and drop, or sprain one of my wrists again, as I did last time. I see him take his phone out of his back pocket and glance at the screen.

"You must be kidding me!"

Straight away he puts it back inside his pocket.

My arms feel nearly numb.

"Oh my God. You're lifting off!"

I look down.

"Yep!"

Still flapping, I tilt my arms slightly outward and drift towards him.

"We're the same height now!" I blurt out, nearly out of breath and soaked in sweat.

"I need to film this," he says.

To give him some space, I turn my palms upward and start flapping away from him.

"Just a sec. I updated my phone this morning and I can't seem to find the video button."

I glance down and suddenly realise I've drifted beyond the edge. It isn't a sheer drop, but it would be enough. One irregular flap and I could tumble down, grabbing at the air, perhaps managing to cling to something.

My heart is racing. Stay calm, I tell myself. You can do this. Easy peasy lemon squeezy.

"Oh—here it is. Ready?"

Knowing how close I've come, I nod, somehow managing to hold back my tears.

Then, I lower myself and land.

"Ow—why did you stop? I could've filmed you a little longer."

Trembling, I walk over and hug him.

Ernest Hilbert

Out in That Gloomy Meadow

All night	*I look*
Down here	*In dirt*
With all	*My books*
But I	*Can't find*
A thing—	*Just why—*
My mind	*So near*
That hurt	*Will fall*
It looks	*So bad*
We want	*To hear*
That fear	*You have*
We want	*To hear*
What did	*You find*
We want	*To hear*
What hid	*Out there*
We want	*To hear*
I found	*A thing*
I can't	*Put back*

Steven Gray

Two Poems

A Room of Heads Without a Face

How often am I seeing a generic
silhouette, it's hanging on the wall,
an executed figurine, a body
of work, not to mention the abstraction
of a democratic principle
that anyone could do it with a spastic
brush, an empty space, and someone so
obtuse they focus on magnetic color
fields. Their dim connections to the
anthropomorphic are a blur, it could be him,
it could be her. The composition lurking
on the edge of our attention, it's
peripheral, inflated, and inferior,
with some nostalgia for the humanist,
like something which is vaguely recollected,
not entirely reconstituted
in the mind of someone who is modern.

You can pay six figures for a stick figure,
it depends who did it, and identity
is everything in the primordial
ooze, the leveling of the mass production,
otherwise we don't stand out. There is
an old nostalgia for identity,
those who have it are celebrities,
the rest of us will wallow in obscurity,
awash in all the shifting shapes
and sizes of a lower common denominator
with its fluctuating luck.

The Broken News

NATIONS APPROVE of Fortress Mountain

Downhill Thrill Divides Women

Five tips for
'A Whole New Being'

Little Evidence for
Purgatory

METROPOLITAN Illness COMES
OUT OF THE BLUE

An Encore Presentation of Guns

FINE JEWELRY Prohibition Style

WHICH WATCH IS THE
EPITOME OF
Dirt-Cheap Gas

Texas Leads Scrutiny
of Satellite Time

. . . to pay you the
highest prices for your
unwanted
Seniors

Believe
IN THE MAGIC OF Elections

Death Toll to Include Women

TAKE AN EXTRA
20% OFF on civilian casualties

MONDAY Undone in London

A Mock Shooting
WITH ICONIC STYLING AND A TRULY INDULGENT
INTERIOR

Man Charged
With UNDENIABLE PRESENCE

SEIZING the
Smartphone for a 'New Being'

SIMPLY INTELLIGENT   migrants flee

SWISS-MADE ELEGANCE MEETS
a cholera outbreak

sleep patterns   starting at $995

Custom Interior Protection   for
Bodies Left in Streets

Agreement's Careful Language on Curbing
Forests

NEW YORK INSPIRED   bite-mark forensics

'Inclusive' House Agenda Must Counter
ARABIAN PERFUMES

Mothers and Daughters Debating   PURE LUXURY

for New Year's Eve, Hotels Pull Out
The Gender Factor

THE ONLY THING BETTER THAN
a Ghost Resort

is   Riding a Bike

Breathing New Life Into
sexual crimes

A Rescue That Has Come With
a   SKELETON TIMEPIECE

I taught her how to ride   RALPH LAUREN

Workers Face Choice: Lose   or Lose

There's no business
like   Hockey

After success as a TV
housewife, a struggle
with   The Silent Treatment

Seizing the   Composer of Operas

to Create   GIFTS we LOVE

Keep the flame lit for   An Attack Underground

Despair About   Pluto

James Sallis

Six Poems

The Surrealist's Day Job

He drives his cart each morning
alongside the canals
and from stair-stepped homes
tarpaper shacks and high-rise condos
from cardboard shelters at the edge of town
they bring theirs out to him

Nothing here he can sell or trade
no real use for most of it
here in this better world of ours

He stacks it all carefully and rolls away
ringing his wee bell
wheels of his cart creaking beneath the weight

All those desires sorrows regrets

Where We Are

Monday, bills arrive
from the other side,
swaddled in small print.

Men in blindfolds
stumble again and again
against our dreams.

Even the microwave
sings to us
in our time of dejection.

In walls we hear
the cries of wire and pipe
begging their freedom.

In the Hour Between Dog and Wolf

The gallery paintings love it
when there are no people
and they're left to be themselves,
when they don't have to
represent, change lives, document,
or matter.

—

In the quiet meadow
you imagine troops advancing, hear
the pound of hooves on bare ground,
mud falling from the treads of tanks.

The great war has come at last.
We will all be heroes.

—

We're still lighting candles
for those who died, he said—
on his break, outside
the church. There's free coffee inside
should you care to join us.

—

I have six children
she said
they are all dead

their names linger
in the dark of night

they call
from other rooms
want things
need them

—

Listen
how sorrowfully
water
falls into the sink.

In the Time of a Dying Wind

The stuffed bear stands by the door
to the hall
removing its stuffing handful by handful
growing by degrees, smiling, smaller

Sadness glides in on
the same wind the hawk rode out against
when its feet found the eagle's nest
found the eagle's young

Out in the kitchen the teapot
speaks shrilly and will not stop
of things I don't care to hear again

Tells me of a loneliness only horizons know

Audition

Someone in a spectacularly bad suit and worse haircut comes in and sits across from me, tells me in a terrible actor's voice that he's my father. Hair sprouts in tiny bouquets from nostrils and ears. He's brought doughnuts. Cheap ones—all icing has fallen to the bottom of the box. He watches as I push the box back across the table. Out of the very bones of sadness he is building this moment.

Freshness

My wife Jill has taken to hiding things from me, often in the freezer. Leftover pizza, the house phone, Oreos, memories, the mystery of who I am. Getting started each morning is a challenge. Where are those personal goals I wrapped so carefully in foil and dated? And the canister from behind the flour, where I kept my youthful cunning?

Carl Landauer

Don't You Know There's a Parade Going On?

Mike Nichols's *Catch-22* (1970) after
Joseph Heller's *Catch-22* (1961)

Just after the credits but before dawn
a dog's bark echoes from the distance, birds
barely introduce their sounds, and unseen
gulls begin to call. With the early sun,
off-screen engines ratchet up.
Shrouded by kicked-up dust and exhaust,
bombers file by one by one,
blowing leaves of grass
sideways at their wheels.
This could be any war film.
Even the officers' conversation
—they're perfectly dressed—
in the bombed-out building
overlooking the field
can't be heard. I know
the insanity must begin
but we're held one moment longer.

Heller excavates the snafu-
ridden experience of war,
knowing
we're all in this business of illusion together
and generals demand the
nicer aerial photograph
where
the bombs explode close together
and surely, we understand
so many countries can't all *be worth dying for.*
Perhaps the fifties sneak in,
loyalty oaths and Communist accusations
you never heard him denying it until we began accusing him
and officers promoted
by an I.B.M. machine with a sense of humor.
Heller's mind working, fevered,
with a mess officer

who was
        not only Vice-Shah of Oran
but also
        the Caliph of Baghdad,
        the Imam of Damascus,
        and the Sheik of Araby,
moving markets the world over.

Nichols returns again and again
        as did Heller
to Yossarian trying to attend
his wounded gunner. Each time
gaining in horror,
the secret gore unwraps,
punctuated only by the share of M & M Enterprises
where the morphine should be.
Nichols uses the almost blinding
light and the wind of those scenes
to announce each transition,
the reedy saxophone music
accompanying Yossarian's dancing
morphs to the wind around
the dying gunner.

The film Yossarian walks the dark
streets of a nightmarish Rome,
Heller's man beating a dog with a whip,
like the horse in Raskolnikov's dream,
reverts to the dream.
But forget the Fellini gestures
and think of the pay-offs, the murders, and disease
of Italian cities newly occupied by American forces
and the real General Mark W. Clark
who by vanity and incompetence paraded
into Naples from the wrong side,
the city's good citizens waiting
at the other end.

Kurt Luchs

Two Poems

Marching

They were marching and they asked me
to join them of course I had
no intention of doing any such thing
but my feet had other ideas

who knew that feet could do the devil's work
whatever rhythm I had on my own
was swallowed along with my conscience
no more offbeats no more jazzy time changes

nobody marches alone there is always
a company and as they march the cry goes up
death to the infidel death to everyone
who isn't marching may our boots

stamp on their faces forever how joyful
the song of those who worship death
and think that it's god you must admit
the legions of death always have the best songs

but then a tune that can be whistled
may be what is required to tramp evil
upon evil and call it good I don't
call it that I call it marching

Helmut

To tease and torment him, we called him
the mutt from hell.
He had names for us also, his six siblings.
It was a household of names,
a household where growing up
was tearing down,
starting with the name.

He was and is the middle child of seven,
a lucky number in any other world
except ours, which would've seemed
like home to the ancient Greeks and Norsemen
leaving axes in each other's skulls.
Blows rained on him from the older children
and he rained them on the younger
as our father pummeled everything in sight
except our mother,

whose favorite weapon was her tongue.
We learned all too well from both of them.

Jesus said the kingdom of heaven
is within you, which is true,
albeit a truth of little use to us
as the other kingdom is within you too
and has complete charge of this realm.

The words of Jesus mean nothing
to a child being beaten down every which way
every day. He's like the uncle
who sees what's going on in your home
and doesn't lift a finger to stop it.
Suffer the little children!
Jesus can go fuck himself.
If he came back today
I'd start building another cross for him.

But I appear to have gotten away
from the subject of my sibling Helmut.
No matter what has happened to you
at a certain point you must decide
who you will choose to be.
Helmut elected to be a husband and father,
not perfect in either role but so much better than
our parents that any comparison seems ludicrous.

His two sons carry the best of him forward,
making music much more successfully
than he was able to make comedy and humor
with his brothers, delightful and doomed
as that attempt was.
He was always the cleverest at thinking of endings,
the hardest part of any comedy sketch.
And now I'm thinking of his,
still a long way off, I hope,
though Alzheimer's has been chipping him
into one of those ancient headless statues.

O my brother, death is stalking each of us
all the time and we don't know the day or the hour
yet when he comes for you
will it still be you that he steals from us?
How wrong it feels to mourn beforehand
but the tears keep coming unbidden
and I have no power to stop them, little brother,
named after some World War II German air ace
who, unlike you, is long forgotten.

Eric Weiskott

Seven Poems

Long Days of Your Own Wherewithal

after Prageeta Sharma[1]

And who is to say the operation will succeed,
the day will brighten out of the southeast like a room,
what we tell Lili and Theo will be OK, will be OK?

Day succeeds night, which succeeds
in convincing you of your own wherewithal
to lift your tremulous voice in song.

The day succeeds only in ending in colors for a healthy cheek.
And who is to say the voice, when it rises this time,
will not be a whispered vow?

Untitled #56

blocked by ulterior poem the one
lodged in gullet and lost

in the aftermath of hurricane
artworks are only as precious

as loss / delicate storm in
late Netherlandish

we have painted the horizon blues
and yellows, scent of vanilla

just before rain- and landfall
where do you go if

before explanation the sea
rears up to devour

why does the lost poem always
a change in attitude or pressure

common to our celebrated
figuration / always late

a style or method of measurement
common to crisis

and moments of lyric, painted
landfall

---

[1] Prageeta Sharma, *Grief Sequence* (Seattle: *Wave*, 2019), 67

Like Paper under Ink

after Edgar Garcia[2]

an obsolete phrase, my
love for you sagging under its own weight

it is incomparable and absolute
to be awakening now

in the dream, we think,
"to have loved and lost"

in the renewed mourning of this-day-of-today
the bare suggestion of flesh

on bedside table, one barrette
and purple comb

each room a discarded phrase
and our awakening to solidity

Autobiographical Lullaby

after Solmaz Sharif[3]

To locate the reference partway down a lefthand page
To notice afterwards the pencil writes brown not leaden so brown blooms on the page in the warm yellow light of the desktop lamp
To purchase a hundred-foot roll of archival three-mil mylar sheeting
To use a hobby knife to trim mylar sheeting to fashion protective folded covers for a quarto leatherbound volume printed in London in 1637, and an octavo leatherbound volume printed in Edinburgh in 1770
To sigh and flip the pillow over
To learn how to do this on youtube
To retire when the clock strikes
To repeat yourself
To grow up in a village on the North Fork of Long Island
To undertake some other kind of mission
To notice afterwards the way the town divides itself through its third street
To sigh and flip Suffolk County red
To undertake a study of the minds of dead people

To locate the reference to the early work of Lisa Jarnot, in which the poet traces syntactical possibilities latent in certain lesser-known lyrics of Bob Dylan
To use a hobby knife to trace the East River detaching Long Island from New York
To repeat yourself
To learn how to do this on youtube
To retire to the antechamber in 1637 or in 1770 certain of the rightness of this, of the rightness of the world, and in expectation of great things such as my love she speaks like silence such as ancient Scottish poems such as a grandfather clock striking such as a pencil sharpened for use such as a leatherbound volume expressing the county such as retirement such as archival three-mil mylar sheeting such as ornate pillows
To grow up and to notice

---

[2] Edgar Garcia, *Boundary Loot* (Scarborough, ME: Punch, 2012), [1].
[3] Bob Dylan, "Love Minus Zero / No Limit," *Bringing It All Back Home* (1965); Lisa Jarnot, *Some Other Kind of Mission* (Providence: *Burning Deck*, 1996); Solmaz Sharif, *Customs* (Minneapolis: *Graywolf*, 2022), 59–60.

to write a book called *Sisyphus the Completist*. It would
include all my recent poems and my college poems.
Each stanza rolls a stone up one side of the same idea:
it would include a poem called "Sisyphus the Completist,"
full of black and violet words.
It would include mourning and epiphany, concluding
will trigger self-awareness in conclusion
international relations and settling accounts. *Sisyphus the Completist*
so you know how weird you are but it no longer matters.

Nabokov felt he had already composed
his future novels. The trick is to
Listen, every box must be checked. Every apology
to one's wife in the evenings, for example, ends the same.
Every morning, you wake up with a stone
in your stomach. The trick is to know when you've reached
Heartbreak Hill, a Beacon Street of the mind.
Newspaper feature reports on research: women marathoners
This seems metaphysically appropriate
stay young but men age an extra ten years.
and biologically dubious.

Sisyphus still has so many academic conference lanyards
to collect, it's crazy. The book would express anxiety
about submitting new work to judgment. It would
include a comment in the form of a question.
Each stanza rolls a stone up one side of the same campus.
Full of vengeful words, I remember
The student union supports
lost souls I knew at [redacted].
Un-Koch My Hippocampus. The trick is to age
Ten years, it takes self-awareness, Ben.

Unfortunately for the lanyard set,
you have to play the minor key
to earn the right to play the major key.
That's what the blues taught me.
Does it seem that your article passes too quickly from one genre to another?
Nabokov's third novel contains a passage
when it doesn't imitate art.
predicting the *Lolita* film adaptation. We only notice life
on niches—you had to be there.
Newspaper reports on research
Sisyphus still has so many references to check,
it's crazy. Each stanza rolls a stone: I want[4]

[4] Vladimir Nabokov, *The Luzhin Defense*, trans. Michael Scammell (New York: Putnam, 1964; repr. New York: Vintage, 1990), 244–48; Priscilla Meyer, "Black and Violet Words: *Despair* and *The Real Life of Sebastian Knight* as Doubles," *Nabokov Studies* 4 (1997): 37–60; Michael Staines, "Running Marathons Can Age Men by Ten Years," *NewsTalk* 7 June 2022 <newstalk.com/news/running-marathons-can-age-men-by-ten-years-1352285>.

On a Ruin

translated from Old English

There are wet ruins and dry ruins.
    A poet knows the difference:
gray lichen and dust,
    vermillion roof and asbestos.
Thirty generations ago,
    this wall held a number of ideas
about English weather.
    It abides. Warriors in bright
byrnies encircled
    the ruins at bathtime.
You know the place:
    where hot springs
surged up from the jewelled heart
    of memory. Now all idle,
a picture of siltation.
    The river floods and tempers
the baths' water, the wall molders,
    even the name is buried.

The Revelator

Time's the revelator
        —Gillian Welch[5]

The solo, as if overdubbed
    from some other song,
            crackles against the chord change
    subsides into its rhythm.
At the turnaround
    time reveals the missed notes
            as intentionally withheld.
    Mandolins belong
to their county,
    an Angeleno's twang
            on air. In this song
    your lover has vanished
into the banjo's arc,
    the guitars are trying
        not to weep,
    and the president is dead.
In the other song
    time reveals only mist.

---

[5] Gillian Welch, "Revelator," *Time (The Revelator)* (2001).

Mike Silverton

Poems in Words

Lucky Pierre, the Werewolf

His striking figure notwithstanding, when the moon is full
late-night shoppers hasten on home. Architectural features cling
to his thoughts. He sleeps with snails.

"We could do with more hairballs."
Slathered in foreboding.
Lucky Pierre was here, was not . . .

Grisly protrusions, ochre secretions—
in a Potemkin village they exist elliptically,
leaving sticky hints.

Lycanthropes, out of malice (some say modesty),
favor opaque over pel
lucid.

Thankless task: sorting teardrops where
werewolves regret with every
drawn breath.

Soft-slippered, eyes half-closed,
whoosh whoosh whoosh,
slam! he goes.

Easy come, easy go.
Lucky Pierre,
he knows where to look.

Lucky Pierre's allure resides in his mind. We add
a few choice gobbets, taking care to keep them tangible (edible,
digestible, friable, risible, flammable, fungible . . .).

Loco Schlomo, Lucky Pierre's board-certified sensei,
recalls successes embroidered with threads
of purest silver and glaucous guts.

When Lucky Pierre's teeth require filing,
dental assistants cower
in closets.

The distant hills resemble a naval blockade, or, in the right light,
upholstery. Werewolves look like
werewolves.

In the interest of public safety, Lucky Pierre's saliva includes
an antiseptic. He's also a shape shifter. Have
another look at your couch.

A werewolf's glance screams *en garde!* Even as I craft
these lines ensconced in my cozy inglenook,
I tremble and perspire.

When Lucky Pierre feels out of sorts, he naps.
Prying him from the pavement proves
a thankless chore.

When the mood strikes, Lucky Pierre boils pumpkins
in commensurately large pots over very large fires. No one
knows why, nor has anyone the courage to ask.

On fine and starry nights Lucky Pierre mounts a bronze stallion
already bestraddled by a bronze war hero.
Here too, best not to ask.

Lucky Pierre's endearments attract gnats and bats.
His indestructible shithouse sits at the center
of an impenetrable maze.

As for those who go about muttering, "Surely everything's something,"
an example must be made! Lucky Pierre loathes
inanities!

How conspicuous is a werewolf? Say, as a manatee in a sand box,
a vampire in a distillery, an iceberg in a dining room,
a Goldberg bereft of variations.

Pop!

When titans stride across the land
poetry must do what it can
to avoid being stepped upon.
Ah, surely not me, the poet cries,
who asks nothing more to eat
than yesterday's scraps, as
soon as is convenient,
of course. Later that day (in the world)
upward illuminations awaken, already having
broken treaties. The eyelid lifts.
Pop!

The Irresolute They

They say they're too artful, also too lazy
to bandage the bloodwort. They are also too artful,
also too lazy to roll about in their terracotta
bathyspheres. George, I'm not the same as I was
moments ago. There go the fakirs into Miriam's house,
or maybe that's a wilderness or something that
zigzags? Wait one minute! What's going on?
Who is this, back from the dead?

Industries rise and industries rise and I'll love me forever,
notwithstanding inaccuracies and this elegant horseman from
behind the stars or maybe Chicago, also too lazy.
And the bloodwort.

In Pairs

Under a carpet lies a secret sky that says goodbye
when one least expects it. Its face of ashes lasts but a moment.

With this mallet the poet subdues livestock, also with suction.
Simple Simon says goodbye too.

Oaken staves strapped to his feet, the poet walks across the gloomy ceiling.
No bigger than a nickel, the poet's effigy likewise finds life good.

The poet observes recidivist loudmouths
in the vestibule of their capabilities.

Six people are getting a drink or something, which
demonstrates that life has its moments.

I forgot about sticking cloves in the mermaid
and putting her somewhere.

The first time you chirped my sweat was so heavy
I dropped to the floor and snuffed out the light.

On especially slippery days
words slide off the poet's pages.

The bellicose imagination's fumes
produce noms de guerre.

It's late afternoon.
The sky is looking at you.

Poem in Words

Be wary of homunculi in unstable stacks,
if only of words.

Beautiful words, a shimmering lyre,
silken promises from hills someone named.

Words: parabola, spiral, magical cat box,
artillery Luger.

Five Quintains

Who is so handy in a pea-soup fog as to locate his wishes for
better weather? Of scythes I have heard the best, Hello!
Surprise!, feeds a need. Conversely, one embraces
tiny flowers and butters each sunny hour
with happy thoughts.

Something like a Utah troubles my head.
Something tells me to water the birds.
Something like massive gerbils mill about in a box
or is it a lifeboat drill? Or something else?
I cannot tell.

Bare feet plop about on my thoughts.
Rates of absorption notwithstanding, I feel better.
Stuffed animals dream their stuffed dreams.
In the sky, fluffy clouds.
Below, in Arles, Arlésiennes.

Banalities, whatever you may think of them, could, and
I doubt you've ever seen them in quite this light,
weigh three-hundred pounds apiece.
In what way is this useful?
Shall I call for help?

The vegetables are cheaper,
the privies stink,
the girls are more willing,
springtime!
(Attributed to Heine, though I cannot confirm.)

The Uprushing Wind Has the Suicide's Earlobes at Right Angles to His Neck.

We awaken sooner or later, but I digress.
Awakened Inuit climb up icicles.
Awakened spelunkers climb up stalagmites.
This is how they exercise. This is how I don't.
I will, of a morning, raise the blinds
to see what my world looks like.
For me, that's enough.
(Little happens as we'd wish it.)
"Finger in band, onion in sand, and so
a wee wifey and garden."

Dead Grandmothers

Nor did I anticipate all this blood
as through an Alpine village passed,
shades of night falling fast,
a youth who bore through snow and ice
an ensign with the strange device,
What Is This About?

Stitches, Not Sutures

Recalling quite suddenly that I must be alive
in order to open and close umbrellas, expressions of grief
neither help nor hinder. We need to show the Cossacks something
else to pillage. Distractions have their place. Kinetics also:
Off the roof at last, immobilized in traction,
I strive to leave the reader in stitches.

Alone, in a Room

My expressions of grief are often mistaken for the unoiled hinges
of a kitsch reproduction of a castle-keep door, as an unwelcome distraction
from "Death and Transfiguration," which I'll soon conduct,
alone, in a room.

La Primavera Blows Her Tromba

The poet's lot, to be brayed upon by the disaffected
as idiots founder and die in their kayaks.
These misfortunes persist even under manhole covers,
even among witnesses to a fascinating incident
copyright restrictions prevent me from describing
(hint: wading up to one's earlobes in yogurt).
La primavera blows her tromba,
spizoopy!

Saint George, Exposed

Dada is Trouble, Dada is Truth, and so a troubling Truth:
as the first and last Dada Exposé, we offer Saint George, or
more precisely, aspects of a life no one knows about. To begin,
Saint George ate insects, in the main, plump beetles.
He flossed with spider webs. One would have thought better,
but no, it's true. Dada says so. Dada knows.
Further, the dragon was a gecko;
the spear, a twig; the mount, a Radio Flyer.
He was four years old.

In Anticipation of Publication

"The cravat, sire, is a tapeworm in repose,
a household pet marking the hours. And, above all,
a cherished companion." No sooner uttered,
thunder crashes along with other disturbances
of a meteorological character. "Pedal faster, mother!
I see enemies everywhere!" Mister Printer Man,
kindly print this poem in theatrical blood.

Just Short of Despair in Three Tercets

I come to you, reader, through granite chewed poetically:
though but a borer of metaphorical rock, I ask for your love
or a merciful gesture or a hint of one's destiny, should you be privy.

I Come to you, reader, glutes flaccid,
teeth elsewhere crafted, likewise knees hinged,
Depend dependent, libido in the wind, prospects sketchy.

I come to you, reader, on an incorrect frequency,
in the wrong boulangerie, picking the wrong pockets
in search of an answer to a question that eludes me.

Foolish Deists

Summer departs. My sighs fill the countryside.
Walnuts drop. I need to explain.
Walnuts drop, yes, and Indians tiptoe all over the nation,
with those untrustworthy Indian smiles. Among them also
a sickly boy who bequeaths his meager belongings—to whom?
Has anyone noticed? Apparently not.
Foolish deists are talking to trees.

Dead Guppies in January

Does the senator really require guppies belly-up
his entire vacation? "I do, and
I also require water in difficult formations."
The FBI's power he loves even more
than water's several applications,
like a beautiful virgin assembled in Heaven.
"Let's see which slob it through our scalps, two,
with a horse in." Excuse me? What?
(A reluctance to answer implies culpability.)
Better than this, pretty apertures.
She raises roses. Sometimes exhaustion
smells like sandalwood.

Speaking of exhaustion, please, enough!
Umbrellas in the tuba? Froth on your lips? Really?
(Look! Crayons where her teeth should be! In primary
colors! This is so wrong!)

The Franklin stove makes cozy crackling sounds,
rogues give up in numbers to the FBI,
the sea is already calmer. The senator is returning to
the Senate. This, at least, is not so wrong.

Standing in Snow, a Poem for January

Do you sometimes awaken feeling disengaged?
Never mind answering.
The affair is rather delicate.
She is dead.
She had a headache.
Her walls were five feet thick.
Her garden was long. Once allowed in,
she stayed all day,
all week,
all month,
all year, fucking forever.
Was that progress?
Don't be silly. But yes, a favorite color,
and while we're about it, a favorite flavor:
standing in snow.

Another January Poem

In my head, a stampede.
I'm reminded of the cupola shipped pick-a-back,
also the luggage (stylish containers one lugs).
I pause by the portal, arms upraised, cloak flapping.
The gale shrieks, the portal claps to
and I am gone

to this line, where I need to ask
when a vista appeared. Did it pop up overnight? Is it
from the shop where I purchase fragrant oil
for my good but smelly people?
One need only add water to a dehydrated vista
to produce the full effect. Mystery solved.

I am now an oligarch with his own moistened vista.
Well-wishers are burdensome, with greater horrors to come!
A deflating childhood! This calls for a patch!

Bargains! Chopped clams! Pillows for pounding!

Wedding Cake

If a man is relieved of eyes, ears, nose and throat
it had best be metaphorical.
It's a question of faith. If this much reduced fellow
is wrapped in a cloak, this too could be metaphorical,
even if the cloak is actually grey.
What does he do? How does he pass the time?
Does he practice the piano?
Is he proposing marriage to a metaphorical belovèd?
If she accepts, if the wedding-cake icing
is sufficiently firm,
the little figures capping the top
can safely walk to the edge
and climb down.

Rendezvous in Two Tercets

How can I carry you without a handle? Go away
on your two good legs before you break
my heart's moving parts,

while I revert to anonymity, spelled without Y's.
Out of spite or out of spit, we find ourselves
at a rendezvous nobody asked for.

Winter Melancholia in Two Quintains

A SWAT team shouts at a sad cold dog
which only serves to make the dog sadder.
The poet steps forward and defunds the police
and anything else displeasing that day.
Such is poetry's clout.

In winter rabbits tend to be empty
and rattle like maracas around in the woods,
with their fingers in their rabbit ears.
In winter trees are often noisy,
except inside where they're often icy.
The poet goes home.

Kites in Two Quatrains and Two Tercets

So, a poem about keeping the pieces, a little glue,
a lot of string, voilà, kites. They go too far,
these kites, looking to the clouds
for one can only guess.

Secrets? Probably not. "No use putting it there.
Or anywhere." Point and purpose
evaporate like dewdrops
in sunlight.

How curious, kite, that you should respond to
oxidation's liminal ruckus. Do kites seek
exits we cannot see?

Would my conceits hold up better in ripstop polyester?
I smell a great moment. Indifferent kites
fly sky-high.

Disclaimer with Exception

A giant schnauzer plays the piano? I think not.
Sunlight streaming in through a window
or a dump truck's load of river rocks? The former.
Poems need not be cruel or irrational.

An exception:
Tennis balls replace your eyes.
Your vision takes in opponents only.

I Have No Answer

Today I am a cloud,
a plaything of the wind.
I am over my house,
I obscure the sky,
then you step outside. "What
 are you doing?" I have no answer.
Clouds can't speak.
We deal with our deficiencies.
Often we prevail.

Forgive the Icicles

I am like a dark cloud, I am like a rest stop busses pull into,
where people take a toilet break. But I do insist that
I am a poet weekdays and weekends. This is non-negotiable.
I once was like a Howard Johnson but am no longer.
Poetry cannot flourish in a mediocre restaurant. The eternal sky
provides intermittently gloomy aspects and is likely
the reason for this depressing poem.
Forgive the icicles.

Banana Poem

Nix on clouds! Too many poems about clouds. Enough!

Mares eat oats and does eat oats
and little lambs eat ivy.
A kid'll eat ivy too,
wouldn't you?
Ignore. Read on.
I'm old.

I'm Chiquita Banana and I come to say
bananas have to ripen in
a certain way.
When they are flecked with brown
and have a golden hue
bananas are the best
and are the best for you.
You can put them in a salad, you
can put them in a pie-yi.
Any way you want to eat them,
it's impossible to beat them. But bananas
like the climate of the very very tropical equator,
so never put bananas in the refrigerator,
no no no NO! NO! NO! NO!

I'd walk a mile for a Camel.

I'm not Chiquita Banana. I don't smoke.
I'm an omnivore sitting in a comfortable desk chair
in a comfortable room belaboring my editor
with such as you see.
Outside it's cold. We just had our driveway
plowed. My shade is drawn,
so I've no idea what's up in the sky.

Poem in Disparate Thirds

Now that I have your attention my requirements disperse. They
go here, they go there, calling to mind an infinity
of multidirectional ball-and-socket joints.
For humankind's preservation we must look
to our defenses, as if to say,
you think the foyer's something?
Step into my parlor.

Fuss as you will with your waxed moustache, it's
fantastical punctuation that grabs your ass,
bro.

I require a mirror.
I'm jumping up and down
with a look I need to see
in order to believe that's me.

Zombies

All are working together, i.e., teamwork,
preparing to go fly kites. The kites, how to put it,
just go. Even the zombies lend a hand.
It is as if one spreads reluctant knees. It is as if
sharpshooters tick kernels off cobs,
turning in time
from glittering gold to crepuscular dun.
As for me, I want you to have my paths of air
in the sky. Have a care
for the kites.

REVIEW | P.J. Blumenthal

Good News Rising From the Grave

Pete, the Photographer & Other Impressions
Marvin Cohen
Tough Poets Press, 2025

Pete, the Photographer & Other Impressions is a posthumous collection of fifteen "pieces" by the prolific New York writer Marvin Cohen who died this year at 93 just days before the vernal equinox. The timing would probably have pleased him. He liked the promise of warmth and light.

I call them "pieces" because, frankly, I don't know how else to label them—except for those he designates as "Dialogues" because they really are dialogues.

Colin Myers, editor of this collection, agrees and suggests "marvins." And yes, they are unique, as unique as the tough Brooklyn guy with the mushy heart who wrote them.

Maybe stream of consciousness forays would be a more suitable description for some of the pieces which at times drift into essayistic, philosophical and even metaphysical modes. One thing all these pieces do have in common: they are downright wacky, as if Marvin Cohen were writing scripts for Olsen and Johnson's "Hellzapoppin". To make matters more difficult when trying to categorize the contents of this book: the dialogues sometimes truly make you think of Plato or Xenophon (if anyone still reads them). Erasmus, a master of the comic/satiric dialogue, comes to mind too. I doubt Marvin Cohen parleyed with any of these predecessors.

"Pete, the Photographer," the title story, and longest piece in the book—you might call it a novella—puts you right in the mood: "The day Peter was born it was so dark that it was night already," we learn in the first sentence. A power blackout in the maternity ward follows, and soon we learn that Peter (who soon will be called "Pete") has bad eyesight, wears thick glasses and is teased at school. A denizen of the land of darkness, an open wound is his heart, he develops a predilection for art but has no special talent. To make matters worse, according to some arcane medical test, doctors have determined that he has no visual memory. Yes, Pete has all the makings of a loser . . .

And then he discovers photography . . . and like a mythological hero on a quest that will benefit us all (the job of all heroes), he is off on the adventure of his life.

Laden with cameras, film, developing equipment (*nota bene*: we are in the pre-digital world), he travels far away to a "vast landscape", all the while, snapping pictures—even of his own shadow. Crocodiles, extinct birds, Arabian leprechauns, spiders, lizards, rainbows are among the marvels he encounters on his way into the unknown until he arrives in a metropolis where he soon becomes a famous photographer. Then comes a scandal, and he is run out of town. More adventures, and next he settles in an antediluvian city whose main attraction is an ancient tower, a tower he will soon come into conflict with . . . verbally. One day the tower collapses. Pete is blamed and must make a hasty retreat. Next stop, an uninhabited island where another tower is the main attraction. Pete, a lonely tower and the ruins of an ancient civilization. That's all there is here. But this morose tower quickly grows possessive, demanding more and more of Pete's attention. Again a confrontation with a tower, and this ancient edifice too collapses. Now Pete constructs a boat and off he goes, sailing the endless sea. Of course his photographic equipment is intact. He drifts and drifts till, driven by curiosity, he descends to the ocean floor—naturally equipped with the appropriate protective diving garb, and with camera in hand—and is off on yet further adventures . . .

Clearly this plot is unconventional to say the least. All Marvin Cohen's plots in this book are. As unconventional as his use of language. He just can't resist being playful. Yes reader, you are in Marvinland where language is the message. There's a constant flow of alliterations ("solitude's lonely solo flight of one's sole soul, alone in all the solar splendor"), endless puns ("this shouldn't be Pete's dust-iny"), cheap jokes and passages you might mistake for rap—though all this was written in the pre-rap era. The author is all over the keyboard: hammering out everything from highfalutin literary parlance to the hard sounds of Brooklyn street-tawk. Some of his puns are only understandable if you savvy his Noo Yawk voice ("to behold its wrath would ore out awe").

Are there other writers to compare him with? Maybe, but just maybe. Elfriede Jelinck's love of verbal juggling comes to mind. Ditto Joyce's. Lautréamont, Henri Michaux, Lewis Carroll veered beyond the edges of fantasy as joyfully as does Marvin Cohen. Or think of Henny Youngman. Perhaps you've heard the name or perhaps not. Marvin most certainly knew it. Youngman was a stand-up nightclub comedian who, while playing on his violin, would fire off endless salvos of one-liners that, told individually, might have elicited groans, but as a conglomerate had his audiences knocking over their martini glasses before dropping from their chairs belly-laughing.

It's hard to label Marvin Cohen's writing. Dadaist is not a good fit. Maybe he was a surrealist. Yes, maybe—but only sometimes. Marvin Cohen is, well, Marvin Cohen.

Some writers strive to keep their language invisible. They remove all verbal obstacles in order to keep a reader's attention on a complex story. Not Marvin Cohen. He wants you to notice his words.

Still, he is never just all play. Like his "Pete," Marvin Cohen is driven by a need to snap pictures of this world in all its facets. In his piece "He, For Want of a Better Name," he narrates the life of a person called . . . "He." This is done in 26 very short chapters titled "A" to "Z," an alphabet of time and existence. Occasionally "he" gets to be called "I" and "you." Naturally, "he" is an Everyman. Yes, "He" is a refreshing contrast to the "me me me!" current in some contemporary literature.

In "How Al Got to the Top," Al, a Mafia lowlife from Brooklyn, is gunned down at the tender age of 32 by another Mafia lowlife. Jesus Christ happens to observe this violence and feels immediate love and compassion for this wasted life. He transports Al's soul to the heavenly realm where Al gets to sit around with God and Jesus and exchange metaphysical vistas.

Nota bene: Marvin Cohen is very interested in exploring those deep questions about ultimate meaning. He frequently seethed at the hypocrisy of religion and was happy to describe himself as an atheist. Still, that never stopped him in his writing from mulling over truly gnawing questions like "what am I doing here?" or "what's this really all about?" In Marvin Cohen's texts, Mr. Death is always nearby, even when unseen.

In "The Skull Left Off by a Man Who of All He Had Done, How is It to Be Valued," two interlocutors are discussing the skull of a deceased acquaintance. (Yes, a little nod to old Yorick, I knew him Horatio). The reader never learns who these two speakers are, but the discussion grows increasingly profound—even though the joking never lets up. One passage, I should add, reminded me very much in style and content of the *Book of Ecclesiastes*. I'm not sure Marvin Cohen would have approved of that comparison.

This very original author was ever searching for the key to the mystery of existence. This especially dominates the final piece in this book: "The Continually Diverging Dialogue." Here, two antipodes endlessly discuss whether material existence or spirituality is a more valid mindset. Sometimes these two characters sound like Abbot and Costello bantering on a vaudeville stage: nonstop dueling with puns, corny jokes and proto-rap riffs. But this is truly a very serious discussion about very serious stuff. I will not reveal who gets the last word.

I would recommend this book not only to readers interested in fresh, original writing but also to theater people. Some of the pieces in this collection would make very good theater, and I hope some daring director takes the hint. It's grown-up theater for grown-up audiences.

Pete, the Photographer and Other Impressions is a keeper. Believe me, Marvin Cohen is a writer whose reputation is only beginning to grow. And more good news: I have heard from Colin Myers that there are still many boxes of unpublished "marvins" out there . . . meaning there will be plenty more to come.

REVIEW | Isabelle Whittall

Soft Lighting
Jared Joseph
Bench Editions, 2025

Reading *Soft Lighting* felt like navigating a maze of memory made of soft clay, forming and reforming bits of it, attempting to find a person. The novel's core is a question: how is it that we might operate interpersonally, interspecifically, or interspatially, let alone *correctly*, when each of us is fated to view the world only from our own perspective? In *Soft Lighting*, Jared Joseph re-creates individual perceptual limitation through writing that limits itself to only the first-person stance. He sets out to write a novel with no setting, which means a novel with no main characters. The book is pure substance, a world created with a big question mark over "creator" (much like ours). How much of our existence is who we are, and how much is what we do? Must personhood be attached to action? Responsibility, relation, and accountability are investigated, positioning today's violence and oppression in a bubble of *why* and *who*. *Soft Lighting* is an experiment, an asking. I found Joseph's authorless world to lack no meaning. Sometimes it is not how we came to be here, but simply that we are here, in this room, where the lighting is soft, and there are some things we just can't make out.

Soft Lighting has no sections, no table of contents; the novel avoids demarcation in its very form. The only separations are between paragraphs, or speakers, all of whom are "I". Each paragraph functions as a synecdoche of the full work, with its own rules and its own ecosystem, repeating or revisiting concepts cyclically with a pattern like an internal palindrome. The novel speaks for itself, since it speaks only to itself. In one conversation between "I" and "I", the speaker asks, "Does this statement in any way reflect the thoughts I was having beforehand?" (98). The question references a concern of inconsistency we might have when thoughts become constrained by the symbolic realm. It is a way of validating the insecurities of any writer or speaker; "I" in this sentence is the speaker of the novel and "I" is also me, and you, and anyone. Through the novel's alien landscape formed by the lens of deeply personal anonymity, questions that move intensely past masks of convention or norm are welcome. *Soft Lighting* is more lawless than most works, and it becomes that by being strictly law-abiding.

Without names or places, Joseph must rely on other meaning-making devices in his novel. Geometric metaphors enhance his larger investigation of relationality and solitude. One "I" describes an oval as the primary life-shape, representing both the closeness of intimacy and the distance of betrayal, and functioning as primally as planetary orbit (123). *Soft Lighting* does follow the shape of an oval, because of the concurrence of intense vulnerability due to being locked in first-person mental space and jilted communication due to talking across or at each other, "I" to "I", no actual translation possible. Elliptical swooping is between us in connection, in individual orbits of life, and in conversation; as another "I" says, "a conversation never really dies, but pauses, as the two inside the conversation separate in space, but there is a thread between us that is unbroken" (163). As well as the space between speakers, Joseph investigates the space between thought and speech, often following "I say" with a reflection on whether what was said was thought, or what was thought was said. The novel's speakers ask, through this separation, through the one-mindedness, if we can ever really communicate and be understood. Although the space between self and other is emphasized, there is suggestive hope, too; Joseph introduces the possibility that we both think the same thing we don't say. One speaker comments that "Sarah wants to ask the question 'why did you stop loving me,' but Sarah will never ask that question, because I will never answer it, and so it isn't allowed" (165). The acceptance that "Sarah" and "I" share a law brings them both into a new sphere, crossing boundaries between each mind's thoughts by acknowledging a rule that spans both, locking the dyad in an ontology of their own making.

Soft Lighting's speakers probe the limits of responsibility in autonomy and relation. Joseph begins his solipsistic project in perhaps the most ambitious territory one can find for it, writing "I"'s who date, grow closer, and eventually engage in physical intimacy, each a lone protagonist in what can seem a necessarily multi-person experience. The discomfort of reading a conversation between me and myself is made vulgarly salient when that conversation becomes sex, and explicit physicality occurs between me and myself, bringing what is arguably the most vulnerable form of relation inward and the most vulnerable solitary act outward. Does physical intimacy require two or more people? Why is it that when reading it between one person, I still saw two people? Joseph writes, in his *Notes* section, that he found the process of writing a novel with no setting to be difficult and frustrating; what about the process of reading it? Why did I find myself needing to ascribe multiple selves and personalities to the "I" present, and did Joseph do the same in his creation process? Relation, here, is probed as a polyvalent process. The repetition of the pronoun "I" in the novel aesthetically evokes a Kantian autonomous rigidity. The direct and continuous exploration of that self in relativity with others, however, continually draws out an inclination, a bend toward the other. Through his form, Joseph touches on the paradox of the Kantian upright symbol; if inclination, as Kant understands it, is necessarily an outward turn away from the self, then in what direction does a self-love go? When I speak to, fall in love with, and have sex with myself, where have I inclined myself out of rigidity, or where have I collapsed?

Where self may be located draws itself out in the novel through an investigation of definition. Joseph asks what is necessary for existence by exploring what makes up a who-ness. "Does a name live while a body dies?" one speaker asks (36). Does it matter how we are remembered or can be referred to, or is the who-ness located in our corporeality? The question of accountability follows from this investigation of who we are: how responsible are we for the actions of our past selves, or our future selves? To whom are we morally obliged? Following the section that delves into intimacy and relationality romantically, a speaker laments "'But we may not have much time together, soon, I don't know when we'll switch', I say . . . 'I'm going to miss us,' I say" (39). I first understood this as a pre-grief of a romantic relationship, but I came to understand it as a grief of the last person the speaker was, and a fear for the next person the speaker will be. On the back cover of *Soft Lighting*, the concern is expressed that "once I've written an autobiography, that autobiographer is a dead person". A new option arises, then, for what dictates existence: perhaps not a label, or a physical existence, but a temporal one. When the we we are now has passed, must it die? Can it, and how might it, continue to exist in our reference of it? Because each version of self has once been born, can it continue to be, even when temporally dissolved? I'm always going to miss me, but I'm always right here.

Joseph has a tendency to break the fourth wall in his writing by asking, near the end of a work, what has really been going on in the journey of writing or reading. In *Soft Lighting*, in one of several eponymous expressions, a speaker asks "'What is this room?' . . . 'What are its rules? I know I can't see anyone well, or myself, but there is still lighting in it, a soft lighting'" (140). Options are considered: maybe the setting is purgatory, maybe it is death, maybe it is life now, maybe it is life in a different time. The irony is that the book does have a setting, and its only setting is soft lighting, a cytoplasm of this questioning organism of a novel, confirming only that our limitations are valid and our confusion is true. The thing about light is it demarcates, and the thing about soft lighting is we can never tell what is being demarcated, not quite, even as we come close. The fog of the novel is dense, but its meaning is brilliant. Joseph closes his novel with a question asked by none of the "I"'s, with no quotation marks, plainly: "What's the difference?" (177). It's about separation, sameness, violence, and peace. Each "I" has told a different story, through a different gender, body, political orientation, backstory, and profession, but each "I" is making and asserting themselves through the softest lighting. Existence is something reached at by each self, and maybe but maybe never grasped. Why are we killing each other, Joseph asks? What is the difference?

REVIEWS IN BRIEF | Jesi Bender

The Witch's Egg
Donya Todd
Avery Hill Publishing, Oct. 2025

SOMETIMES I AM A GOD
SOMETIMES I AM A GATEWAY
SOMETIMES I AM A GHOST

A Lisa Frank *Holy Mountain*. Or *The Labyrinth* starring the cast of *Adventure Time*.

The Witch's Egg is an epic queer love story between a catwitch and a troubled birdgirl who is forbidden from anything joyful. Despite birdgirl's hesitancy, they come together and lay an egg. In *Eraserhead*-level anxious anticipation of their child, the birdgirl fears their baby is a "maggoty worm" with "speckled throat" and "the sorrowed song he sings brings an end to all things." The lovers quarrel over whether or not to destroy what they've created and the remaining pages follow the catwitch as she absconds with the egg and journeys on trippy Odyssey to find safety.

These pages are filled with magic and originality. The artwork is truly beautiful, a horrible macabre juxtaposed with bright rainbow colors. The graphics are often rendered in a minimalist way but made complex by a great amount of detail. I love her color theory and line work but perhaps the best element of Todd's art would be her flow, how she manipulates elements on the page to move you around the page to magical and dizzying effect.

If you come from the writer world and like Akwaeke Emezi, Joanna Ruocco, or Azareen Van der Vliet Oloomi, I'd suggest you check out this graphic novel. If you're from the art world, you'll enjoy this book if you are fans of Takashi Murakami, Harry Clarke, or Kay Nielsen.

Throughout *The Witch's Egg*, trials of love (including self-love) are underscored by a constant underlying fear that inside the core of you is something horrible and rotting that will open its eyes and ruin everything you love. It is filled with haunting symbols, equals turns at hope and horror, and a dread inherited from traumatic childhood that love won't be enough. In the end, though, Dodd shows her readers that there is a magic alive in love, even when that love dies.

In my dreams, in the end
I love you until I am
laid in the wormy dark.

Little Neck
Darcie Dennigan
Fonograf, 2025

"I am saying *tomorrow* to the starving part of me."

Little Neck is an enigmatic little book (only 100 pages) that employs the best of Gothic literature and creates a vacillating portrait of a young woman from birth to death and back again (again and again and . . .).

The narrator wakes up at the home of sisters Rita and Rosmarge, owners of Marguerite Concrete, tombstone carvers in the quaint and haunted New England town of Little Neck. At the point of discovery, she's bleeding and her blood leaves a trail throughout the rest of the novel, reminding the reader both of life and of its loss. We learn that, as a baby, the narrator was found in Rose Head cemetery. She is raised there by a mysterious groundskeeper until a fateful night where she attempts to dig up bindweed at a grave that simply reads 'Pearl'. Like Pearl in *The Scarlet Letter*, this dead woman holds an otherworldly power over the narrator, and represents a liberty unknown to the protagonist. The narrator cuts herself digging up the weeds at Pearl's grave and is suddenly moved to Rita and Rosmarge's care—leaving the reader to unravel the mystery around the narrator's origins and her seemingly inherent connection to death.

Dennigan uses flowers as symbols to mirror different characters based on their fragrance and appearance. The aforementioned bindweed, for example, is seen growing on graves in Rose Head. The narrator remarks that it is very pretty and sweet but strangles everything else. When she tries to cut it out, it is incredibly difficult to kill and only multiplies in division. Flowers also remind readers of the precarity of living things while consistently imbuing the pages with something tactile and sensuous. They are often placed next to dirt, dust or rock, to emphasize their difference obviously but to also illustrate their symbiotic nature, how they feed each other reciprocally through growth and decay.

Little Neck doesn't choose a lane between sex and death; instead, like all good Gothics, it intertwines them freely. Likewise, familial relationships are very complex and only further complicate the strong death and sexual instincts of the characters. The narrator dreams of the groundskeeper, the only parental figure in her life, and thinks "I have to break his skin with my teeth." She sees her transfer to Marguerite Concrete as punishment and she lets the resentment fester inside.

> ". . .and I grow it myself. I grow it the summer of trouble. Its seed is a rock. This rock is cold and tough. I make myself stand in the high grass in the paupers' part. Then I push the rock far up in me."

The rock, this 'seed', is seen as a punishment for arousing the 'keeper' and, in turn, for being aroused by him. It is the jail of Marguerite Concrete, it is the jail of a child. A tombstone she lives within and lives within her. In some sense, she, as a child and as a woman, is pregnant with herself. It is the responsibility she faces as she lusts for both her keeper and her death. Eros and Thanatos dancing together in an open grave on a Rose's Head.

This narrative, and indeed the narrator, lives in repetition. At first, it can seem excessive but Dennigan utilizes this Gothic trope only to further underscore *Little Neck*'s themes of generational trauma. The repetition becomes a meter of grief, and how, by its nature, mourning is an act of reliving. As Dennigan puts it, "[t]he bereaved want to say the same things over and over again until something different is at the end of what they say."

This haunting novel's short, simple sentences, told in a building echo, ultimately pack a powerful punch. Pay attention to names, like Viti for example, and how the Latin derivatives of vita (life) or vitis (vine) inform you about those characters. Find roots in the repeated phrases. The word 'flesh', for example, is used often to reflect both the animal and the alien, desires and decay. A Brontë novel by way of postmodernism, *Little Neck* is perfect for those who love haunted things like family myths and tragic love stories.

Yes I Am Human I Know You Were Wondering
Erin Dorney
Autofocus, 2025

At first glance, Erin Dorney's collection *Yes I Am Human I Know You Were Wondering* possesses several things that would scare me away: influencers, trendy yoga, and it's a COVID book (and I've not encountered many successful COVID books yet). Leafing through the book, however, it was Dorney's nature-inspired collages that drew me in. They have a simple graphic quality that places natural elements in concert with spare phrasings, creating their own asemic poetry.

"I can't decide what body part to use as the thread that stitches me through time and space . . ."

Throughout this work, Dorney weaves together texts ranging from Wikipedia fragments to John Grisham to her own thoughts to create an epistolary dialogue with YouTube influencer Adriene Mishler of *Yoga with Adriene* fame. These one way letters to a face on the screen examine false intimacy and the reflexive tendency to try and find kinship in digital spaces. Dorney's exploration is in a quiet but unexpected way. Her voice is equal parts humor and contemplative, sometimes both at once, and each poem is paired with full-color collaging of natural textures and text, which lends both a grounding and an enigmatic air. Side-by-side, the colorful earth-bound art against the black-and-white emails to a nature rendered in pixels subtly creates tension while also expanding the beauty of Dorney's assemblages of image and word.

"You say, *notice how you feel*, and I assure you, I've been trying."

Overall, Dorney's *Yes I Am Human I Know You Were Wondering* is a fun, relatable contemplation of modern life and the pursuit of connection, through flawed bodies or flawed online mediums, and how, if nothing else, it is our mind and its never-ending pursuit for meaning that persists across all plains, across all times and environments.

REVIEW | Greg Bem

Cassandra at point-blank range
Sandra Moussempès
Translated from the French by Carrie Chappell and Amanda Murphy
Diálogos, 2025

> Poetry is a forest filled with precious wonders—
> that was my view of things
> (from "Symmetrical group of simultaneous emotions," page 91)

Following the 2015 English translation of *Sunny Girls*, Paris-based Sandra Moussempès's new release is a masterwork in abstract feminist poetry. *Cassandra at point-blank range* is an exciting new collection that is teeming with inspiration from a wide swath of historic feminine champions, as well as the everyday, film-like experiences of the poet herself. Translated with an astute attention to detail, and crisp, continuous tonality, Carrie Chappell and Amanda Murphy have offered us a glimpse into the amorphous and readily engaged mind of Moussempès across a patchwork of fever dream spaces, where reality twists and turns, and language is the cohesive element binding shared experience, necessary history, and the grim but defiant inquiry of conflict and resistance, together.

> The time when ghosts emerge from every mirror
> Like tree roots interlaced by a memory
> (from "Language & pruning shears," page 159)

Cassandra is far from a simple or easily approachable book. It is a trove of ideas, often swirling amongst each other. Each poem blends into the next. The poet contributes an idea, which is revisited across new source material and other inspiring contexts. The poet is the observer, is the watcher, is the witness, both by choice and circumstance. There is a power to this historic take on the poet as a seer and archivist of shared experience, alongside the reclaimed power of the voice of the woman poet and individual women brought into center collectively. And through every moment that moves beyond the figure, beyond the character, there are the graying peripheries of movement that fill time, fill space, and reveal a brittle, challenging landscape through which we all must travel. There is thus a subtext, literal and ethereal, of grimness, a necessary fabric of reality that sits between us. It is sordid, unkempt, and rough. It is difficult to accept, but in many cases must be sat through, moved through, burdened by.

> Poetry is an idea of the black sky and
> Red thoughts that disturb it
> Speculation becomes a tentacle there
> (from "Repainting a sentence fragment," page 225)

And what of Cassandra? As an homage, a mirror, and a reference point, this figure sets the stage and remains alongside it throughout the book, as anchor and as amplifier. Cassandra, the mythic Trojan seer cursed by Apollo to speak the truth but never be believed, is a symbol of the poetry itself and the prophetic behavior of the poet whose writing must be cast across shadow and light. Vision and witness is hallucinatory as it becomes a multifaceted, singular voice. In this space, in this collection, poetry is where observation, memory, and defiance meet. Readers are gifted with an opportunity to move through the voice of Moussempès and emerge past difficulty and conflict into moments of reflection and growth. But the poet doesn't force this change, is never didactic; we are instead pushed forward into her ether to explore on our own terms. Critically engaging, this is a feminist poetry that is as postmodern to the reader as it is confessional to the poet, as bound to time as it is widespread in its presentation.

> Her face brightens as the dream progresses and ends
> up disappearing completely
> (from "Downsizes models of red mirrors," page 203)

The book contains a variety of sequences, opening up new layers of readability and making this a significant collection of Moussempès's work. Each sequence contains up to 16 poems, and sequence titles include "Unidentified feminine objects," "Symmetrical group of simultaneous emotions," "Scissors & nighttime sky," "Black pink face," "House of liquid sentences," "Cassandra at point-blank range," "Soundscape at Venice Beach," "Madness and veranda," and "Spouses and decibel forms." *Cassandra* may be emerging out of the French, but it has significant roots in the United States and other parts of Europe.

Many of the images from the book are derived from otherworldly times and places, which cascade across 2025 like a freshly opened archive.

70s-era California scenes and settings, potentially connected to and seemingly limitlessly embodying films from that era, dominate the poet's channeling. Other feminist poetics from previous generations, including Shelley, Woolf, Plath, and Dickinson, are centered. And yet this centering is a phantasmagoria: images we may believe until they shapeshift, blend in and out of focus, enter and leave scene.

> They are not ready to glisten in the void either or to
> move in their bikinis, to go over meters of thoughts
> between scalpeled memories and prefabricated
> psychic homes
> (from "The cloister," page 25)

A poignant sequence across hundreds of pages that crests with each page flip: a dreamlike vision of what the poet has observed, processed, and transformed into the purity and messiness of poetic thought. History, while not imposed upon the reader, is a real character within each poem, offering its own subtextual layers through which we may approach, learn, and grow.

Cassandra surprises us with how it presents each image, each idea, each person, in a way that fleets objectification. Reference points are fluid and in flux, mentions or allusions are real and brilliant while at the same time subtle and peripheral themselves. If we are to imagine the true form a historic, feminist collective takes, it moves away from solidity into the fragment of radical inclusion. Of course the book doesn't tell us that and as I read it, I began a series of questions of myself, as a reader, as a learner, as one open to immersion and a personal fragmentation of being, identity, and readership.

> I have entered into the spirit of the poem
> That I covet
> One minute later I am disarmed
> (from "Process," page 141)

Some of the most blinding moments are seemingly small phrases of transgression and contradiction that scatter across the book like a binding agent, a seasoning, or a blessing. Moussempès does not shy away from a blend of objectivist-style image making, quiet reflections, and loud observations. This range results in an intellectual spirit that holds the book together in a completely separate way; a series of logical arguments indicative of the poet's own growth, that the poet herself isn't objectified, neutral, or set in a fantasy space of stability.

This may be the most arresting quality of this collection, that the poet has been deconstructed by herself for herself, and for the reader. To what end? It takes a reading of the book to understand; but we are afforded an intimacy and privacy that are rarely normalized in the fictitious fancies of most contemporary poetry. We are given Moussempès, a poet who is a human being, whose life and works are composed in the realms of past and present human beings, who is as active in her exploration as we can be in ours.

REVIEW | Charles Holdefer

The Girlie Playhouse
V.N. Alexander
Heresy Press, 2026

Follow your bliss, but don't expect to be understood. Worse: you might be pilloried. Such are the stakes in V.N. Alexander's latest novel, *The Girlie Playhouse*, a tale of exotic dancers who try to find a place in a world where they are met with incomprehension or bad faith.

The title refers to a cabaret where the narrator, Pixie, dances nude. The story centers on another dancer, Trixie, whose appearance and performances fascinate Pixie. She avows, "My entire life has been an expression of my peculiar love for girls with meretricious charms."

The story opens with the cabaret under attack by outsiders who want to close it down. The Gideon Angels, a feminist group of Carrie Nationesque killjoys, inspire protests by "misguided, albeit well-meaning" student activists from the local university's "Oppression Studies Department."

Thus the battle lines are drawn. At first blush, the above description, putting apparently infantilized "girlies" with cheesy names on one side, and dour moral enforcers on the other, seems to promise a broad satire. And that is, in fact, one feature of the novel. At the same time, however, *The Girlie Playhouse* raises more complicated questions about performance and personal autonomy.

Alexander pushes back at received images of dance venues as merely tawdry or exploitive, grim places for desperate women with nowhere else to go. Pixie's story is not devoid of risks—violence against women figures in the plot—but these characters assert agency. Pixie says that her method "is to complicate the issue rather than clarify," which is a sentiment that implicitly reflects the author's approach, too. The male gaze, she claims, can also serve her purposes: "while the breath of the men constantly threatens to extinguish, it actually feeds my flame."

Exotic dancing, for Pixie, is not just a job, but a need. She'll dance naked on her porch under the gaze of a blackbird on a maple tree because, for her, "Any pair of eyes will do." This aspect of self announced itself early. She recollects being scolded by her auntie, when she was only six years old:

> "Stop that prancing around like a little harlot, you gypsy girl. Where is your modesty?" [. . .]
>
> I stamped my tiny foot and demanded, "What was I doing wrong?"
>
> "It's not what you're doing. It's what everyone'll think."
>
> "I don't care what they think."

This pattern persists into her adult life, and is corroborated by her friend Trixie, in the context of Trixie's relationship with her boyfriend Max. Max is a regular customer at the Girlie Playhouse. He recently won the lottery, thereby freeing him of financial worry. He's hopelessly smitten with Trixie, and his good luck continues when Trixie returns his affections. What more could he want?

As it turns out, a lot more: namely, control. He challenges the need for Trixie to continue dancing.

> "Don't tell me you want to be a stripper. I thought it was just the money."
>
> Trixie looked at him with bitterness. "You're not making sense."
>
> "You're the one who's not making sense. You don't have to strip anymore."
>
> "I never had to before," she said.
>
> "What do you get, Trixie, what do you get out of being at a strip club that you couldn't get dancing somewhere else?"
>
> "I like it."

The ensuing discussion, in which Pixie participates, addresses the question that hovers over much of the story. Why? Why does she like it? Max defensively poses the question in reference to another man:

> "Why do you need to dance for him?"
>
> "It's not for him," replied Trixie, groping for her point. "It's at him."
>
> "Oh, I see at him. Well, that makes perfect sense." Max laughed, tickled with the idea that her argument was weak. "Pixie, now you tell me, do you dance at or for your customers?"
>
> I hesitated for a few minutes, biting my thumbnail, considering this delicate point.
>
> "Through," I said finally. "Through."

This conversation does indeed complicate the issue. A reader could parse this as a sad testimony to how much the patriarchal gaze has colonized the female psyche, resulting in a sociosexual "captive mind." Or a reader can conclude that dancing *through* the gaze of others is an empowering move, surfing across a liminal space on a wave of desire. Or a reader, particularly a reader weary of theorizing, can conclude that our pleasures are polymorphous—yes indeed—so enough said. Sometimes a cigar is just a mirror ball.

I found these ambiguities interesting. Elsewhere, Pixie says up front: "there is a phenomenal pattern in the hazy chaos of events, one that cannot be explained entirely by psychological factors."

In any event, realistic convention isn't a priority here. When not dancing at the Girlie Playhouse, Pixie lives quietly by herself in a snug garden cottage, tending wildflowers. She leads a pastoral, fairy-tale life, where money isn't an issue.

Sex, when it occurs (not that often) is also refracted. Alexander's satirical strategy is to describe it with somewhat prim or florid language, the opposite of a striptease reveal. For instance, in a voyeuristic scene, Pixie watches Trixie as Max "resolutely possessed the coquette."

For all its playfulness, the emotional core of the novel—its ideology, if you must—seems to be to a concern about the ills that arise when someone decides for someone else. I'll avoid spoilers, but the novel is tenacious on that point. Full of surprises, *The Girlie Playhouse* subverts cliché. V.N. Alexander is a serious stylist who is not afraid to ruffle feathers.

REVIEW | David Winner

The Encouragement of Others
Magnus Mills
Self-published, 2024

Another possible title for Magnus Mills' most recent novel, *The Encouragement of Others*, might be *The Absence of Explanation*. The lack of context for the characters and their landscape is typical of Mills, who was a fence builder and a bus driver before turning to fiction with the Booker Prize-shortlisted *The Restraint of Beasts* (1998). *Encouragement* is like a canvas left intentionally part blank. We don't know our protagonist's name, nor where he came from. We do learn that it's not "the north," where the novel takes place, nor "the south," where everyone assumes that he must be from. Neither is necessarily Britain, though Mills is an English writer and people in the novel speak English and drink in pubs. We also don't know where our protagonist sleeps at night, nor what he does for a living. Actually, almost everyone in the novel, except for those in the pub business, seems to be ne'er-do-wells, perhaps because "the north," we learn, is so prosperous that most people need not be employed.

Part of Mills' residual brilliance is to compel readers to follow his toned-down enigmatic narratives on their own terms. In fiction-writing workshops many years ago, we would frequently demand that fictions have "more of this character" or "more of that character" as if each person who showed up on the page needed to be equally fleshed out. It's interesting to imagine how Mills' work might have been greeted in one of those of classes. More of . . .well . . . everything.

The novel does have a plot. The unnamed narrator takes his sailboat back and forth across a body of water to two very different pubs: The White Swan, which is crowded and features a noise rock band that never actually gets around to performing in a back room, and the always empty The Black Swan, whose two featured beers, the special and the reserve, turn out to be the same.

Soon, the narrator abandons his prized sailboat for the New Standard Sailing Dinghy urged upon him by two not very friendly characters, Jenkins and Louise.

Another mystery is why Mills, who after the Booker-shortlisting seemed to have taken up permanent residence at Bloomsbury, has chosen to self-publish. Is the UK publishing industry no longer imaginative enough to appreciate him? Is he interested in writing and publishing without the hassle of agents and editors?

His early more renowned novels were also opaque, though quite a bit more dramatic. The two Scottish fence-makers from *The Restraint of Beasts* go to England and meet the violent Hall Brothers, leading to dark happenings. And the two rival teams of pioneers in *Explorers of the New Century* (2005) run into intense difficulties trying to reach the AFB, agreed-upon furthest point. Those earlier novels also have more easily legible systems of metaphor: the literal as well as metaphoric beasts, the relatively innocent-seeming exploration getting to look more and more like violent colonialism.

The New Standard Sailing Dinghy, so efficient as to practically sail itself, does begin to dominate. At one point, an enormous flotilla of them crosses the body of water. And the narrator is appointed by Jenkins to do some sort of PR for them. Is this a cautionary tale about over-mechanization like self-driving cars, the body of water in the novel a contemporary San Francisco? No, it doesn't really feel weighted like that. There is real harm, menace and metaphor among fence-builders and explorers, but *Encouragement* has a much lighter feel.

At the very end, as our protagonist seems to be failing at his new gig, he has a surprisingly pleasant interaction with Louise. I won't play spoiler here except to say that one of the novel's constant tropes gets repeated and the hugely entertaining novel is suddenly over, leaving me imagining that chorus of undergraduate workshoppers yelling more, more, more!!!

REVIEW | Ellen Harrold

It Is Still Beautiful to Hear the Heart Beat
Margo Berdeshevsky
Salmon Poetry, 2025

Observation is a deliberate act, enforcing a new context to the actions of the person who is being observed. We cannot control what we see of other people, nor can we relinquish the power of observation without ridding ourselves of the sense that we use to navigate the world. Most people will, knowingly or not, observe someone during a moment where they believe they have total privacy. This changes the nature of that moment, regardless of how either party reacts. Margo Berdeshevsky plucks at these tenuous divisions between isolation and intimacy in her latest collection, *It Is Still Beautiful to Hear the Heart Beat*. Composed of lyrical poetry, narrative vignettes, and philosophical reflections, this collection explores systemic violence as a force and an action. The magnitude of its implementation renders such cruelty to a state akin to the divine, a veneer punctuated by flesh and blood.

Visceral reality is inescapable with Berdeshevsky's vivid prose. Over the course of the collection's four acts, you walk the razor's edge between wonder and despair, realising how tenuous our existence is in the face of global interest. Poems such as 'Postcards to the Body Politic' explore the dichotomy between our tangible ability to affect the world around us and our limited ability to change the course of history.

> "If a body meet a body. Where the body of the
> state falls. Or, because what not-to-
> be-trusted gods—refuse to fall. . . . *twirling*
> *on the horse, blowing kisses—*
> *indefinitely into the grey future, and if this*
> *entertainment were to continue.* Body"

So, we are left with the aftermath, the states of healing and decay that follow in the wake of suffering. The collection does not follow a linear path, ebbing and flowing, much like scar tissue or the news cycle. We move between action and aftermath, the innermost thought and political consensus. Berdeshevsky's fluid prose adapts itself to each perspective, using the contrast between simple and lyrical language. These distinct approaches are reflected in the simplicity of poems such as 'Cain—After—And After'. In the aftermath of his brother's death, Cain makes sense of the new existence he has created with his acts of violence, even as he recognises the discrepancy in control when compared to the divine being that instigated the conflict. Vulnerability and grief seep through the bareness of his words, belied by the pause of a person reconsidering their instincts with every word.

> "I—who never killed, but pulled a root from the good
> brown soil—learned from you who loved blood,
> better."

When compared with 'After Forgetting How', a poem that considers the background noise of a physical and political landscape, we see a much more intricate use of language, emulating both the complexity of the information radiating through every living moment and the perceived distance from the rest of the world.

> "enough to trust. True believers. Sun swords through.
> And the din of protest like
> birds that announce both storm and wings with their
> hundred damaged eyes—"

Our ability to act is questioned but not ceded. *It Is Still Beautiful to Hear the Heart Beat* is actively in conversation with itself, intertwining and challenging each piece with equal conviction. The nuance brought forth in each poem invites the reader to bring their own experiences to their understanding of power. How we can be both perpetrator and victim, unaware of our place in the suffering of others, without empathy and critical thought? The duality of personal experiences and how these patterns repeat themselves on an international scale is a highlight in the formatting of this collection. By placing poems such as 'Chorus of One' alongside 'Those Are The Pearls That Were His Eyes. Look! *' Berdeshevsky considers how imbalances of power enact themselves upon the individual and the community, how those states of violence are inseparable as a force of dehumanisation. By committing an act of violence, one has classed a subset of human beings to be acceptable targets for this, and future acts.

> "I am despondent, she whispers.
> My culture died, and no one came to the funeral."

> "Reorder the page of names, Sequence revered and
> Replaced"

Coming away from this collection, I believe that Berdeshevsky has given equal weight to reality and possibility. Her work is marked by nuance and an appreciation for beauty in the face of pain.

Christopher Boucher

Wheres v. Graves

We'd been working hard on *Exacting Clam 20* for weeks, but that Saturday we broke early to attend the Clamball finals. I wasn't the biggest Clamball fan myself, but my colleague Mar Doyle had been talking up the match all week as we set type together. "It's going to be a *bloodbath*!" she shouted at me that Friday while arranging a stanza on the opposite page.

"A bloodbath doesn't sound very fun," I said, lining up two quotation marks.

"Editorially, I'm saying," Mar said. "These two teams are just very evenly matched."

"Who's in it again?" I shouted from my quote.

"Long Days of Your Own Wherewithals versus Good News Rising From the Graves."

"And you're rooting for . . . ?"

She grinned and made a fist. "Wheres all the way baby!"

So around four p.m. on Saturday afternoon, a big group of us—me and Mar, our colleague Emily Why, a few of the authors and some phrases from the issue, remember when the pine-scented room and Sunrise, the outermost circle —walked out to the page 133 stadium. Even before we reached it, though, we could hear the thrum of language in the distance. Then we saw the tailgating phrases—retired to Canutillo as a relic equal cooking up hotdogs on a grill, a generous celery stalk pounding a beer.

We found our seats right before the first sentence. Mar'd purchased a block right at midpage, so we could see everything: the shining clam, the nervous ink, the punctuation on the sidelines. The atmosphere was the word charged—you could have cut the word tension with the word knife.

One of the reasons I'd never gotten into Clamball, though, was because I don't totally understand the rules. I knew the clam—or was it the *word* clam?—was carried by issue phrases from one end of the page to the other, editing themselves to make meaning while the defending team tried to check or demean them. It was the penalties that confused me. What constituted 'meaning,' exactly? Was fighting allowed or wasn't it? And how could you tell if a phrase was off sides?

I would have asked Mar these questions, but before I could the copyeditors raised their red pens to bring the phrases midfield. "Here we go Wherewithals, here we go!" Mar began singing. "Here we go Wherewithals, here we go!" The chief copyeditor held the clam above the fold, then dropped it—the game was underway. The Graves won the drop and read the clam down the page, passing to the Flogger and then It Is Still Beautiful to Hear the (clam's) Heart Beat. Should be accepting of life's vicissitudes tried to edit Homegrown Tender Meat with Lime Butter—and clam—but Lime Butter dodged Heart Beat and The Encouragement of Others. "No no," muttered Mar. "Tackle the Butter! Get Butter!" But Lime Butter speedread into the margin, and just like that it was one clam to nothing.

"No!" groaned Mar, falling to her seat.

"Not a great start, Marry!" quipped Sunrise.

"Shut up," Mar said. "Shake it off Wheres!"

And the Wherewithals tried to, reading the clam back up the side of the page—the numinous clam is cyclical, the shouting clam to spit its righteous wrath—but the Graves read their formation, intercepted, and counter-read past the fold. This time, though, a benevolent eagle planted a reversal and checked the Flogger right into his own bench.

In the stands, meanwhile, the word wave began and the pine-scented room went to concessions and came back with a round of beers and snacks. "Plenty of game left," Why assured Mar, and Mar took a swig from her beer. By that point, I think our whole group just wanted her to see her team win.

But it was a tight contest—the clam going back and forth, with neither team giving a paragraph—through the first reading and the second. Late in the third, though, the Wheres' alone and ever changing took advantage of a bad transition and skimmed the clam up the far margin to even the score. A fight broke out near the page number, the Flogger and alone, both phrases swinging letters, until alone dragged the Flogger to the page.

With only three minutes' reading time left, though, the Graves' coach a writhing green vine started signaling cryptically from the margin. "What's that?" asked Why, pointing to You wake up with a stone in your stomach. "What are they doing?" Stone, we realized, was changing tense—from wake to woke—right there on the field. Every Grave on the page, we now saw, was following suit, shifting from present to past. Suddenly everything is was: it *was* still beautiful to hear the heart beat, the author *was* all over the keyboard. While the Wherewithals tried to adjust, the Graves peppered them with endings—clammy in the face of pain, he made sure to cherish the clam—in an attempt to finish the match.

But this turned out to be the Graves' mistake. Seeing the endings, the Wheres' coach to indulge in smug admonishment began shouting something to his players. "Start over!" he seemed to be saying. "Start over!"

"Is he saying 'start over'?" asked Why.

"Yes! Here we go," said Mar quietly.

"I don't understand," said Sunrise.

"They're going to run a new beginning." Mar leaned forward in her seat.

Soon I understood: To counter the endings, the Wheres were flooding the page with beginnings: Now don't clam me wrong, Waiting for the clam excitedly, Observation is a deliberate clam, we'd been working hard on *Exacting Clam 20* for weeks. This caused the score, in turn, to shift back to what it was at the start: zero zero all.

The opposing phrases looked clamiffled. "What?" shouted a writhing green vine from the Graves' sideline. "Copies, what?"

But it was too late. In all the confusion, the Wheres forward a very drunk, self-pitying Truman had picked up the clam and bolted for the margin. "Look at Truman!" shouted Doyle. Truman evaded one grave phrase, then two. Mar leapt to her feet. "Go Truman Go! Go!" we shouted. "Go Truman!" Truman read past Lime Butter and juked the Flogger. Wouldn't it be nice to be cured? made one last leap for him, but Truman denoumented him and spiked the clam into the footer as reading time expired, and we leapt to our feet and roared in victory.

Matthew Wolfman

The Mirror Knew

A mirror blinked, the clock withdrew,
The ceiling wept a shade of blue,
A cactus whispered rendezvous,
And time dissolved like sugar glue.

A zebra rode a kangaroo,
Down avenues of mist and hue,
Where jellyfish recited screw you,
To stars that blinked déjà vu.

The moon wore shoes of quiet rue,
She danced with spoons in a sky askew,
The clouds, monks of bold kung fu,
Performed baptisms in shampoo.

I kissed a ghost named Thank You Too,
She floated past my lost canoe,
She fed me grapes that softly flew,
Then told me, Child, be always true.

A doorbell barked, a snowflake grew
A beard of steel, like a point of view.
Hit the ground, made up of misused glue,
Breathed haikus written just for you.

A fountain sang of cashew stew,
Of tissues torn by twigs of yew,
While unicorns with eyes that drew
Wrote manifestos in bamboo.

The sun came out in a tutu,
She sipped soft rain and sweet fondue,
And winked and said, What will you do
When dreams come dressed real and true?

A thousand fish in a pink canoe
Rehearsed a symphony that flew and flew,
The sky split wide, let insights through,
And whispered, softly, None of it's new.

But still, the mirror knew the hue,
The one that bleeds through all we do,
The thread between the false and you,
The ever-living, ever-true.

Contributors

Corina Bardoff is a writer and librarian currently living in New Jersey. Her fiction has appeared in *Storm Cellar, Menacing Hedge, Hysterical, Cream City Review*, and elsewhere.

Greg Bem is a poet, librarian, and labor activist in Spokane, Washington. He writes book reviews for places like *Rain Taxi, International Examiner, North of Oxford*, and *Exacting Clam*.

Jesi Bender is an artist from Upstate New York. She is the author of the novels *Child of Light* (Whisk(ey) Tit, 2025) and *The Book of the Last Word (WT, 2019)*, the plays *Crux* (Sagging Meniscus, 2026) and *Kinderkrankenhaus* (SM, 2021), and the poetry collection *Dangerous Women* (dancing girl press, 2022). Her shorter work can be seen in *Denver Quarterly, FENCE*, and *Sleepingfish*, among other places.

P.J. Blumenthal is an American writer living in Munich, Germany. He is the author of *Self Portraits* (SM, 2026), *Winston Hewlett's Impotence* (SM, 2024), and a nonfiction book on feral man, *Kaspar Hausers Geschwister* (Franz Steiner Verlag, 2018).

Israel Bonilla lives in Guadalajara, Jalisco. He is author of the story collection *Sleep Decades* (Malarkey Books, 2024) and the micro-chapbook *Landscapes* (Ghost City Press, 2021). His work has appeared in *Your Impossible Voice, Firmament, Minor Literature[s], Berfrois, King Ludd's Rag*, and elsewhere.

Christopher Boucher is the author of the novels *How to Keep Your Volkswagen Alive* (Melville House, 2011), *Golden Delicious* (MH, 2016), and *Big Giant Floating Head* (MH, 2019). He teaches writing and literature at Boston College and is Managing Editor of *Post Road Magazine*.

Ian Boulton is a UK-based writer. He has been a regular contributor to *Exacting Clam, The Rusty Nail, Notes From The Underground, Literary Juice, Sentinel Literary Quarterly* and others.

Caroline Clark has published three books: *Saying Yes In Russian* (Agenda Editions, 2012); *Sovetica* (CB editions, 2021) and Own Sweet Time (CB, 2022). Her next book, *What Lies Ahead and Other Essays*, will be published by Black Herald Press in 2026. She lives in Lewes, UK, and works as a community interpreter.

Marvin Cohen (1931–2025) was the author of many novels, plays, and collections of essays, stories, and poems. He lived in Manhattan's East Village.

Sarah Daly is an American writer whose fiction, poetry, and drama have appeared in fifty-one literary journals including *The Molotov Cocktail, Bright Flash Literary Review, Cardinal Sins*, and *New Feathers*.

Gina DeMartino, writer and artist, recently graduated with her BA in Visual Arts at Montclair State University. Through her acrylic paper collages, she curates colorful adventures of queer relationships and self portraits exploring both uncertainty and acceptance of the self.

Mike Fox's stories have been nominated for Best of Net and the Pushcart Prize, listed in *Best British and Irish Flash Fiction* (BIFFY50), and included in *Best British Stories 2018* (Salt), His story, *The Violet Eye*, was published by Nightjar Press as a limited edition chapbook. His new collection, *Things Grown Distant*, featuring photographic illustrations by Nicholas Royle, is available to order from Confingo Publishing.

Julian George's work has appeared in *Fictionable, Minor Literatures, Exacting Clam, Naugatuck River Review, Perfect Sound Forever, New World Writing, Slag Glass City, Ambit, Panoplyzine, The Journal of Music, Film Comment, The London Magazine, Cineaste* and *Art Review*. His novella, *Bebe* (CB editions), was published in 2023.

Jake Goldsmith is a writer with cystic fibrosis and the founder of The Barbellion Prize, a book prize for ill and disabled authors. He is the author of the essay collections *In Extremis* (SM, 2025) and *In Hospital Environments* (SM, 2024) and the memoir *Neither Weak Nor Obtuse* (SM, 2022). He lives in Suffolk, England.

Leigh Gore makes collages from images found in magazines, calendars, and other ephemeral sources, physical assemblages from discarded objects, and pottery, from clay. Born and raised in Trinidad, she lives in New York City.

Tyler C. Gore's essays, stories, and reviews have appeared in many of the fine, high-quality journals preferred by discerning readers like you. He is the author of *My Life of Crime: Essays and Other Entertainments*, a delightful book that you should definitely buy. He is also, from time to time, a graphic designer and digital artist. He lives, as he dreams—in Brooklyn.

Steven Gray lived in San Francisco for many years and read his work all over town. In 2020 he moved to the coastline of Connecticut. His poetry and prose have appeared in many publications, and his literary reviews are at litseen.com.

Ellen Harrold (She/Her) is an Irish artist and writer as well as editor-in-chief of Metachrosis Literary. She uses drawing, text, and textiles to explore physics, anatomy, and ecology through creative abstraction. She has published poetry in English and Irish in magazines such as *Shearsman, Channel*, and *Skylight 47*.

Ernest Hilbert is the author of the poetry collections *Sixty Sonnets, All of You on the Good Earth, Caligulan*—selected as winner of the 2017 Poets' Prize—and *Last One Out*. His fifth book, *Storm Swimmer*, was selected by Rowan Ricardo Phillips as the winner of the 2022 Vassar Miller Prize and appeared in 2023. He lives in Philadelphia.

Charles Holdefer's new novel is *Move the Mountain* (SM, 2027).

Ulrica Hume is the author of the novel *An Uncertain Age* and the story collection *House of Miracles*. Her work appears online, in literary journals, and in anthologies.
Carl Landauer, visiting scholar with Berkeley's Institute for South Asia Studies and contributing editor for *Poetry Flash*, taught history at Yale, Stanford, and McGill. He is the author of a book of poems on film adaptions of literature, *The Reel and the Paperback: Refracted Ekphrases* (SM 2027). His poems have appeared in *Kenyon Review, Exacting Clam, VerseVille, Poetry Flash, Santa Clara Review, Bangalore Review, Great Cities: London*, and the Mary McCarthy Society website.
Alice Lowe's creative nonfiction has been published this past year in *Broken Teacup, Burningword, Masque & Spectacle, Painted Pebble Lit Mag, Griffel, In Short, Drifting Sands*, and *Eckleburg*. She has been twice cited in *Best American Essays*. Alice writes about life, literature, food and family in San Diego, California.
Kurt Luchs is the author of *Tributaries* (SM, 2025), *Death Row Row Row Your Boat* (SM, 2024), *Falling in the Direction of Up* (SM, 2021), *One of These Things Is Not Like the Other* (Finishing Line Press, 2019), and *It's Funny Until Someone Loses an Eye (Then It's* Really *Funny)* (SM, 2017). He lives in Michigan.
Gary McDowell is the author/editor of seven books, most recently *Aflame* (White Pine Press, 2020), winner of the 2019 White Pine Press Poetry Prize. His poems and essays have appeared in dozens of literary magazines, including *The American Poetry Review, The Nation, Ploughshares, Poetry Northwest*, and *West Branch*. He is Professor of English at Belmont University in Nashville, TN, where he lives with his family.
Kat Meads' most recent book is *While Visiting Babette* (SM, 2025).
Jim Meirose's novels include *Sunday Dinner with Father Dwyer* (Optional Books), *Le Overgivers au Club de la Résurrection* (Mannequin Haus), *No and Maybe—Maybe and No* (Pski's Porch), *Audio Bookies* (LJMcD Communications), *Et Tu* (C22 press), *Game 5* (Soyos Books), and *Game 4* (Ranger Press).
Sergii Pershyn is a Ukrainian-American writer previously based in New York City who is currently working on his debut novel in Madrid. Sergii began writing following a career in financial public relations. His short works appeared in *The New York Times*' Metropolitan Diary section.
James Sallis (1944–2026) was the author of eighteen novels, multiple collections of stories and essays, six collections of poetry, a biography of writer Chester Himes, and a translation of Raymond Queneau's novel Saint Glinglin. His most recent books are *Bright Segments: The Complete Short Fiction* and the novel *Sarah Jane*.
Mike Silverton is the author of *New and Used Poems and Objects* (SM, 2026), *Yoga for Pickpockets* (SM, 2024), *Trios* (SM, 2023), and *Anvil on a Shoestring* (SM, 2022).
Cevin Soling is a writer, award-winning filmmaker, and chart-topping musician.
Julian Stannard currently teaches English Literature and Creative Writing at the University of Winchester. He taught for many years at the University of Genoa. He has written about Genoa and Liguria in his poetry. *Sottoripa: Genoese Poems*—a bilingual project—was published in 2018 by Canneto. In 2024 he was awarded the Lerici Shelley Prize for his contribution to Anglo-Ligurian literature. His *New And Selected Poems* (Salt, 2025) contains many of his Italian poems. A satirical novel—*The University of Bliss*—was published by Sagging Meniscus Press in 2024.
Selin Tamtekin is a British-Turkish novelist and art writer based in London. Her art writing has appeared in *Cornucopia Magazine, The Markaz Review, T24*, and elsewhere. Her two novels, written under the pseudonym Deniz Goran, are *The Turkish Diplomat's Daughter* (2007) and *The Fugitive of Gezi Park* (Ortac Press, 2023).
Thomas Walton is the author of *Unsavory Thoughts* (SM, 2025), *Good Morning Bone Crusher!* (Spuyten Duyvil 2021), *All the Useless Things Are Mine* (SM, 2020), *The World Is All That Does Befall Us* (Ravenna Press, 2019), and, with Elizabeth Cooperman, *The Last Mosaic* (SM, 2018).
Eric Weiskott is a poet and scholar of poetry and poetics. His debut book of poetry is *Cycle of Dreams* (punctum books, 2024). Eric's poems appear in *Fence, Texas Review*, and *Inverted Syntax*. He lives in Massachusetts.
David Wheldon died in January 2021 at the age of seventy. He was born in 1950 in the mining village of Moira, Leicestershire. He graduated in medicine from Bristol University. He was the author of four novels, a short story collection, and several collections of poetry. A short story collection, *The Guiltless Bystander*, appeared posthumously in 2021. His two early novels were reissued by Valancourt USA in 2024.
Isabelle Whittall is pursuing a Bachelor of Arts in Philosophy and Political Science at the University of British Columbia (UBC). She co-hosts the radio show *Hail! Discordia!* on CiTR 101.9fm, and is Editor-in-Chief of UBC's *Journal of Philosophical Enquiries*. Her work has been published in *Discorder Magazine* and *The Sundress Blog* by Sundress Publications.
David Winner is the author of *Master Lovers* (nonfiction, Outpost 19, 2023) and the novels *Enemy Combatant* (Tablo, 2021), Tyler's Last (O19, 2015), and *The Cannibal of Guadalajara* (Gival Press, 2010). His work has appeared in *The Village Voice, Fiction, The Iowa Review, The Millions* and *The Kenyon Review*. He is a senior editor at *StatORec* magazine and a regular contributor to *The Brooklyn Rail*.
Matthew Wolfman spent thirty years working in advertising in the UK and then escaped to Andalucia, Spain, to write short stories, poems and hike in the mountains. He has lived in Gaucín for twelve years and has contributed stories and poems to ten collections of *Escritores de Gaucín*.

www.ingramcontent.com/pod-product-compliance
Lightning Source LLC
LaVergne TN
LVHW081324110826
845149LV00007B/1589

* 9 7 8 1 9 6 3 8 4 6 7 0 6 *